D1564424

A NURSE'S STORY OF ADDICTION AND RECOVERY

Patricia Holloran

While *Impaired* is based on real events, some names and other details have been changed for the sake of privacy.

Published by Kaplan Publishing, a division of Kaplan, Inc.
1 Liberty Plaza, 24th Floor
New York, NY 10006

Printed in the United States of America

Library of Congress Cataloging-in-Publication Data

Holloran, Patricia.
Impaired : a nurse's story of addiction and recovery / Patricia Holloran.
p. cm.
ISBN 978-1-4277-9862-6
1. Holloran, Patricia. 2. Nurses--United States--Biography.
3. Women drug addicts--United States--Biography. I. Title.
RT37.H576A3 2009
610.73092--dc22
[B]

2008048322

10 9 8 7 6 5 4 3 2 1

ISBN-13: 978-1-4277-9862-6

Kaplan Publishing books are available at special quantity discounts to use for sales promotions, employee premiums, or educational purposes. Please email our Special Sales Department to order or for more information at kaplanpublishing@kaplan.com, or write to Kaplan Publishing, 1 Liberty Plaza, 24th Floor, New York, NY 10006.

In honor of all nurses who are in the grip of addiction,
struggling with the fear and confusion of new recovery,
experiencing another miracle of recovery,
or imparting the experience, strength,
and hope of a recovery long embraced

CONTENTS

PROFILE OF A CHEMICALLY DEPENDENT NURSE vii

PROLOGUE ix

PART ONE:
FROM DENIAL TO ACCEPTANCE

1. Impaired 3
2. Humiliation 21
3. And Now for the Bad News 35
4. Fear 39
5. Institutionalized 41
6. Repentance 49
7. Denial 53
8. Disease 65
9. Legalese 73
10. Walls and Secrets 87
11. Kindred 93
12. Turmoil 101
13. Religion 105
14. Legalese Part Deux 109
15. Deliverance 117
16. Sponsor-Angel 121
17. Emerging 125
18. Quack 129
19. The Great Oak 135
20. Losing It 143
21. Willingness 147

22. The Passionate Process 153
23. Hurting 157
24. Laboring 167
25. The Morning of January 22 179
26. The Hearing 187
27. The Prosecution 207
28. In Closing 221
29. Celebration 227
30. Baggage 231
31. Judgment 235

PART TWO:
FROM ACCEPTANCE TO TRANSCENDENCE

32. Disclosure 247
33. Confession 255
34. Healing 259
35. It's All about Me 263
36. "F" Words 265
37. Sweet Pee 273
38. Blessings in Disguise 287
39. Eyesight 293
40. Emptiness 297
41. The Answer 305
42. Back to Normal? 309
43. Giving Back 313

EPILOGUE 327

THE PEARL 331

ACKNOWLEDGMENTS 333

READER'S GUIDE 335

ABOUT THE AUTHOR 337

PROFILE OF A CHEMICALLY DEPENDENT NURSE

A chemically dependent nurse...

- Is a high academic achiever who usually graduates in the upper one-third of her or his class.
- Has advanced degrees and ambition, and is achievement oriented.
- Is quite accomplished in her or his field.
- Has a demanding and responsible job.
- Is highly respected for excellent work; is not a borderline performer.
- Is talented and a doer; is respected by colleagues and loved by clients and patients.
- Continues, despite her or his addiction, to feel responsible about work, and tries to meet work responsibilities.
- Has a conventional life attitude and a traditional background.
- Becomes dependent usually only in adult life.
- Does not usually have a history of childhood or adolescent delinquency problems.
- Does not generally resort to street crime to obtain drugs.
- Is likely to have a history of chemical dependency in her or his family.
- May have alcohol as his/her drug of choice

- Is at higher risk if working in critical care areas or if the nurse is male.
- Keeps her or his chemical usage solitary, not social.
- Does not initially use for "kicks."
- Experiences physical or emotional pain as the precipitating factor in her or his use.
- Is demanding of herself or himself.
- Has a tendency to deny or ignore tension, depression, boredom, or unhappiness.

— Adapted from the Nurses in Recovery website

PROLOGUE

I STARED WEARILY at my unfinished nurse's notes. The stool I was sitting on was really uncomfortable. I wiggled around until my posterior found a hollow it could be happy in, convinced that the stool had been purposely designed for discomfort.

I was exhausted and I just wanted to go home. It was Friday at 7:00 A.M., the end of my shift, on June 28, 1996. For the past several hours, I had been assisting with the labor and delivery of a beautiful baby boy.

I glanced over to the room where the baby and his mother were bonding. The father and grandparents were gathered around them, laughing and crying in their joy. I stretched, wiggled again, and reflected for a moment on how much I loved the work I had chosen. I loved being a nurse. In my twenty-four years as a registered nurse, I had worked in coronary care, IV therapy, and intensive care. They were all great areas, and I had gained a wealth of experience in them, but nothing was as fulfilling to me as working in labor and delivery.

Each baby is a gift from God to the world, the very definition of the word *miracle*. The enjoyment and gratification I experienced while helping a mother cope with the pain and tediousness of labor were unparalleled. To see the parents experience unmitigated joy and express amazement as their baby entered the world was truly a gift.

I had been at this hospital only since September of 1995, but for the past thirteen years, I had worked nights. I liked the atmosphere of working the night shift, and the people I worked with. Fewer staff were scheduled to work then, so we were forced to cooperate effectively as a team. Also, we were able to function more independently because we didn't have to cater to the whims of the supervisors, who were there only during the day. Last but not least, I was able to make more money on the night shift.

My hours suited my family, too. Either my husband or I could be home with our children if they were sick, and I was generally available whenever they needed me. It was important to me that my kids knew that one of us was always there for them.

AS I RESUMED WRITING my nurse's notes, the words ran together before my eyes. I was having a hard time concentrating. I had had only had three or four hours of sleep in the last twenty-four hours. With my father in ICU, I hadn't had the time. And with all my responsibilities, my need for sleep was usually the last thing I considered as I plodded along through my day.

The day shift of nurses, technicians, and housekeepers slowly drifted in to the unit, laughing and talking. They tried to engage me in conversation, but all I wanted to do was finish my work, go home, and sleep!

Nearly done with my notes, I raised my head and saw the assistant nurse-manager of our department walking in my direction. Another woman, in an attractive beige suit, accompanied her. The assistant nurse-manager stopped and pointed to me, and the woman in the beige suit continued to walk in my direction. Hoping against hope that I wasn't the target of their attention, I put my head back down to finish my paperwork.

"Hello. Patricia?"

My whole body grew icy cold. I looked up, smiled, and said, "Yes?"

She did not smile in return. "I'm Linda Spivak, the vice president of Nursing Services. I need for you to come downstairs with me."

"Please let me finish my charting," I replied, my hand shaking as I finished my last note and signed my name. I didn't know that this would be the last time I would write up any notes or do any nursing for a long time. I didn't know yet how profoundly my life was about to change.

PART ONE

From Denial to Acceptance

Addiction is the only disease that tries to convince you that you don't have it.

CHAPTER I

Impaired

My legs could barely hold me as I got down off of the stool and began to follow the woman in the beige suit. I couldn't bear to look at my coworkers as I was escorted out of the unit. I just looked straight ahead at the beige suit. My legs carried me, but they weren't part of my body. I had no control over where they were taking me. Everything suddenly seemed surreal. The truth is, I should have seen this coming.

Three years earlier, my husband, Fred, suffered a series of unexpected job losses due to buyouts and company shake-ups. Each time there was a job loss, he was able to get another job because of his stellar reputation and contacts. The last time, however, was more devastating. The company that provided support to his direct mail advertising business was not willing to continue.

"Patty, it's a done deal. They aren't going to do it," Fred told me when he called from the office. I could hear the distress in his voice.

"Oh, God. This sucks. How are you doing?"

"Eh . . . pissed off. Well, back to unemployment."

"Are you coming home?"

"I'm gonna go out with Earle."

"Okay. Just be careful."

"I will. I love you. We'll get through this."

I hung up the phone and started to cry: for him, for me, for every single thing I could think of. I lay on the bed. I don't know how long I lay there. I couldn't believe that we were going through this again.

That night, we briefly talked about how we would handle his job loss. We didn't need to talk about it, really. It was a foregone conclusion. The only solution was that I would take on more hours, and Fred would handle things at home. My husband was a great father, and he liked to cook. From then on, we would both work as hard as we could, not only to make ends meet, but also to keep the household, and our family, going. The next day, I asked my manager to give me as many empty shifts as she could. Resentment began to build deep inside of me, but there was no one to blame. I was like a bow pulled taut but without aim to direct the arrow.

Not long after, in 1994, in the new age of managed care, many hospitals altered their budgets in response to the projected decrease in reimbursements from the HMOs. At the hospital where I worked they called it "reengineering." Each department was required to cut their budgets by twenty-five percent, which translated into the loss of jobs for nurses. The remaining nursing staff was forced to carry a heavier workload of patients, yet expected to deliver the same level of care. The job was made more difficult, and even dangerous, with the hiring of unlicensed personnel to carry out tasks that normally one needed a nurse's license to do. True, a "nurse's aide" taking a baby's vital signs could accurately report the number of heartbeats or respirations, but she was not experienced enough to recognize the subtle changes that could signal a problem and, if undetected, spell disaster for the newborn. Of course, if any harm came to the baby, the nurse supervising the nurse's aide, who was already multitasking her own heavy workload, would be the one held responsible, and her license put in jeopardy.

We felt totally powerless over the situation, but most of us needed our jobs; I know I did. So we did the best we could as the stress level continued to rise.

I wasn't sleeping well. I had lost the ability to know what being tired felt like. I was in a state of perpetual, yet functional fatigue—or so I thought. I slowly developed many of the classic symptoms of clinical depression, but I did not recognize them, or I ignored them. But I couldn't ignore the migraine headaches I was experiencing. I had suffered from them for most of my adult life.

Around that time, a new product came onto the pharmaceutical market: a drug called Stadol Nasal Spray, which was specifically formulated to be absorbed in the nasal passages for the treatment of migraine headaches. A doctor prescribed it for my migraines, and it worked very well. Now, instead of suffering from a migraine for three days, I had to endure it for only three hours. Stadol had all of the properties of a narcotic, but its chemical properties prevented it from being considered a "physically addictive" substance, and therefore it was not controlled by the FDA. However, the euphoria I felt after taking it was as good as that produced by any narcotic I had ever taken. Soon, I was using the drug to cope when the exhaustion and anxiety became intolerable.

In the injectable form, Stadol is the most widely used pain medication for women in labor. Milligram for milligram, it is ten times stronger than morphine. As a labor and delivery nurse, I frequently provided the drug to my patients as part of their care. I wondered if I would get the same effect with the injectable Stadol. Since I am a diabetic and use insulin, I did not have a problem with needles. The dose that was ordered for a patient was less than was in the vial. After supplying a patient with her dose, I saved what was left in the vial. I put it in my pocket until I got home, or nearly home, and injected the remainder into the muscle in my thigh. The effects were even better than sniffing it. I used the injectable Stadol three to four times a week for several weeks. I had no idea what

I had unleashed in myself. My burgeoning addiction was beginning to dictate my actions, but I did not know that.

Fred was able to find another job in his field. I felt relieved that some of the pressure was off me. I cut back my hours to my usual three nights a week. I continued to take the Stadol, however. I refilled my prescription and continued to take it from work. I always told myself I would stop tomorrow, and I truly believed that.

IN THE FALL OF 1994, my nurse manager had the difficult task of sitting me down to tell me that my performance at work was declining.

"This is really hard for me, Patty," she started, "but, your behavior has been, um... bizarre."

"Bizarre? What do you mean bizarre?"

"Well, sometimes your colleagues can't find you, your charts are missing information. You left a pushing labor patient alone in a room..."

Shaking and crying, I tried to defend myself against these incredible accusations. I had no idea anyone had seen anything wrong with my nursing. I was confident that I was providing the same excellent patient care as I always had done.

"I've never left any patient alone! I had to go to the bathroom, so I told whoever was in charge to watch her for me!" This was the truth! I was shocked that anyone would accuse me of compromising the safety of a patient. My patients always came first.

"Well, that's not what I heard."

"Who's complaining? I need to have some specifics if I can address any of this."

"I'm not going to tell you that." She sighed. "Patty, you just need to improve your performance. All of this is shocking to me as well. You are one of our best, most experienced nurses. People trust your instincts and judgment. But lately I'm disturbed by what I'm hearing."

I told her what Fred and I had been through over the past few years, how scared I was about our finances, how anxious and depressed I had become. She listened sympathetically as I rambled on and on, crying the whole time.

I omitted any mention of the Stadol, of course, and she never mentioned it. I don't know if she knew. But, I knew God was punishing me for taking the drug from the hospital for my own use. I promised myself I would never do it again.

She advised me to take some time off to "get some help." I had never been to a mental health professional before, but I agreed to take a week off and see someone. I made an appointment with a psychiatrist who worked for the hospital. I felt a weight lift from my shoulders as I admitted to myself that I needed help. I desperately wanted to feel better and was eager to tell the psychiatrist how I had been feeling, and all that was going on in my life.

I did not tell Fred that I had been given the week off. On the three nights I was scheduled to work that week, I made up excuses for staying home. I told him that I called in sick due to a migraine or that it was slow at work and they offered me the night off.

ON THE DAY OF the appointment, the psychiatrist ushered me into her small office. I sat down in an office chair, wondering where the traditional therapist's couch was hidden. The psychiatrist's stick-straight posture and lack of a smile or the suggestion of empathy made me suddenly cautious. *Will she report back to my boss?*

"So, what's going on?" she said.

"My job performance is declining at work," I said. I then told her, in an abbreviated way, how stressed, anxious, and depressed I had been feeling, and about my family's financial problems and my need to work overtime. After about ten minutes, she interrupted me. "I am not surprised you're depressed, considering how they're decimating the whole staff by this reengineering process. I'm surprised I'm not treating the whole hospital!" she exclaimed.

True, it had been nerve-racking to wonder if we were going to be left with enough staff to do our jobs, and how much our workloads would increase. But I realized this psychiatrist had assumed that the reengineering was the only reason I was depressed. I was sure that job stress was one of the contributing factors to my recent poor performance, but she and I never got around to talking about the stress I was experiencing at home. I took this to mean that she didn't consider it a legitimate concern, and that I should continue to do what my family expected of me. The whole appointment took only fifteen minutes. After she made her comment about the hospital, she wrote out prescriptions for Prozac, an antidepressant, and Ativan, for anxiety, and asked me to return in two weeks.

And like that I was "cured."

At the time, I was happy to follow her directions, happy that this was going to be so easy, happy to know I was soon going to feel better.

I returned to work the following week, and waited for the medications to work their magic. Prozac takes weeks to ease depression. The Ativan, therefore, was supposed to eliminate my anxiety until the Prozac kicked in, but it made me feel apathetically euphoric. I developed a slight case of amnesia while under its influence and had trouble remembering what I had done the previous day or which patients I had taken care of. However, the apathetic euphoria made me not care that I couldn't remember blocks of time. I was simply relieved that I was feeling better. I was following my doctor's orders.

THREE WEEKS LATER, my nurse-manager brought me into her office and issued another warning. My coworkers were once again complaining that I had left things unfinished and been uncooperative. I didn't know this was happening. I had been feeling better, so I'd assumed I was doing a better job, too. None of the people who were reportedly complaining about me had given me any indication they were unhappy with my work or my attitude. Or, if they had, I had failed to take note.

In spite of the Ativan, my anxiety returned and soon became intolerable. The psychiatrist increased my dose, which only amplified the apathy and amnesia. My anxiety was alleviated, but my self-perception became increasingly altered. To me, the Ativan made everything better. I was able to cope at home and at work, and I was finally sleeping better. The psychiatrist told me to keep taking the Ativan until the Prozac took hold.

Over the winter, I received two more warnings from my nurse-manager. I did not know it at the time, but Ativan had become a major part of the problem. It was not the solution. I cut back on the Ativan, but increased my use of Stadol, using my prescription for migraines to obtain it and getting however much of it I could sneak away from the unit. By this point I had moved from simply taking home whatever was left in the vials after administering the drug to a patient, to withdrawing whole vials of Stadol for myself directly from the Pyxis, an automated medication-dispensing machine much like an ATM that requires a username and password for access. It was risky, but the drug, I felt, was the only thing that could truly ease my anxiety.

One day, Fred found a few vials of Stadol in my closet, hidden in a box of sanitary pads. When he asked about them, I told him I had brought them home by accident.

"It's nothing. It's not controlled or anything. It's just that when we're really busy and we give a patient only half the vial, we drop the rest in our pocket for the next dose. That's all. It happens to everyone."

"Why didn't you just throw them away when you realized you'd brought them home?"

"Because I didn't want you to see them in the garbage and jump to conclusions, like you're doing now."

"I hope you're telling me the truth, Patty."

"You are always so suspicious and negative."

"Don't start that again."

I walked away to end the conversation. Soon after, he left for work, and that was the end of that — for the time being.

In May of 1995, my father came to live with us. Eight years before, suffering from severe rheumatoid arthritis, he had moved to Alabama, where the warm weather helped him feel better. For a while he was fairly independent, but he was now becoming increasingly disabled as the arthritis progressed, and had decided to move back to Connecticut. He could still attend to most his daily needs, and could even drive his own car, but he no longer felt comfortable living alone. When he asked if he could stay with us until he was able to enter elderly housing designed for the handicapped, I agreed.

The communication problem between my husband and me, which had increased over the past few years, now reached a new level, something neither one of us fully admitted or understood. The fact that my father would be coming to live with us for a while was a monkey wrench thrown into an already malfunctioning and unhealthy machine.

While growing up, I was taught that families "take care of their own," and that sometimes this requires a lot of sacrifice. Just before my father arrived, the arguments my husband and I had been having about him became more frequent.

"This is too hard on you and on this family," Fred argued. "Why didn't you even ask me? This involves me, too, you know."

"How does this affect you?" I shouted back. "You won't have to do anything! He can take care of himself. You know, it's going to be really hard for him to leave Alabama. He loves it down there. But he needs to be around his family. It'll be no different than when he comes up here for a visit. And anyway, we'll get him into elderly housing as soon as we can. Besides, he can't stay with anyone else. We are the only ones who have the room. My sister and brothers can't take him in. Could I really say no to him? Could you?"

"I bet he hasn't even filled out the senior housing application yet."

"I don't know. If he hasn't, I'll take care of that when he gets here."

"It will take months to get him into housing. He just expected you to say yes. He's taking you for granted."

"I'm his daughter. Of course I'll take care of him. It's my responsibility. Just like I hope our kids will help us out when we need them. How do *you* think we can do it better?"

"I'm just saying…"

And around and around we went. Fred couldn't see my side, and I didn't understand his strong objections. The whole thing made us angrier and more distant. The hardest part was hiding all the anger from the kids, and eventually from my father.

IT WAS WONDERFUL for all of us — me, my sister, Kristin, and my brothers, Mark, John, and Tim — to have our father back in Connecticut, close to us. We loved him very much and had missed him when he lived so far away — at Christmastime, his birthdays, his grandchildren's birthdays. He used to play the guitar, but his rheumatoid arthritis no longer allowed him to stretch his fingers to produce the chords. He was able to play the electric organ, however. Singing and playing, surrounded by his children, were the things about him I had missed the most. I also missed just hugging him.

My father seemed resolved that moving in with us was the right decision. He frequently thanked us for our help and said, "One of the best things in life is to have such a good family." He had a deep spirituality and a remarkable understanding of our Catholic faith. I loved talking to him and learning from him. He had been a good father, and I was willing to do just about anything to help make these years as comfortable for him as possible.

We knew he had loved living in Alabama, and that his decision to move back north had been a very difficult one. I wanted him to feel as welcome as possible, to give him time to adjust and settle in, so I did not pressure him into finding his own place right away. I knew that when he felt better, and less depressed about leaving Alabama, my siblings and I would help find the right place for him. At least, that was the plan.

SO NOW I HAD even more responsibilities. When I came home in the morning, I had to make sure there was food for my father to prepare himself breakfast and lunch. I arranged for new doctors to take over his care, and many times in those first few weeks I had to drive him to his doctor's appointments. When I finally got to bed, I would be so overtired I couldn't fall asleep. After about three or four hours of sleep, I would get up to prepare supper for everyone, eat my own meal, clean up, and go back to bed for a couple of hours. All through it, I pretended to myself and to everyone else that I was okay, that I could do this.

My relationship with my husband became increasingly strained and distant as our respective resentments grew. I resented how little help he was giving me with the day-to-day tasks that had recently multiplied and how little emotional support he was providing me. Fred seemed so distant to me. We barely had any conversations without it leading to an argument. I did not complain. I did not want to hear any "I told you so's." He always seemed angry and unapproachable. Fred resented my father's presence and how much of my time he was taking away from our family. I am sure that I was the same way to him. The less we talked, the less we fought. Therefore, I was happy to be at work when Fred was home, and I did not go out of my way to spend time with him.

About a month after my father moved in with us, the well-thought-out plan for his future suddenly changed. One day, while trying to rise up out of a low chair at a doctor's office, he screamed in pain. He could not move his leg; nor could it support his weight. He could barely stand the pain during the car ride as I drove him to the ER. We found out that he had torn the tendon that supports the main muscle in the front of his right leg. Since this is also the muscle that holds the kneecap in place, the injury had caused a fracture to his kneecap.

He had surgery to reattach the muscle and repair the kneecap, but due to years of his taking Prednisone for his arthritis, the tendon or the kneecap never fully healed. His legs had become progressively weaker in the last few years, so this new injury would now render him even more disabled.

After surgery, he spent several days in the hospital, and then three months in a rehabilitation facility, but still, he was unable to regain full use of his leg. To make matters worse, he developed an infection that caused his knee to fill with fluid that had to be drained daily. The infection was so resistant it wouldn't clear up, and could be kept in check only with the use of strong antibiotics.

WHILE MY FATHER WAS in the rehab facility, I was terminated from my job. One morning when I was punching out, I noticed that the nurse-manager had arrived earlier than usual. She pulled me aside and asked me to meet her in her office.

What now? I thought to myself.

When I entered the office, a human resources representative was also there. Together, they presented me with another list of complaints about me.

"All of these incidents have brought us to the point that we have no choice but to terminate you from employment," my manager said bluntly.

"*What?*" I cried out. "You know me as one of the best nurses here! I oriented *you*! I've been here for twelve years. I think I have a right to have my side be heard." I began crying in anger. I was terrified.

"Here is the list of reports and complaints," the nurse-manager continued.

I looked over the paper she'd handed me. Among the complaints, there was a vial of Demerol missing under my name in the Pyxis. I had removed it for a patient, but she changed her mind about taking it. This potent narcotic was not accounted for in the patient's chart as given, so it appeared as though I had taken it for myself. But I did not take the Demerol. It should have been documented as given in the chart or discarded with a witness and documented in the Pyxis.

There was no mention of missing Stadol. At the time, it was not considered a controlled substance, so each vial did not need to be accounted for when it was removed from the Pyxis.

"I took the Demerol out for a patient who could not decide whether she wanted it. I taped it to the counter with a label on it. After a half an hour, Irene asked me if I was going to use it, and I told her probably not, and she discarded it. I didn't know she didn't account for it in the Pyxis. I trusted her to do that. Besides, I am allergic to Demerol! Ask her! Ask Irene!"

The nurse-manager looked toward the HR person, whose expression was stony.

"What about the monitor paper running out on the patient who was in early labor? Weren't you watching her?"

"I was watching the central monitoring at the desk because it was such a busy night. I had several patients at the same time. That patient was sleeping. The monitor tracing was fine! The baby's heart rate was normal. You know there's no alarm to let anyone know that the paper's run out unless you're in the room." I glanced over at the HR person because she may not have known that, and I was hoping it make a difference in her decision.

"That's not the point. You neglected your patient..."

"Did the patient complain?"

"Not that we know of, but she needed a C-section later that day."

"And that's my fault?"

There were other complaints: of my not being cooperative, not spending enough time with patients, spending too much time with patients, and so on. My head was spinning.

"Who made these accusations?" I demanded. "No one I work with ever indicated that they weren't happy working with me."

"Several people."

"Who? *Who?*"

"It's not your business to know."

I tried to address each of the items listed on the report, but it was pointless.

"Patricia, you are terminated," The HR person said. "I am not going to allow any more of these hysterics. You will no longer work here *ever* again."

I buried my face in my hands, wracked with choking sobs.

I declined their offer to go to the Employee Assistance Program (EAP) to talk with someone. What good would that do if I was being fired anyway?

Devastated, I walked out of the office alone, afraid to go home and face my family. I had been terminated from the job I loved, and would be separated from the people I considered my other family. I called Fred and asked him not to leave for work until I got home.

WHEN I TOLD MY husband and kids, they were just as devastated

"Does this have anything to do with those vials of Stadol I found?" Fred asked.

"No! They never said anything about that. They didn't mention that any Stadol was missing at all! They didn't even mention the word *Stadol.* Here... here is the list of complaints. I think this happened because four of us were competing for the night charge position. The other three were trying to make me look bad."

My boys, ages 16, 13, and 10, were shocked and scared. My youngest son burst into tears. I will never forget the look of fear in his eyes.

What was I going to do now? I could barely function. My husband was angry and scared. He tried to be comforting, but I saw him as so much of the problem that I could not accept his gestures of consolation.

I went to visit my father at the rehab facility, I told him about my job. The look of disbelief and fatherly love in his eyes is something I will never forget.

I had a long telephone conversation with my mother and stepfather. They were as surprised, shocked, and saddened as everyone else. They knew how much I loved my job. Their unconditional love and support had always been there for me.

I spent the summer in a perpetual state of anxiety and fear. No matter what I did, the fear never went away. I ran out of the Ativan and did not go back to the psychiatrist to renew the prescription. Frequently that summer we went to the beach or to my mom's pool. I was determined that my kids have a good summer. Fortunately they were old enough to entertain themselves, and they had their friends. When I was alone, I spent my time watching TV to distract myself from the punched-in-the-gut feeling I carried around with me always. Any physical activity felt like trudging through mud.

I WAS SO AFRAID that I would not get another job because I had been fired. The only thing I wanted to do was obstetrics. Finally, in September, I was hired at a hospital closer to my home, in their obstetrics unit. I was so relieved! I would work four nights a week with full benefits. Everything would be okay now. I knew that it would take time for me to settle in, but this was the solution to all my problems. I would be the best nurse ever.

When I began the new job, I stopped taking the Prozac. After all, my problems were behind me. I didn't need it.

MY DAD CAME HOME from the rehab facility on Friday, October 13, 1995. I had to make sure that we had all the equipment he would need to facilitate his mobility, such as a huge portable trapeze contraption over his bed, a bar around the toilet, a wheelchair, and a bedside commode. We hoped that physical therapy would restore his strength enough for him to regain some of that independence that he had once enjoyed. In fact, things did not work as well as we hoped. There was very little progress. His future was uncertain.

I had to help my dad even more now. After working from 11:00 P.M. to 7:30 A.M., I'd come home to prepare his breakfast and lunch. I would remove the dressing from his knee, inject his knee with an IV needle to drain the fluid, and replace the dressing and ACE bandage. I'd accompany him to the bathroom, and since he had no strength in his leg, I had to lift him on and off the toilet.

We had a nurse's aide come in once a day, but she was there for only two hours in the morning, to help him wash himself. If he had to use the bathroom after she'd left, I would have to get up and help him. And I still had to get him to his doctor's appointments. I alone was there to lift him from his wheelchair and into my van and, once we arrived at the doctor's office, get him from the van and back in to the wheelchair, and then repeat the whole process. He tried as hard as he could to help with his good leg, but I was still left with a lot of heavy lifting.

Nothing had really changed. I was right back to taking care of everyone but myself. Between seeing to my children's needs and taking care of my father, my sleeping was pretty much reduced to a series of short naps, and I found it difficult to fall asleep after being awakened over and over again.

The signs and symptoms of depression escalated once again. I desperately missed my old job. I was even more angry and resentful at everyone: at my dad for his neediness; at my brothers and sister because they couldn't do more to help; and at my husband for not being more sensitive to what I was going through. Still, I buried these resentments as far down as they would go as I put on my happy "I'm okay" face. I could not reveal these feelings to anyone because I thought not only that I *could* handle it all but that I *should* handle it all. In fact, I thought I *was* handling it all! I was a nurse for Christ's sake!

All through this I also experienced tremendous guilt over my anger and resentment: it wasn't my dad's fault he was ailing, and my siblings didn't know what they could do to help. I had imposed this unfair burden on our family. Nobody knew how angry, resentful, sad, and tired I was because I kept this information from everyone — especially myself. I didn't even know I was drowning again.

I thought, if I could just get more sleep, everything would be better. A lot of people take care of their elderly parents, right? It's not easy, but isn't this what I am supposed to do?

I remembered my grandmother taking care of my great-grandfather in their home, and my mother taking care of my grandmother at home. I loved my father, and he needed me. I continued to convince myself that I could do it all. Moreover, I had my new job; I should be feeling *grateful*, not resentful. Because of this, I took care to ensure that my work performance was excellent. I could not have what happened over the previous summer happen again.

Every pressure cooker has a valve that releases pressure so the pot won't explode. Once again I found my release valve: my prescription of Stadol Nasal Spray. With my anxiety and inability to sleep, I needed it. The narcotic-like effect helped me get to sleep quickly, and I began to use Stadol to fall back to sleep after my dad had woken me up during the day. I was overjoyed because I was able to get more sleep. Not only did the Stadol help me sleep, but it helped me get through the day, and it eased all of those frustrations that I believed would magically disappear the day my dad was no longer living with us. I was confident that I could stop whenever I wanted to. But for now it was helping me cope. I would simply stop taking it when my situation was less demanding at home. I started to feel human again. It was the perfect solution. The drug was short-acting, so there was virtually no hangover, and it did not have the amnesiac side effects as Ativan had. It left me feeling euphoric, but not apathetic.

ONCE AGAIN, ON TOP of my nasal spray prescription, I began taking home whatever Stadol remained in the vials I administered to patients. It seemed to make sense. The injectable Stadol worked much faster than the nasal spray—five minutes as opposed to fifteen—and I wouldn't have to call my doctor's office for so many prescriptions. I couldn't possibly become addicted to it. All of the literature stated that it was *not* physically addicting.

My abuse of Stadol picked up right where I left it off three months before, but now the escalation of my addiction was truly beyond my control. Over and over, I convinced myself *just this one time; it will be okay.* Again, at first, I took it only once in a while. But before long, I was taking home whole vials of Stadol for my own use, and using the drug in increasing amounts, and progressed to using it intravenously, injecting it into a vein, rather than merely injecting it into my thigh muscle. I augmented my supply by getting my prescription for the nasal spray whenever I felt it was safe enough not to arouse suspicion. I did not recognize that I had become obsessed with the drug, and that most of my thoughts now centered on where and how I was going to obtain it.

Over the next six to eight months, my intake increased to several vials a day. I didn't think *anyone* knew or suspected. My husband occasionally found a vial, but once again I explained that I had inadvertently taken it home, as did most nurses. And once again, he appeared to believe me.

On June 5th, My father was admitted to the hospital to have his prosthetic knee replaced in an effort to clear the infection. On the day of surgery, he suffered respiratory arrest and was placed in an induced coma on a ventilator in the intensive care unit. He was not in my care, but the stress and lack of sleep I experienced weren't any less. I was the nurse in the family, so I was the one expected to interact with the physicians and explain everything to my brothers and sister, and to my cousins, aunts, uncles, mother, and stepfather. I needed my Stadol to cope with all of this, and with the pain of seeing my father so helpless and sick. But still, I felt I was in control.

Your best thinking got you here.

CHAPTER 2

Humiliation

But now, as I followed the beige suit down the hall, that illusion began to shatter. I tried not to act too nervous, or jump to any conclusions, as I rode the elevator with Linda Spivak, the vice president of Nursing Services. I was afraid they'd found out that *someone* had been stealing Stadol from the Pyxis, and I couldn't think beyond that.

When we got to the ground floor, I followed her beige suit silently past the administrative offices and to a small conference room, where two men were seated far apart at a round table. Once I was inside, Ms. Spivak walked back out, closing the door behind her.

The man closest to me stood up, extended his hand, and announced, "Hello, Patricia. I'm John, and this is Dick, and we are from the Department of Consumer Protection, Drug Control Division. Will you please sit down?"

John gestured to the chair I was to sit in between the two men. As the room began to spin, I sat, or rather fell, into the chair.

"You are free to leave this room whenever you like," John said ominously. "We are not holding you against your will." They handed me their business cards.

My thoughts raced: *I need to think. I need a plan, and I have to be convincing!*

I glanced to my right, at the man named John, and in a millisecond I knew what to do: *I'll just look confused and deny everything.* They would ask me some questions about the missing Stadol, and…well… I would simply tell them I had no idea what they were talking about. They would then thank me for my help and let me go home.

I felt in the jacket pocket of my scrub uniform for the four or five vials of Stadol I had there, secretly berating myself for not having hidden them in my bra, as I usually did. I became more fearful: What if they asked me to empty my pockets? What would they do if they found the stuff on me? What were my rights? My heart was pounding so hard I could actually hear the valves closing with each beat, as if I were listening with a stethoscope.

John continued. "The pharmacy department at this hospital reported several weeks ago that there was a large amount of Stadol missing from the department where you work, Patricia. Also during our investigation, Percocet was found to be unaccounted for. Your supervisors were made aware of this. Since Stadol is not yet a controlled substance, and is in a general use drawer, they have been doing random inventories to pinpoint when this would have occurred. We found that many times when that drawer was accessed for Motrin, Tylenol, or Pitocin, Stadol was also taken, or when Stadol was signed out, there would be more missing than a given patient needed. Your name, Patricia, was the common denominator."

I was sure I could convince these two men that I could not possibly have anything to do with this situation. After all, I was an excellent nurse and had been so for more than twenty years. I was a law-abiding person. I was a hard worker and a smart woman. People loved me, loved to work with me, and often told me that they depended on my skills and intuition. So how could anyone accuse *me*? And besides, if my husband had believed what I told him about the vials of Stadol he'd found at home, surely I could convince these two men I didn't know what they were talking about. They would let me go home, and then I would not take another molecule of Stadol for the rest of my life.

But then John placed a printout in front of me. What I saw made me nauseated: it was a report of the Pyxis activity over the last few weeks. My name was highlighted in bright yellow over and over again, on page after page after page.

As I stared at the report, I tried terribly hard to look confused, and to absorb the information in front of me. As I planned my next move to convince these guys they had the wrong gal, my mouth went dry, my heart started beating even faster and harder, and I broke out in a cold sweat. But I was *not* going to give in. *I am innocent until proven guilty*, I assured myself.

"I... I don't know what is going on here. Someone must have stolen my PIN number!"

John leaned forward and, with an expression of exasperation, stated firmly and deliberately, and with a trace of sarcasm, "Pat, nobody stole your PIN. We have cross-referenced who was working on the nights the Stadol went missing, and nobody else was consistently working all of those nights. It was only on the night shift that this happened. The Stadol was never diverted when you were not on. Besides, if you suspected that someone had stolen your banking PIN number, wouldn't you have reported it? Come *on* now."

As quickly as it formed, my plan unraveled. I could no longer pretend. I couldn't fight it any longer. The months of lying and the charade of excuses had to end. They already knew it was me; there was no doubt in their minds. My head was spinning; the room was spinning; my abdomen was cramping; my cold sweat got colder and sweatier. I felt weightless, like I was spiraling down a bottomless abyss, as the reality of what was happening began to sink in.

I found myself silently praying to God as the tears began to flow, *Please, please, if they let me go, I promise I will never do this again. Dad is in the hospital now, so I don't need it anymore. I will just stop. This is a bad dream. It can't be happening.*

My hands began shaking. I did not know if my blood sugar was crashing. The glucometer I used for my diabetes was in my purse, under the table. I retrieved it. Racked with tears, and while the two men silently watched, I went through the motions of checking myself. I soon learned that my blood sugar was okay.

I knew I couldn't deny taking—*diverting* was the word they used—the Stadol from the Pyxis. I knew and they knew that I was guilty of that. But as for the Percocet tablets, I had no clue how they'd gotten thrown into the mix. I never took any Percocets. Maybe I got them out for someone else and she didn't chart them. I was trying hard to think logically about what that scenario might have been, but I couldn't. I could barely breathe because of the pure terror I was experiencing at that moment. I could not think, period.

With tears streaming down my face, I slowly and reluctantly nodded my head when they asked me one more time if I had taken the Stadol. Then they again asked me about the Percocet. I told them that it was probably a charting error, which of course, they did not believe. Just like at my former hospital, since the drugs had been taken out under my name, there was no way I could prove them wrong. I gave up trying to convince them about the Percocet. It was pointless. I sat there crying quietly, terrified even beyond my own comprehension, and wishing that I could run from this room, escape, run away, disappear. I hoped I would receive just a warning. I would promise to be good.

After a few seconds, Dick leaned forward, looked right into my eyes, and said to me, "Patricia, you have a problem and need help."

I stared blankly back at him, stupefied. It was fine for *him* to say that, for *him* to believe that, but *I* knew it wasn't true. I became indignant. They could accuse me of diverting, but they weren't going to pin an "addict" label on me.

My head was throbbing and my thoughts were racing. *I really don't need the Stadol. It just helped me get back to sleep and cope with taking care of Dad. I just needed to get caught. I'll be okay now. I'll stop. How could I have been so stupid! Why didn't I just stop? I have jeopardized everything in my life that is important to me! I'll plead with them. I'll promise NEVER to do this again. I'll even promise to get an evaluation, or see a shrink again.*

"I won't do this anymore!" I choked out the words as the tears rolled down my face. "Please believe me!"

John, unmoved by my emotional outburst, said, "Patricia, we need to have some sort of statement from you. You need to tell us your side. If you cooperate with us, everything will be all right. We will submit a report to the Department of Health, and when they see that you are willing to cooperate, they will look upon this more favorably. And Patricia, we will be submitting a report whether or not you provide us with a statement."

I didn't respond immediately, or make any indication I would compose anything. I was afraid that they might be trying to trick me into officially admitting something that I did not want or need to admit to. If I provided them with some sort of "confession," I thought I could be arrested. I began to think I might need the help of someone who knew what to do in cases like this, but who? I was filled with too much humiliation, disgrace, and fear — and the fatigue from being awake all night — to compose all on my own any statement as important as this. I did not want to incriminate myself, so I resisted. I am forever grateful for the only two sane neuronal synapses that stayed connected at that moment.

"Do I need a lawyer?" I asked. They didn't answer my question directly, saying that it was up to me. Then they did an about-turn and said they would give me an opportunity to think about my statement over the weekend. They said that this being Friday, they wouldn't submit a report until at least Monday, and that they would call me.

"So what happens after that?" I blubbered.

"When we get your statement, we will submit the entire report to the Department of Health, who will review it to see if you need a hearing before the Connecticut State Board of Nurse Examiners.

The nursing board! Oh my God! I was in serious trouble. I was at risk of losing my nursing license! My license was the most important thing to me next to my family. It was my first love. I began shaking again.

Could they take my license right now? Would the board of nursing revoke my license as soon as they got the report? Could I ever work as a nurse again? Was the hospital going to press charges? Was I going to be arrested? Were the state police outside this room waiting? My mind raced.

I did not know what to do. I felt utterly uninformed. I didn't know any of the rules, and was too scared to ask. I tried to think of whom I might turn to. I could think of no one who could help me, nobody I would be willing to tell about this terrible thing I'd done. I did not want to reveal this to my husband, family, or even my friend Dede. I knew of no nurse who had ever experienced this. I was utterly alone!

Dick handed me another business card. Across the top were the words NURSES FOR NURSES, and underneath this were the first names and phone numbers of several people.

"This is a group of nurses who can help you, Pat." His tone was now soft and fatherly. "They have been through this themselves. It would be a really good idea if you gave them a call."

Other people have been through this? There is even a support group? I did not recognize any of the names listed on the card, but I found myself feeling just a little less alone. In my acute and hysterical need to have this all go away, I now hoped that this group would tell me how to get this case dropped, would convince me that this was just a scare tactic. Then I could go on as before — but without the Stadol.

But what if this was just a group of pitifully addicted nurses? If so, I didn't want anything to do with them. I did not want to be associated with a group of ne'er-do-well nurses.

John and Dick finished their job and got up to leave. They wished me luck and said they would contact me after the weekend.

Soon Linda Spivak came back into the room. She sat down across from me and gave me the next chapter of bad news. She seemed genuinely concerned and sorry about what she was about to say.

“Patricia, you are suspended as of today. There will be a hospital board hearing next week to determine if you will be terminated.”

I thought I had already reached a critical mass of fear and terror, but now I was in a full paralyzing panic.

I cried and begged, “I can’t go through another summer like last year’s! I won’t do this again! I really need this job to support my family.” I clung to the fact that she’d said they were only suspending me, not terminating me for good.

She continued: “The hospital considers this a very serious matter. We don’t intend to press charges, however.”

This provided a little relief. My mind raced again.

Why hadn’t I been more careful? Why hadn’t I just stopped? I should have had more self-control! Every time I went to work I made a promise to myself that I wouldn’t walk off with any Stadol again, but by the time I headed out of the hospital to go home, some Stadol always ended up in my pocket.

Gently and kindly Linda continued: “Pat, I am reluctant to send you home without your first speaking to someone from the Employee Assistance Program. You need to talk to someone. You do have a problem that you need to address. You need to be evaluated by a professional. Is it all right if I call over there and see if a counselor is available?”

I reluctantly agreed to let her call the EAP office. I certainly was not addicted to anything, but I *did* need to talk to someone. I needed to convince this “professional” that I wasn’t addicted, just depressed, and that I would stop taking the Stadol now. I just needed to be put back on my Prozac and Ativan. I needed a job.

After placing the call, Linda informed me that someone would be available at EAP in about ten minutes. I agreed to go there.

"Are you sure that you don't want to call your husband?"

"Yes, I'm sure. I will after I go to EAP."

The thought of telling Fred right then was horrifying. It was something I just could not bring myself to do.

"Take care of yourself, Patty. You are a very good nurse, but you need help right now." She said she would be in contact with me to inform me of the hospital board's decision.

I SLOWLY WALKED OUT of the conference room in a daze. I was completely alone. The EAP offices were on the other side of town; I would have to drive there. As I approached the back door to the parking lot, my pace quickened. I threw open the door and ran to my van. My throat was constricted. I was gasping for breath. The mental and emotional pain was excruciating. The craving for relief was overwhelming. I climbed into the van and, with shaking fingers, pulled a vial of Stadol from my pocket, found a vein, and injected the whole thing.

Almost immediately, my muscles relaxed, and my breathing came easier. The blessed euphoria and the dulled sensibility that replaced the pain washed over me like warm sunlight. I started up the van and backed out of the parking space.

As I pulled out into the city traffic I thought, *They've allowed me to get in my car and drive! Even though they'd just accused me of stealing drugs and telling me that I had "a problem." Knowing that I have been awake all night, and that I am severely emotionally distressed, no one offered to drive me?* I shouldn't have been behind the wheel. How did they know if I was actually going to go to EAP? I had considered not going. I wanted to flee. What if I were suicidal? What if I overdosed? I was a danger to myself and others.

I looked out at the beautiful early summer day. I saw people carrying on with their everyday routines and activities, but I felt like a stranger, an alien. How could they be so lighthearted and energetic when I was so terrified?

I wished I wasn't me. I wished time could move at an accelerated pace, move me to the future, past this, so that I wouldn't have to feel all of this anguish. I didn't want to die, but I didn't really want to be alive either. For the first time in my life, I understood how someone could contemplate suicide as an alternative. With that thought, I pulled over, jumped out of the van, and vomited on the side of the road.

When the retching stopped, I slowly climbed back into the van. I stared straight ahead, not seeing. Reluctantly, painfully, I realized that there was no other way than just to continue on. I had a family—children whom I loved and who loved me, who needed me. Somehow, I had to figure this out, but how? How could I convince Linda that I would be okay now? If she wanted me to pay them back for all the Stadol that I took, then I would do that.

WHEN I ARRIVED AT the building where the EAP offices were located, I screamed to God inside my head. *Please, Jesus, I don't know what to do! Help me! You know my heart! You know that I am sorry and that I will try my hardest. Just help me to... to... live through this.*

The halls seemed long and empty. I followed the signs to EAP. I kept making left-hand turns, like I was going in circles, but soon I found it. I went to the desk and asked for the counselor with whom I was supposed to meet. With the enthusiasm of a slug, the receptionist informed me that she was not there. I impatiently informed her that the counselor was supposed to be there to meet me, and that it was very important. Sluglike, the receptionist agreed to page her.

I sat down on a hard chair and waited for about a half hour, with my head leaning against the wall, trying to fight the overwhelming need to sleep. Finally a motherly looking woman with a warm smile appeared, apologizing profusely. She introduced herself as the EAP counselor, and led me into her office. As soon as she closed the door, she turned around, took my hand, and helped me to a chair. She looked directly at me and gently asked me what had happened.

The floodgates opened, and the story of the last few years came out in one long run-on sentence.

When I was finished speaking, she leaned forward and said in a tone that was so nonjudgmental, so soothing, I felt comforted and validated, "The last few months have been particularly tough for you. So, it sounds like you were self-medicating," This woman seemed to understand that I had had a *reason* to take the Stadol. Finally I had someone on my side. She would listen, she would help me. She would make Linda Spivak understand that I was sorry for what I had done, that they just needed to give me a few days off, and then I could return to work. This person would be the answer to my prayers, and then I could get on with my life.

"Patty, you need to understand why you needed to take a drug to cope. The best thing for you now, and what you really need, is to get into a program, a drug treatment program. Also, the nursing board looks favorably on a nurse who completes a treatment program."

My hopes of an instant acquittal by the hospital's board of directors and a return to work were suddenly dashed.

Nurses are notorious for diagnosing and treating ourselves, something that is unwise, but common. So the counselor's explanation was acceptable to me. I had been self-medicating—self-treating my symptoms of anxiety and depression.

I was beginning to relax in this woman's presence. Her explanation of the situation didn't make me feel as I had with the Drug Control agents: like a criminal. She really seemed to care. I trusted her. I would do anything to preserve my nursing license, so if she was advising me that the nursing board wanted me to go to drug treatment, then that is what I would do.

She began making phone calls to my insurance company, and found out that they approved a program about twenty miles away, at the Institute of Living (IOL) in Hartford.

The feeling of unreality returned as I watched her dial the phone and speak with the intake person for the IOL's Addiction Recovery Services. She handed the phone to me. I expected the same compassion and empathy, but the voice on the other end of the phone was the complete opposite of the EAP counselor.

In a very hurried manner a woman who introduced herself as Nora, a substance abuse counselor, explained to me that they had a twenty-day program, Monday through Friday, 9:00 A.M. to 2:00 P.M., and that I should start as soon as possible. I responded by saying that I would start right after the Fourth of July holiday, which was the following Thursday.

She responded as if I were a recalcitrant child: "You have to make a decision to enter a treatment program as soon as possible, Patricia. Either admit you have a problem or not."

Her tone and her words startled me, leaving me stunned. *Is she working on commission?* I thought to myself. I was already feeling so low, so despondent about what I had done, that I thought I couldn't feel any worse, until this wicked witch of the west chastised me over the phone. I *was* willing to go to a treatment program, but I just needed time to think, time to digest all I had just been through.

Angry, I responded, "I will start right after the holiday. I just need to talk to my family first. I will be in touch with you!"

"Well, you have to call as soon as possible, Patricia," she said with an intolerant sigh.

If attending this rehab program had not been so important to my retaining my nursing license, I would *never* have gone there after talking to this woman.

As I put the receiver down, the anger began welling up, *Oh brother! Twenty days and I'm not even an addict!* Stadol isn't physically addictive; all the literature I read supported that. It wasn't even controlled by the FDA, so how could *I* be an addict?

And who did this woman think she was talking to? She'd never even met me! If this was what treatment was going to be like, then I wasn't going to be happy. But I was *not* going to lose my nursing license. I would go through the motions, just enough to make everybody happy, and then the nursing board would think that everything was hunky-dory. I would grin and bear it for my career. I had made the biggest mistake of my life, and had been foolish to think I could continue to get away with it, but now I would behave.

THE EAP COUNSELOR interrupted my thoughts by softly and tenderly asking if there was anyone she could call for me.

"No, no one," I replied softly. No one could find out, at least not right now, if ever. It was my problem and I would have to deal with the consequences. I could not burden my family or friends.

WHEN I GOT HOME, our dog, Oreo, greeted me with her usual unrestrained delight. It felt so reassuring to pet her, look into those big brown, trusting eyes and know that whatever I had been through, she would never stop loving me. At that moment she was a stabilizing constant, a reminder of a normalcy I had left behind hours ago. She helped bring me back to reality. I had to do the right thing, whether it was as simple as taking care of her or as difficult as taking care of my very uncertain future.

I went to the refrigerator to get her something to eat, and the light didn't go on. We didn't have any electricity. I figured it had something to do with the work that the power company was doing on the street in front of the house, so I went out to ask when they would be restoring the power. The workers informed me that they hadn't turned off the power, but that my circuit breakers had probably been tripped.

It was a warm day, so when I went back into the house, I took off my shoes and socks. I couldn't stand wearing them anymore after all night and all morning. I then went downstairs into the dark cellar. I walked to the far end of the cellar, where the circuit breakers were located, and turned them back on. As I turned around, I felt a sudden, ripping pain in my left foot. I lifted my foot and found to my horror that there was a hacksaw blade sticking out of it! In the dark, I had stepped on it in my bare feet.

"Holy shit!" I removed it and flung it toward the wall. My foot was bleeding profusely. I hobbled upstairs, my trusted canine friend licking up the blood behind me. I grabbed an entire roll of paper towels, ripped off several, and applied pressure to the wound. I started to feel very light-headed and sat and put my head down on the kitchen table. *Please, God, don't let me pass out.*

After a few minutes, my head cleared, and the bleeding slowed enough that I could inspect the wound. It was a significant injury and needed attention. It was about three inches long and half an inch deep. I covered it as best I could with the rest of the paper towels and limped back to the van. I drove right back to the building I had just left, where there was a MediQuick clinic.

One hour and five stitches later, I was again heading home, but this time the beautiful day seemed more like a dream sequence — colors too bright and noises too annoyingly loud.

Finally, back home, I changed my clothes and flopped down on the bed. I had experienced every negative human emotion possible in the span of just a few hours. The fear was intolerable. I got up and injected another vial of Stadol. I didn't care. I even thought about taking more. I needed to escape. I went back to bed, and lay there awaiting the all-too-familiar feeling of tranquility that would transcend the fear. It soon was there: the relaxation, the sense that "all is right with the world," and even the feeling of courage. I could and would save my career, even if I had to bullshit my way through it. It was the best I had felt all that day and I welcomed the relief. Finally I drifted off to sleep.

The Chinese word for crisis is made up of two words — crisis and opportunity.

CHAPTER 3

And Now for the Bad News

I AWOKE TO A VAGUE, UNEASY feeling. As I rolled from my side onto my back, I knew that something terrible had happened. Suddenly an infusion of ice cold fear spread from my chest to the tips of my fingers, as the events of that morning came crashing back into my consciousness.

What do I do now? The anxiety was intolerable. I started to shake uncontrollably as I sat up and reached for the syringe and a vial of Stadol I'd left under the mattress. I injected some more. I am not even sure if I paid any attention to the amount. I glanced at the clock. It was 1:30 in the afternoon. I had slept only one and a half hours.

Before I had fallen asleep, I had placed the Nurses for Nurses card Dick had given me on the nightstand. I reached for it now. On the bottom were a name and a number to call for information. I wanted to crawl under the covers and assume a fetal position, but God must have been directing my shaky hand as I dialed the number.

"Hello?" a male voice answered. I almost hung up.

"Hi...um...my name is...I mean...Pat. (*Deep breath*)...I'm calling because I need information on Nurses for Nurses."

"Is this for you?" he asked.

"Yes," I reluctantly admitted.

"Were you confronted at work?"

"Uh huh," I replied, trying to sound calm and rational.

"Were you confronted today?"

"Uh-huh," I said, starting to cry again.

"How are you doing?" he asked.

"Not too well considering..."

"I hate it when they confront people on a Friday. It leaves them hanging over the weekend, especially if they are really sick and need detox. Do you need detox?"

I told him that it was Stadol, so I didn't need detox, and that I was going to start the day program at the Institute of Living.

He replied reassuringly: "That's really good, Pat. You are starting out on the right path. You are going to have to go through a lot of shit, but do all the right stuff and it will all be worth it. I know how hard this is, and that you can't possibly see that now, but you will."

Since my whole focus was directed toward preserving my nursing license, I was anxious to get on with the process. I needed to get this resolved, and put this nightmare behind me.

"How long does it take to get a hearing before the nursing board?" I said.

"About six months."

Six months! I had thought the whole thing would take only a couple of weeks! I'd thought that I would be called up to tell my side of the story, that I would sign a promise not to do it anymore, that they would see I wasn't a drug addict, but was just going through a difficult time. I would tell them that my father was in the hospital, and I didn't have to take care of him anymore. I knew that I was a good nurse. I had no "black" marks on my record, so they should let me continue with my career.

"Why does it take so long?" I asked.

He explained: "Pat, this is a major process. You see, the Drug Control guys are the cops, the Health Department is the prosecution, and the nursing board is the judge. They will be issuing you a statement of charges that you will have to answer to, so you may be getting some scary stuff in the mail from the Health Department."

It took me a few minutes to absorb all of this information. My knowledge of the workings of any legal matters was extremely limited, and because of the lack of sleep and the unremitting anxiety (not to mention, the Stadol), I was having an increasingly difficult time concentrating.

He continued: "Did you sign anything?"

"No. I didn't want to sign anything without someone giving me advice, like a lawyer or something," I responded, not knowing if I had done the right or the wrong thing.

"Oooh, I'm so proud of you for not signing anything. When you are that stressed, you may give them more information than they need, and dig yourself a deeper hole. A lawyer is a good idea. Did you have anyone in mind?"

"I know that there is a lawyer who represents nurses," I said. I didn't quite know how I had this information. I'd probably heard of her through a lawyer friend of mine, Judy, who works outside of nursing.

He continued: "There are really only two lawyers in this state who know how to represent nurses before the nursing board: Martha and Marilyn."

Marilyn's name was the one that sounded the most familiar, so I told him that I would talk to her.

"Good idea. She's really good, and she's a great person. You'll love her. Do you want me to call her for you? I can do that and then call you right back, if that would make it a little easier for you."

"Thank you. I really appreciate that."

When we hung up, I injected more Stadol. He called me back in about ten minutes. He told me that Marilyn Pellett would be happy to meet with me, but that she was going on vacation and wouldn't be back until the following Sunday, but there were a couple of things she wanted me to do before she returned. I was to tell Drug Control that I would be talking to her and that we would get back to them regarding a statement. Also, if any of that "scary stuff" came in the mail, I was to save it for her.

The spark of hope that I felt when the Drug Control agent handed me the Nurses for Nurses card had now increased a smidgen. This guy was so willing to help me! Even though I didn't deserve any help from anyone because I had done a despicable thing; I had stolen drugs from where I worked for my own use, and I had no excuse for this behavior.

"Does your husband know?" the man on the other end of the line asked quietly.

I started to cry again. "No. I can't tell him. A least not now. I'm afraid he'll leave me."

"Go to a Nurses for Nurses meeting. They can help you figure things out. They can help you tell your family, because we've all been where you are right now."

WHILE I WAS IN my bedroom, our three boys, now ages 17, 14, and 11, came home at the same time and were laughing and talking in the other part of the house. This was the first day of their summer vacation. I lay back down so they would think I was still sleeping. They were used to finding me sleeping during the day. I heard them each stop by the bedroom door, and then quietly walk away as they checked on me.

Oh my God! How can I ever tell them about this? *Especially after last year.*

I wasn't looking forward to *my* summer with eager anticipation. It looked like yet another one filled with anxiety, fear, and debilitating depression. They did not deserve this. They had a right to have a happy, carefree summer. I would keep this to myself for as long as I could. It was my job to be a good parent. I was not going to abdicate that responsibility. I deserved every inch of what I was feeling, but I was not going to burden them. I was going to be their mom, nothing less.

Stay out of your head.
There is no adult supervision there.

CHAPTER 4

Fear

I DID NOT TELL MY HUSBAND. *How could I tell anybody?* I was too embarrassed, humiliated, and ashamed. This was not the Patty everyone knew and loved. This was a Patty no one knew. I was not about to reveal the other Patty: the thief, the liar, the drug abuser. No one would ever have trusted me again.

Because I was a nurse, the burden was even more oppressive. I should have been more responsible! *I should have known better!* A nurse I worked with a few years before had been caught diverting Percocet. She was fired. At the time, I thought that she got exactly what she deserved, and I was fairly vocal in my contempt for her. Now people would think that way about me — *but not if I kept it a secret!*

What I feared most was abandonment by my husband. I was sure he would leave me and take the kids. How could he live with a drug addict? It had already been a difficult year for us. I felt estranged from him, although I knew that I loved him; that had never changed. He had many wonderful qualities, but we just couldn't communicate in a loving way anymore, so I decided that telling him was out of the question. I had one very close friend, Dede, who was like a sister to me and with whom I used to work. I considered telling her, but how could I tell her if my own husband didn't know? No, I would not tell anyone.

I was living in two different but very real worlds. I had my "public" world of being the competent and confident wife, mother, daughter, sister-in-law, nurse, and friend; and then there was my "secret" world of drug abuse and the mess my life was in because of it.

The fear was the worst part. It was ever-present, pervasive, and invasive. It startled me awake in the middle of the night, leaving me feeling like I had just avoided drowning, breaking through the surface of the water and gasping for breath. At other times, it came in waves as debilitating and tormenting as if I were watching my child get hit by a car, leaving me drenched in sweat and feeling like I had been punched in the gut. Smaller, undulating waves of fear and panic tortured me all day, every day, never letting up.

Paradoxically, the fear was also a motivating force. It eventually caused me to stop using the Stadol. I had gotten a refill for my nasal spray prescription the day after I was confronted, which I used at those times when the anxiety was too much to take, but by the following Wednesday, July 3, I had run out of that supply and was afraid to refill it because I was sure that Drug Control was keeping track of my refills. That was the last time I ever used any Stadol.

The fear of losing my nursing license also made me get into treatment. That fear was like a hot flame lapping behind me, moving me forward. I couldn't see the light, but I could feel the heat.

Bring the body, and the mind will follow.

CHAPTER 5

Institutionalized

THE FOURTH OF JULY HOLIDAY was spent with the usual hot dogs, hamburgers, and family. Since I couldn't participate in any activities because of my injured foot, I sat around and watched my kids splash around in the pool, and cheered on the annual family Wiffle ball game. Fred was busy playing games with the kids and visiting with our extended family. Our interactions went no further than, "Can I get you anything?" "How's your foot?" and "Are you ready to go?" There was no tension. I enjoyed the family and the food. Everything felt normal. My problems seemed far away, but that night the fear returned, and I awoke repeatedly, breaking the surface of the water, gasping.

The following morning, I knew what I had to do—I had to march myself up to Hartford to save my nursing career, and enroll in the Chemical Dependency Program at the Institute of Living. Lucky for me, my husband had to work, in spite of the holiday weekend, and the kids were all at their friends' houses.

As I was about to make the call to IOL, the phone rang. I picked up the receiver and then wished I had let the answering machine get it. It was Linda Spivak. She asked if I could come down to the hospital to meet with her.

Well, good, I thought to myself when I'd hung up. *I can tell her that*

I am going into treatment. That is what they want, right? I'll ask her if I can please keep my job.

WHEN I ARRIVED, I was escorted into the same room where I had been confronted just one week before. Linda and the assistant nurse-manager, Debbie, were sitting at the round table.

"Patty, how are you doing, and what happened to your foot?" Linda asked.

I explained my foot injury and informed them that I was on my way to the Institute of Living to set myself up for treatment.

"Good," they both said, but Debbie looked sad, and Linda wasn't smiling.

"The board of directors has decided to terminate you, Patty. I am so sorry," Linda said.

I started to cry. *How can we live without my paycheck?*

Debbie tearfully asked if I had anything in my locker that she could get for me.

"Just my work shoes," I replied. In a few minutes she returned with a bag with my shoes in it.

I left that same room, clutching my shoes, jobless, and alone, again. I hobbled out into the sunshine in another surreal daze, but now I did not have the comfort of Stadol to soothe my nerves.

I thought about having a drink. I had never had a problem with alcohol. There was some beer in the refrigerator, but I was too nauseated to drink.

I had to save my license! I wouldn't be able to get another job if I lost my nursing license! I was not looking forward to talking to Nora at the Institute of Living. I finally dialed the phone and got the information I needed. She informed me that we could do the intake interview just as soon as I got there. She gave me directions and told me to report to the Donnelly Building. She said she would arrange the appointment with the receptionist, so all I had to do was give her my name and tell her whom I was there to see. She made it sound so easy.

I DROVE THROUGH HARTFORD'S maze of one-way streets. The directions Nora had given me were pretty good, and I found IOL fairly easily. The guard at the front gate gave me a map of the facility and directed me to the Donnelly Building.

I entered a world surrounded by a ten-foot-high brick wall that literally and figuratively separated "us" and "them." Separated by a brick wall, separated by mental illness, hidden, out of sight, different, not "normal," not one of "us." But I was not one of "them"; I didn't have a mental illness or an emotional problem or, God forbid, a *drug addiction*.

IOL has a fairly large campus, consisting of about 15 buildings, some of them were very old, and some fairly new. One building looked like an insane asylum and reminded me of a *Twilight Zone* episode in which a newly crazy woman is led into a building and out of sight forever. I negotiated the narrow one-way road, first to the right, then to the left, and then to the right again, as it wound around the various buildings and the large expansive lawns. I was surprised by the size of the place. In the middle of Hartford, it was a city unto itself. *(Welcome to Looneyville.)*

That surreal feeling reemerged as I walked into the Donnelly Building and approached the reception desk. I gave the receptionist my name and I told her I was there to meet with Nora. With knitted brow, she put on the half-glasses hanging around her neck and, blinking rapidly, she looked over the list of names in front of her.

"I don't see your name here, Patricia. Who is it you are to meet with again?" she asked in a sing-song voice as she smiled and blinkity-blinked over the top of her glasses. Others behind the desk turned to observe us.

"N-Nora," I repeated, trying to sound calm. *She's probably pushing some button under the desk to alert the guards.*

"I don't believe I know who that is. Let me have you sit over here, and I will get someone to help you." Her tone was a little too patronizing for my comfort as she smiled the smile of someone used to dealing with patients in a loony bin.

"Follow me, dear," she said. *Get the straitjacket! We've got a keeper!*

She brought me to a very small, windowless room. I sat in a wooden chair, *no shackles in sight*, and another woman, who looked to be in her mid-twenties, joined me there. She smiled and asked me, in the same sing-song voice as the other woman, why I was there and what she could do to help me. I told her I was there to meet Nora. She smiled the loony bin smile, cocked her head like a chicken, blinkity-blinked, and scrutinized me for a minute.

"Does Nora work here?"

No. She's sitting right next to me. Can't you see her?

My anxiety level was increasing by leaps and bounds, to the point of panic. I wanted to leave. I was feeling paranoid and claustrophobic. I was dizzy from hyperventilating, but I knew I would not leave because I was going to do what I needed to do to keep my nursing license. Finally, I managed to convey to this woman why I was there.

"Oh dear, you are supposed to be in another building. Please wait right here, and I'll call the director of Addiction Recovery Services and find out if she can come over to see you." She walked quickly out of the little room and returned in a few minutes. "I'm really sorry for the confusion. Please wait here, and they will be over right away."

The panic was beginning to subside somewhat. I was pretty sure that no one was going to put me in a rubber room.

Eventually, two different women joined me. One woman was short, about thirty years old, with red hair. She unsmilingly introduced herself as Nora.

"I was waiting for you at the Braceland Building," she announced.

"You told me to go to Donnelly," I replied, confused.

"This is in-patient over here," she replied, as if I was supposed to know that fact.

"I've never been here."

"Don't worry about that," the other woman piped in, smiling. "We're just glad you're here. Tell us what's happened." This woman was older and had an air of authority about her. She looked like Judge Judy, from TV. I learned she was the director of the program.

My voice began to tremble as I tried to relate the facts to them. "I was caught diverting Stadol from the hospital where I work. I was using it to help me sleep, because I was taking care of my father and working nights full-time..." I talked faster and faster as I tried to win the race with my tears, but my voice shook and the tears fell anyway. Looking at my lap, I tried to continue. "I've never done anything like this before. I've never been in trouble or ever taken any drugs."

"How could you possibly rationalize this, Patricia?" Nora interrupted so suddenly that the director and I both jumped. "What made you think you could get away with this? You're a nurse! You should know better!"

I sat for a second in stunned bewilderment at her sudden outburst. She was asking me to analyze and explain my actions. I wanted to give her an answer. I wanted to give her a clever, responsible, and rational answer. I searched for the words as my mouth gaped open. None came. The excuse "I was trying to sleep" seemed so inadequate. I tried to draw from some nursing knowledge for any explanation. I was blank. I had no excuse for the inexcusable, dreadful thing I had done. My mouth closed as I looked at her contemptuous expression, and I knew that no answer would be satisfactory. She had already judged me, and *any* answer would only sound like a lame excuse to her, because, even *I* knew that I *should* have known better.

"I...I don't...I was only..." was all that I could utter as I buried my face in my hands.

The director quickly placed a hand on Nora's knee and shot her a disapproving look. "Not now," she said to Nora. She then directed her attention to me.

"You are in the right place, Pat," the director assured me. "Start coming to treatment next week and you will start to feel better about all of this, and you'll begin to figure it all out. You are not a bad person, nor does this mean that you are a bad nurse," she explained, glancing at Nora again. "You just need help right now. Everyone needs help in his or her life at some point. There is absolutely nothing wrong with that. You are doing the right thing."

I began to feel a little calmer. Nora didn't utter another word. I decided to maintain eye contact only with the director. She continued: "Did Drug Control confront you?"

"Yes."

"Then you are going to have to face the nursing board."

"I know."

"There is an excellent chance that your license won't be revoked since this is your first offense. As long as you do all of the right things, the board will look favorably on you."

What I'd been hoping for was that she would say that because I'd taken Stadol, I would not have to worry about the nursing board. But she didn't even mention, or seemed concerned with, the type of drug I'd taken. Didn't she realize that I was not actually a drug addict? That it was only Stadol, which was not even on the FDA Schedule of Controlled Substances?

"Have you given any thought to hiring a lawyer?"

"I'm going to be talking to Marilyn Pellett," I said, making the name sound more like a question.

At the mention of Marilyn's name, her face lit up. "Good!" she replied with enthusiasm. "She's wonderful, and will explain everything to you as far as the board is concerned. You'll really have someone in your corner if you hire her."

This Marilyn person was intriguing me. Maybe she would be the voice of reason. Maybe she would know that using the Stadol, even stealing Stadol, did not make me a drug addict. She would make the nursing board see what a good nurse I was.

On Monday morning, bright and early, I would report for treatment at the Braceland Building, right across the yard. Maybe that would make everyone happy.

WHEN I GOT HOME, I was so exhausted I did not want to do, see, or say anything. The boys were all home, asking what was for supper as soon as I came in the door. When Fred came home, I acted as if nothing unusual had happened. He knew nothing about the termination and thought I was home just because of my foot injury.

"How was your day?" he asked me. "And how is your foot?"

"Still a little sore."

"Did you see your father today?"

"No. I'm going to call there tonight to see if anything is new."

I made supper. We ate. We talked of this and that. We watched TV. The boys went out to be with their friends for a while. I called the hospital. Dad had been transferred back to a regular room. He seemed to be improving.

I was the only one who knew what I'd done that day. The only one who knew that I had been fired and that I was about to be a patient in a psych hospital for drug abuse. I had to be strong. I could not disrupt our life.

I began fashioning an explanation for my husband. I figured I would simply inform him that I was working the day shift for a while because of my foot injury. *That might just work!* It would only be until I found a way to tell him the truth, to buy me some time. I did not know what I was going to say about the absent paychecks. I would cross that bridge when I came to it.

I had to omit the real truth. If I disclosed it to him, he would be confused and hurt, and demand an explanation, an analysis of my behavior, like that woman Nora had. Besides, I knew I wouldn't be able to form the words to explain the situation to him anyway. When he was hurt or confused, he had a tendency to exaggerate things, to imagine the worst possible scenario. I could barely stand the guilt and shame I was feeling now; telling him I'd been terminated for stealing a drug from work would have been an unbearable experience.

I was so confused and afraid and felt so defenseless that I wanted to avoid *any* confrontation. I was walking on the edge of a cliff, trying not to lose my footing. In telling Fred, and enduring the unpleasant scene that was sure to follow, I was afraid I would lose my footing, crash, and not have the will or the ability to get up. I needed to be strong. I needed to avoid what I perceived to be real danger to my mental well-being, and the only way I could do this was by keeping the secret, by keeping people, especially Fred, in the dark.

Surrender means following the direction
God's finger is pointing.

CHAPTER 6

Repentance

ON MONDAY MORNING, July 8, 1996, I began my recovery. I did not know this when I woke up at six that morning. Even though I did not have to be at IOL until nine o'clock, I had to carry out the charade of going to work. Since I normally wore street clothes to work, and changed into scrubs at the hospital, it was easy to carry off the lie. With time to kill, I went to seven o'clock Mass.

Inside the church a few people were reciting the rosary, or saying the Stations of the Cross. I had been raised in the Catholic Church, and so this all was very familiar and comforting to me. I sat in a pew near the back. Above the altar was a large painting of the Crucifixion. It was just like the one in the church I had attended in my hometown. As a child, the painting had fascinated and scared me. It appeared as though no matter where I sat, the eyes of Christ were looking at me. Those knowing eyes were judging me, reminding me that they always saw what I was doing. I had no secrets from them.

Christ's sacrifice meant that He died *for* me. Since Jesus sacrificed His life for us, I believed we should never hesitate to sacrifice ourselves, especially for our families. "Part of being a good Catholic means that we are to sacrifice our own earthly happiness for the happiness of others," a nun once told me. This is how I processed being Christian, or Christ-like. Anything less meant that you were a selfish, self-serving person.

In the weeks preceding the confrontation by the Drug Control agents, I *had* prayed to and become angry at God. Why wasn't He changing the circumstances of my life, so that I wouldn't have to take the Stadol? I was doing all the sacrificing I could stand! I was trying to take care of my father in the best way I knew how, because I loved him but also because now it was *my duty* as his daughter. Couldn't He see how tired I was, how little sleep I was getting? Couldn't He see how hard I was trying to do it all, with very little help? If He saw, then He should understand why I needed the Stadol: to sleep, to endure the sacrifice, *until He changed things!*

Now, kneeling in church with my hands tightly folded and my eyes tightly shut, I was unable to form any prayer except *I'm sorry.* In the midst of my repentance, as I turned my gaze back to the painting above the altar, I experienced an awakening. I looked up at that face and saw compassion. I looked into those eyes and saw tenderness and mercy. And suddenly I realized that I had been bargaining with God for so long I had mistaken it for prayer. As I continued to gaze, I grasped the notion of my pride. I had wanted things *my* way. I'd been too proud to admit that I was overwhelmed. I had been proud of my sacrifices, as if I'd been trying to prove to the world how wonderful I was. I'd liked hearing people say, "I don't know how you do it." I'd been too proud to admit that *I needed to inject myself with a mind-altering substance to help me get through every single day.*

My pride—and now my fall. I needed God to help me get up. But where did I start? What did I do? I had no answers within myself. With tears streaming down my face, I asked Him to please point me in the right direction. It was as simple as that. Here and now I realized that the compassionate face, those merciful eyes, would never lead me astray.

As the Mass was ending, I continued to stare at the painting repeating the same silent prayer, *Please, just point me in the right direction.*

He already had laid out a path for me to follow. It would be laborious, arduous, and strenuous, but He would always be there right beside me whenever I felt afraid or lost my way. He would show Himself to be the "Lamp unto my feet, and a light unto my path."

The pain is the arrow coming out,
not the arrow going in.

CHAPTER 7

Denial

ONCE AGAIN, I NEGOTIATED my way through the Hartford streets to IOL. I was lucky to find a parking spot in a small lot near the Braceland Building. As I looked over at the building, I felt a huge wave of anxiety and fear. The promises I had made in church, and the feeling of general well-being, had vanished, and I again started to think in bargaining terms. I started to hyperventilate.

I won't stay the whole time, I thought to myself. *They will clearly see that I'm just a nurse who was going through a difficult time, who needs to come here to make it look good to the nursing board.... Well, you'd better get out of the damn car if you are going to save your license.*

After another five minutes, I finally had one foot out of the van. I had to hold onto the door handle until the dizziness from my hyperventilating wore off. I walked over to the building and reached for the handle of the front door. Then I turned to walk away.

I can't do this!

I turned back, opened the door, and entered a small gray lobby. Directly in front of me were two elevators.

I'm going home now.

Next to the elevators was a sign reading, ADDICTION RECOVERY SERVICES — 3RD FLOOR. I pushed the elevator button. The doors opened immediately. I entered the elevator and rode it to the third floor. The doors opened on to a wide hallway.

Well, even though this is a waste of my time, I'll go ahead and make an appearance.

My legs felt like rubber. Looking to my left, I saw a door with a sign that read, CHEMICAL DEPENDENCY UNIT. My heightened anxiety altered my ability to process information at a glance, so it took me a moment to realize that this was where I was to go. Momentarily I felt lost.

I proceeded through the door and walked down the hall past three or four offices, a break room, and a couple of pay telephones. The hall expanded into a large area with a glass-enclosed office in the corner of the room and a circle of mismatched but comfortable-looking chairs and couches, with a large coffee table in the middle. Entering this sitting area meant joining the six or seven people already waiting there. Most of them were pretty young, in their early twenties or late teens. They seemed to know each other and were laughing and fooling around like a bunch of teenagers would. Others were sitting watching them or reading the paper or looking bored or appearing very self-conscious. I slowly and reluctantly walked over to the circle of chairs and sat down.

The panic became more intense. *Is this the group of people I'm supposed to be with? None of them are like me.* Maybe I was in the wrong place; the right place at the wrong time; or maybe my paperwork hadn't arrived yet for those in charge to know I was there. There was no one to greet me, or ask me if I needed help. There didn't seem to be anyone in authority to let me know if I *was* in the right place or with the right group. Then on a large erasable board against the wall, under the heading NEWCOMERS, WELCOME, I spotted my name.

Welcome to what? I wondered. *Who the hell wants to be welcomed here?*

At nine o'clock sharp a woman emerged from the glass-enclosed office and told us to come with her. I followed the group a short distance down another hall into a large room, which also had a circle of chairs, but much less comfortable than those in the waiting area. Over the next few minutes, a few more people joined our group, bringing the number up to about fifteen.

My first ever group meeting commenced with the recitation of the Serenity Prayer. I didn't know all of the words, so I remained silent as the rest of the room recited, "God, grant me the serenity to accept the things I cannot change, the courage to change the things I can, and the wisdom to know the difference." It struck me that I had neither serenity nor courage, and my wisdom was questionable.

The woman who led us into the room introduced herself and said that she was a counselor. Taking turns, everyone began to introduce themselves to the group.

"Hi. I'm Mary, and I'm an alcoholic."

"Hi. I'm John, and I'm an addict."

A new wave of panic overcame me. *I can't say that I'm an addict. I'm a nurse. I know what addiction is. And I don't have it.* I was the last person in the circle who had to introduce herself. I had picked a spot away from others, but strangely, as my turn came closer, I felt a need to belong to the group, to fit in, because, for better or worse, this was the group I was in. I didn't want to feel like an outsider. The nurse in me was saying, *Maybe* I *could help them understand* their *problem*. I wanted to belong, but I knew I was different. I was not one of *them,* and when they heard my story, I was certain they would agree, and empathize with my plight.

With all of these conflicting, self-protective feelings, I quickly decided: *Fine, I'll say I'm an addict, but I'll know in my own mind that it's not true. That's what's really important: what I know to be reality.*

My turn came.

"Hi. My name is Patty, and I'm an addict."

When God presents the truth, the real truth, opens your eyes and lowers the wall of denial, it can be a most terrifying experience. When I uttered that statement, the truth was instantly indisputable. The room, the people, disappeared from my view. I heard a whooshing sound in my head, as I struggled not to faint or run screaming from the room. The waves of fear were drowning me as I sat gasping for breath. I felt as exposed as a raw burn. No one in the room was aware of what I was experiencing at that moment; it was all on the inside. I sat as still as I could, because I knew that if I moved, I would begin to shake uncontrollably.

I'm an addict. I AM AN ADDICT! The painful reality kept repeating and repeating itself in my mind. The self-preserving wall of denial sprang back up just as quickly as it had gone down, but not all the way. All of the rationalizations as to why I could *not* be an addict reentered my mind, but the truth remained.

After a few seconds, my muscles began to relax. The rawness and the fear were subsiding, replaced by numb detachment. I was in the room, but lost in my own world. I looked around at the others. Maybe, just maybe, I did not even know what addiction was. I suddenly felt stupid. In one quick moment my life had been ripped from my control and I did not know what to do! If I walked out of that room the truth would not change, and if I stayed — then what?

My prayer came to me, *God, please point me in the right direction.* I stayed in that room. The numbness and vulnerability were gradually being replaced with a surprising, but fragile sense of relief.

THIS WAS AN ECLECTIC group of people, all different looks and ethnicities. The majority were women who had been mandated to attend the program and stay clean, or go to jail. Some of their children had been removed from them and placed in foster care. Of this group were the teenage ones I'd seen earlier, who were living in a group home in lieu of jail. There were a couple of men whose job-mandated random urine samples had turned up positive for drugs, forcing them to attend the program in order to keep their jobs. There was an older woman whose family had encouraged her to attend because of her excessive drinking. And there were a couple of people who had been arrested on DUI charges and mandated to attend.

Our group was asked to reveal how we had spent our weekend and how we had managed to stay clean. The facilitator was randomly choosing people to share how many meetings they normally attended, what friends they hung around with, and what tools of recovery they were able to use in difficult situations. For much of this first discussion, I couldn't relate. Many people in the group, especially the younger ones, had used street drugs, participating in an entire subculture of drugs as their way of associating with others. Drug dealers, stealing, and homelessness peppered their accounts of their past behaviors, and they spoke of taking care not to associate with the same people, places, and things that might trigger a relapse.

I felt like I was in a foreign country. I had nothing in common with the rest of this group. There was no one I could relate to here, who might understand, a contemporary of mine, another nurse. I was different from these people. I had used my drug in secret and for a whole different reason. I had isolated myself from everyone because I was using. I hadn't had a group of friends with whom I sat around and did drugs. I hadn't had a dealer, nor was I homeless. True, I had stolen my drug from the hospital, but I hadn't stolen money from my family or any little old lady's purse to obtain it. And I was already distanced from my drug; I had been terminated from my job and thus my supply. I didn't need to be detoxed because Stadol is not a physically addictive drug. I might have been an addict, I thought, but I wasn't as bad an addict as these people.

I WAS HAPPY WHEN the meeting ended, and we were able to take a break. The feelings of relief and calmness I had experienced earlier were gone. I needed air. I followed the group back out to the waiting area and sat in one of the comfortable chairs. The sudden and shocking insight that I was an addict was now really sinking in. I wanted to scream.

Again, I began thinking of plausible excuses I could use to leave. I wasn't coming up with anything. I sat with head lowered, tears stinging my eyes.

At ten-thirty, a man in his mid-forties emerged from the glass-enclosed office and told us to follow him. We walked back into the same room we all had just come from. I didn't know if I could tolerate sitting in that room for another hour. My back was stiff and my ankles were swelling. My injured foot was starting to throb, and my mood was beginning to sour. Looking at the schedule, I saw that this meeting was going to last an hour and a half.

The counselor for this group was named Charlie. My first impression of him was that he had very good posture and looked like a professor. He had thinning red hair, but still enough to cover his head, and he wore half-glasses for reading the names on the roster. The more "experienced" addicts seemed to like him, and indicated that they were glad he was leading the group.

According to the schedule, this group discussion was to be focused more on a particular aspect of recovery. Charlie began by introducing himself. Again, we went around the room introducing ourselves, and stating that we were drug addicts, alcoholics, or both.

"Hi. I'm Patty and I'm an addict," I said with a knot in my throat when my turn came around.

Charlie stood up, walked to the board, and wrote the word *denial*. He asked if anyone knew what it meant. A few people raised their hands, and he called on them.

"It's when you're not admitting something," a woman said from the other side of the room.

"To yourself or to someone else?" Charlie asked.

Several voices responded at once.

"Both."

"Either one."

"Someone else."

"Yourself."

"The denial we are talking about here," Charlie said, "is the denial we can have if we can't or don't want to admit something to ourselves. Do you think you've denied the fact that you are addicts?"

Many voices again responded together — some agreeing, some not.

"I knew I was usin'," one of the young mothers responded, "but I didn't know I was addicted, ya know, getting a habit."

"I thought an addict was someone who was really dirty, homeless, smelly, no teeth, ya know," another woman said. "I wasn't like that, so, that helped me deny."

Charlie explained: "There are five stages people have to go through to accept something they don't like about themselves, or if something bad happens in their lives, like a life-threatening disease or the death of someone close to them. These are: denial, anger, bargaining, depression, and acceptance."

I slouched and yawned as immediate boredom set in. *Oh God… Nursing 101 again.*

Suddenly, as if reading my mind, Charlie looked directly at me and said, "Even though you may know these five steps, it doesn't make it any easier to go through them." I gave him a weak smile. "So the first stage we are going to discuss is denial." He turned around to me again and asked, "What group of people do you think have the worst problem with denial, Patricia?"

"Probably nurses?" I shyly responded.

He smiled and said, "That's right, Patricia, but not just nurses, all healthcare providers." I had the feeling that most of this discussion was going to be directed at me.

As Charlie continued, I pondered my own denial. I thought back over the last year or so. The progression of my use of the Stadol had been so insidious, so pernicious. I was always so sure I was in control, that I could stop at any time, even though I never did. I frequently found myself looking up Stadol in the *Physician's Desk Reference* (PDR). Since such an authoritative resource stated that the chance of physical addiction was less than 1 percent, I always concluded that it was impossible for me to become an addict.

I truly thought that to be an addict you had to start using much earlier in life, like in your teens or early twenties. But I was in my mid-forties. Yes, I drank socially, had smoked pot a while back, and had taken prescribed narcotics for pain control, but never with any problems. Plus I came from an intact, nuclear, loving, church-centered family that did not have any issues with alcohol or drug abuse. Naturally I concluded that I did not have the organic ability ever to become an addict. I was immune.

I'd also always thought that addicts continued to use their drug only because they didn't want to experience the unpleasant side effects of withdrawal. And since I didn't need to use my drug to forestall withdrawal symptoms, I figured I couldn't possibly be in that unending loop of need. I also thought that once addicts went through treatment, all their troubles were behind them and they were cured. To continue for them to use, therefore, was owing to nothing more than their irresponsibility and lack of moral fiber.

The next layer of my wall of denial was coming down, and for the first time I realized how my obsession had grown slowly over time. While I was using, each day my obsession had become my first and central consideration. My willpower was never strong enough to get me to stop. It had nothing to do with physical dependence. The essence of my addiction had been just that: the obsession.

DURING OUR LUNCH BREAK, I called home to see how the boys were doing. As far as they were concerned, I was at work. It was not unusual for me to call them to see how they were. They told me that they were doing fine, and I made sure I knew where each of them was and what he was up to. I was reassured that things appeared relatively quiet on the home front, but Michael, my youngest, seemed to be getting a cold; he was coughing a lot. I was worried about him, which fed my guilt.

After lunch, I met with Charlie, who had been assigned as my counselor. He asked me a bunch of questions about my history of drug use and abuse, and probed for psychosocial stuff about my family and relationships. I told him I was afraid to tell my husband about my problem.

"How long have you been married?" he asked.

"Almost twenty-two years," I responded.

"You don't think that your husband will be supportive?"

"I don't know that, but I do know that he'll be angry."

"You mean that you've been married to this man for twenty-two years and you don't know if you can tell him? Are you afraid he'll hurt you, Patty?"

"No. I'm just afraid of his anger. He may leave me and take the kids." I started to cry.

"We have a family educational group on Thursday. Maybe he could come to that."

I thanked Charlie and told him I would think about it, but I knew I was going to keep my secret from Fred.

Charlie continued: "You know, Patricia, even though you have not had a problem with alcohol in the past, this is a program of complete abstinence. You have to stay away from anything that is mind-altering." This seemed really stupid to me. How could I have drunk socially all my life and now not be able to drink at all? But I figured I'd better follow the rules if I was going to keep my nursing license, which was still my primary motivation for being there. Besides, I knew that alcohol was not something I would crave.

THAT AFTERNOON, WE SPLIT into two groups by sex, and I joined the women in a much smaller room, with yet another counselor, to discuss women's issues. This was primarily a gripe session about spouses and lovers, which deteriorated into discussions about sex and the associated silliness that can be connected with it. I looked around the room at these women and again felt so out of place. I didn't belong here. Still, that I was an addict was really sinking in and taking hold. Perhaps my feeling out of place was my way of rebelling against the truth. I wanted to yell and scream to chase away this intense fear and rage, guilt and shame.

What have I done? What have I done?

Finally, two o'clock rolled around and I bolted out of there. I got in my car and started to cry. The crying became screaming and yelling. *This is not what my life is supposed to be all about! Drug rehab! Drug treatment! Recovery from addiction to drugs! I hate this! I hate myself! I can't possibly do this for a month! This is too much to ask! I'll just do this week and then I'll think of some excuse, or convince them that I'm better and don't need all of this. I haven't used any Stadol for a week now—that should prove something to them!*

By the time I'd pulled into my driveway, my voice was hoarse, my eyes were bloodshot, and I was exhausted. My son Michael stared at me as I ran into the bathroom mumbling about having had a bad day at work. As I drew a hot bath, I recognized a strong urge within me for a hit of Stadol and began thinking of places in the house it might be hidden, but I knew that I had used up my supply after I was confronted at work. I lowered myself into the soothing, enveloping warmth of the hot water.

Please point me in the right direction, God.

"Mommy, are you okay?" Michael anxiously asked through the bathroom door.

"Yeah, honey. I'll be out in a minute. It was just a really busy day," I reassured him.

When I emerged from the bathroom, I made myself calm down and put on my happy face. I cuddled with Michael on the couch for a little, to further reassure him that I was fine. He did Jim Carrey imitations that made me laugh. As I fixed supper, I glanced out the window at Ricky and Shaun playing Keep-Away with Oreo. I cracked up as they deliberately tried to confuse her. When Fred came home, he put his briefcase down and joined the trio in the backyard.

I thought about how weird it was that my family didn't know what I had done all day. But I still felt I was doing the right thing by keeping it a secret from them. After all, I was the mommy! My kids needed to feel secure, and it was my job to make sure they were. Their lives would be so disrupted if they knew. I needed to protect them. Besides, I knew I wouldn't be able to look them in the face if they knew. I'd have been so ashamed.

If one person tells you you're a duck, don't worry; but if ten people tell you you're a duck, you better start looking for feathers around your ass.

CHAPTER 8

Disease

IN SPITE OF MY NEAR nervous breakdown that first day, for the rest of the week I continued to get up early, go to Mass, and attend treatment. The program functioned on a rotating schedule of topics. The whole thing took twenty days to complete, but anyone could join in at any time, as long as they finished the entire twenty days. The typical day started out with a meeting to discuss things in general related to our recovery progress, or lack of it. The gathering after that would have a more specific topic, such as relapse or spirituality. After lunch, the group would be divided by men and women on some days; other days we would stay together to learn about various aspects of addiction, such as how a particular drug affected the brain.

As I listened to them share their experiences, I found myself getting to know some of the people in the group. Some talked about having left their small children alone when they went to buy their drugs. Others spoke of stealing from family and friends, committing robbery and larceny, trading food stamps, or whatever it took to obtain their drug. They related the shame they felt when their children found them in the middle of shooting up or snorting, and the devastation when the Department of Children and Families worker came to take their children away from them. One mother told us about not being able to bring her newborn son home with her from the hospital because of her drug abuse. Others described the repeated traffic accidents, arrests, and blackouts they'd experienced from drinking. Many suffered divorces, and losses of jobs and families. Yet, in spite of all the negative consequences they had suffered, they hadn't been able to stop using.

Although the specific events in our lives had been different, as I listened to their stories, I became conscious of what I had in common with them. I was finally accepting the truth that I had been utterly unable to stop using on my own.

Now I realized how much the question of when and how I would obtain my Stadol used to occupy most of my waking hours. I had constantly eyed the Pyxis machine. When no one was near it, I would quickly punch in my username and enter my PIN. I would indicate that I was withdrawing something for staff use, such as Tylenol, but would actually take Stadol. And I was ecstatic when I needed to enter the machine to get Stadol legitimately, for a laboring mom: after taking one for her, I could then take one (or two or six) for myself. And when people were around, I was always thinking up excuses for withdrawing from the Pyxis, such as, "I just need some Pitocin for the induction that's coming in."

When I got out of the hospital with the Stadol, I'd always feel euphoric and victorious. Obtaining it, I now saw, had been part of the "high." If I knew I was going to have a few days off, I would try to get enough to hold me over until the next time I worked. If I ran out, I'd rely on my prescription of Stadol Nasal Spray to tide me over. And I'd frequently call my doctor for refills.

I also remembered how, at home, I'd become very creative about where to hide the Stadol. I would have anxiety attacks about someone finding it, and would therefore hide it in different places. I became preoccupied with how much I administered to myself, how it made me feel, and when I could take it again.

As a result of using the drug, I had gradually and increasingly became intolerant of any of the unpleasant feelings that are part of normal life, numbing myself when I was angry, tired, scared, or even just bored. Though I took the drug to help me fall asleep, I found that it also helped me feel euphoric enough to get my housework or errands done, when the ever-present fatigue that was constantly with me got in the way.

Like the others in my group, the whole time I was using I thought I was in control, when really it was the Stadol that was in control. Our stories were different; the compulsion was the same.

People in the group were discussing "yets." *What the hell was a "yet"?* I kept my mouth shut and listened, learning that part of my denial, part of what had kept me thinking I was not an addict, was my not fitting the "picture," or having the consequences, of a drug addict. I had had a false sense of security. I'd assumed that since I'd never been arrested, since my children hadn't been taken from me, and since I'd never overdosed and ended up in the ER, I did not have the qualifications of a drug addict. There was always a line that I didn't cross, one that convinced me that I was in control of my drug use, which fed the denial. The truth is that those things hadn't happened to me "yet."

One of the lines I'd crossed was taking Stadol from the Pyxis solely for my own use. If the fellows from Drug Control hadn't confronted me when they did, I surely would have continued. I would have harmed someone — a patient, myself, or someone I loved. I had also had thoughts of forging prescriptions; after all, I had easy access to some physicians' DEA numbers, which are granted to those medical professionals who have prescribing authority. In those early days of treatment, I came to realize that prescription writing had been a very, *very* close "yet" for me, one that probably would have gotten me arrested.

I used to think that I would never inject Stadol intravenously, but I did. I just wanted to see how it would feel. The effects were immediate. I used the drug intravenously for a while until one day, when I thought I was going to pass out in the bathroom. I went back to injecting it into the muscle in my thigh until the day I was caught by Drug Control, at which point I resumed my intravenous use.

TWO AREAS PROVOKED some envy between the other members of the group and me. One day, a group member said, "At least you didn't have to pay for your drugs. You could get them right where you worked." After some discussion, we all decided that I *had* paid, by losing my job and thus my income. At that point I became a little envious when I realized others in the group still had their welfare checks coming in, while I had nothing. Meanwhile the others were also resentful that my source of drugs had had an inherent quality control; that is, they hadn't been cut with anything harmful, and the purity and amounts were always uniform. At this point we all learned that the type of drug, or how we obtained it, wasn't that important. Anyone could overdose, regardless of his or her drug of choice. Drug abuse, no matter how you looked at it, was a lose-lose proposition.

In the course of the therapy, I was learning a lot about myself and about addiction in general. Never in my nursing education or during my nursing career had I learned about what it *really* meant to be an addict. Yes, I had been told that it is a disease, but I had never truly accepted that "theory." I thought that once someone went through treatment for a month or so their problem was solved. I thought that they would no longer experience cravings, and that any desire to return to the drug was purely the result of their being weak-willed or selfish or lacking moral fiber. This was not so much an aspect of denial as of misinformation. These negative attitudes about addiction were commonplace in the nurses I knew. Contempt for addicts was pervasive among nurses, including me. The subject was virtually ignored in my career, which had no doubt led to the collective attitude that since we were health professionals, we knew better. How could I have been so judgmental about something I knew so little about? But the social stigma of drug use outweighed any real knowledge of addiction. Being a nurse had also helped amplify the belief that I could self-medicate without considering the risks. Being a nurse was a liability, not an asset, when it came to drug abuse.

All that I was learning was opening my eyes and helping me understand some of the whys regarding my own drift into substance abuse, but the reality that I was, indeed, a drug addict was still a horrifying thought. What could be worse than that?

At one of the group sessions in that first week, Charlie started off the group with the words that would be the beginning of a change in my attitude toward addiction in general, and myself in particular.

"It is a progressive and fatal disease," he said.

A disease, yeah, right. Here we go again.

"Patty, you're a diabetic, right?" Charlie continued.

"Yes, I am," I replied, not really knowing where he was going with this.

"Do you feel guilty about having diabetes?"

"No, it's not my fault that I have it."

"Do you feel the same about your addiction?"

I thought for a moment. "No, because it was something I *did*, an action I carried out, over and over again. If I say it wasn't my fault, that's just an excuse for my behavior, like I didn't know how to be responsible."

"Think about it," Charlie emphasized. "Do you feel like you *really* had a choice? How much of your day was used up, wasted, filled with the obsessive preoccupation with Stadol, let alone with your actually using it? Once you become an addict, your brain has changed. You become compulsive. Compulsions overwhelm all other motivations"

My rational self felt that I had had a choice; but then there was a compulsive, irrational part of me that just couldn't stop, that maybe didn't have a choice. Charlie was right. Maybe this was the real disease, this compulsion. Maybe, I really couldn't control it any more *than I could control my glucose levels*. I had the *disease* of addiction. I tried to let this sink in.

"Think of it in those terms, Pat. Think of it as you do your diabetes. Diabetes is a change in your body's ability to metabolize carbohydrates. You didn't have any control over getting diabetes. Addiction actually changes the chemistry of your brain. Once these changes began to occur, you had no control over them, either. You aren't responsible for the fact that you have diabetes or addiction, but you *are* responsible for your management of them. You are not responsible for your addiction, but you are responsible for your recovery."

I had diabetes, the disease of diabetes. It wasn't my fault that I was a diabetic. But did I dare think that addiction was as much a disease as diabetes?

My opinion of addiction as a disease began to solidify as I compared it with my diabetes. My diabetes required a daily regimen, to which I had to adhere to prevent the short-term effects of elevated or low blood sugar, both of which could render me unconscious or precipitate a visit to the ER, or, God forbid, sudden death. I also had to adhere to the regimen to prevent the long-term chronic effects of heart damage and kidney disease.

Addiction, being a disease, also required a regimen. The short-term effects could be loss of job and family, overdose, or death. The long-term effects were liver disease, kidney disease, brain damage, or death.

Behind the walls of IOL I was learning that I had a disease. The medicine for my diabetes was diet and insulin, and (yuck) exercise. The medicine for my addiction was practicing the "12 Steps of Recovery," attending Narcotics Anonymous (NA) and Nurses for Nurses meetings, obtaining a sponsor, and staying away from *any* drugs, including alcohol. I had the choice to take the medicine, or not. I wasn't a bad person trying to get good; I was a sick person trying to get well.

Step one, my first dose of medicine: We admitted that we were *powerless over drugs*, and that our lives had become unmanageable. This saying from the 12-step program was just what I needed to hear. Much to my amazement, by the end of my first week, I was actually looking forward to going to the Institute of Living, to drug rehabilitation treatment. I told Charlie that being confronted was the worst thing and yet also the best thing that had ever happened to me. I was beginning to experience a feeling of resolution, the beginning to an end of a bad time in my life. I was gaining a new respect for the concept of a life crisis, and what it *really* took to work through it. But I was only beginning to understand; I knew there was still "a lot of shit to go through."

"WHEN I HEAL," A song sung by Sandi Patty, caught my attention one day. I must have had that CD for over a year, but she was singing the words to me one morning and it became the "anthem" for my recovery. Everything about that song spoke to me of secrets and regrets, but also of hope and healing. I had been, as the song says, "shooting arrows in the darkness" every time I injected myself with my drug. I had to face "all that I had been running from." I had to allow my illness to be "driven from the darkness" so that the healing could begin. I thought of the day I was confronted at work: I had foolishly taken off my shoes and gone into the dark cellar, where, in the darkness, I had injured myself. I couldn't see the blood or the injury, but I could feel the pain. But feeling the pain wasn't enough. I had to see the injury, and I could only see the damage in the light. It was only then that I knew I needed to take care of it so it would heal properly.

The same was true for my addiction. I had been in the dark for a long time, continuing to injure myself and feeling the pain. I had to come into the light to really see the damage, so that I could heal.

There are times when my heart is uneasy with fear.
The answers are nowhere in sight.
Then I hear a sweet voice whisper soft in my ear,
'Everything's gonna be all right.' —Fred Carter, Jr.

CHAPTER 9

Legalese

I WAS BEGINNING TO understand recovery, and was beginning to understand what it meant to be involved with my recovery, but this did not alleviate the total panic I faced whenever I thought about my nursing license. The counselors at IOL told me that many nurses had gone through their program, but none of these counselors was able to tell me what to expect from the board of nursing. Charlie (bless his heart) told me that I just had to let them know that I was enrolled in the addiction recovery program, and that my urine toxicologies were free of any evidence of drugs. He said it was necessary for him to prepare a report for them about my progress, and that I *shouldn't have anything to worry about.*

But I was very worried. I knew he was trying to be helpful, but I still wasn't getting any practical advice, all the questions swirling around in my head weren't being answered: *When* was I going to have to face them? *Who* would let me know? Was I was allowed to work as a nurse at this point? Every day I waited for that "scary stuff in the mail." What was I supposed to do when it came? What would they do after they sent it? And the scariest question of all: What if my husband found it? The waves of fear lapped at me whenever I thought about my first love, my nursing license, and I would spend yet another sleepless night in pure terror of losing it.

Most of my identity had always been wrapped up in my being a nurse. I couldn't imagine doing anything else. I hadn't been to a Nurses for Nurses meeting; I hadn't been to *any* other support groups; the thought of walking into an Alcoholics Anonymous or Narcotics Anonymous meeting was too terrifying. To voluntarily walk into such a meeting would be the crumbling of the last brick in my wall of denial. I figured if I never walked into one of those "rooms," I could still delude myself enough to think I really wasn't one of "those" people. I wasn't doing myself any favors with this way of thinking, though: perhaps in one of those "rooms" lay some of the answers I was seeking.

I could no longer put off calling Marilyn Pellett, the lawyer. Drug Control had agreed to wait for my statement until I'd spoken with her, but I was having a hard time reconciling myself to the fact that I even needed a lawyer. The last thing I wanted to do was talk to some lawyerly person who would try to fit me into her busy lawyer's schedule. And I didn't want to have to explain to yet another authority figure about my drug theft and addiction. The prospect of facing another possibly patronizing, judgmental, and disapproving person made me want to avoid the whole damn thing. I could not face another Nora. So I had been putting it off all week, hoping that someone at IOL could give me the answers I needed.

ONE DAY, AFTER MASS, I decided to take a slower road to group therapy than the interstate, since I had some time to kill. It was a beautiful morning, and I wanted to enjoy the trip. When I was about halfway to Hartford, I abruptly pulled into a parking lot where I'd spotted a pay phone. I got out of the car and pulled Marilyn's number from my wallet.

I stared at the phone and swallowed hard. I guess I knew I would lose the one scrap of courage I possessed if I didn't call her at that moment.

After a couple of rings, a woman answered the phone.

I thought I had the wrong number. I had expected more of a professional response, such as, "Attorney Pellett's office. How may I help you?" My singular moment of courage was dwindling. *Please, God, point me in the right direction.*

"Hi...um...I'm looking for Marilyn Pellett?" I nervously replied, with the pitch of my voice getting higher and higher with each word.

"I'm Marilyn" was the answer.

"Um...hi...I'm Patty. Someone from Nurses for Nurses talked to you a couple of weeks ago about me, and he said you were going on vacation, but to call you after you got back on Sunday. I'm sorry it took me so long."

"Hi!" she exclaimed. "I'm so happy you've called me."

So happy I've called her? Where was the lawyerly attitude? Where was the judgment? The disapproval?

"Don't worry, Patty. Everything's going to be all right."

Everything's going to be all right? Did I really hear that?

"Patty? Are you still there?" I heard Marilyn say.

"Yes...yes...I'm still here," I answered. I was too stunned and dazed by what she'd just said to talk. Her "everything's going to be all right" reverberated in my head, then traveled to my heart and soul, and I began to cry with joy and relief.

"Are you okay?" she asked.

"Yeah, I'm really okay," I chokingly replied.

We talked a little more and she explained her consultation fee and asked me if and when I wanted to meet with her.

"As soon as possible," I quickly responded, and we settled on a date and time.

"I'm looking forward to meeting you, Patty," she said.

"Thank you" was all I could manage to respond. I was filled with gratitude toward Marilyn, and toward God. "Everything's going to be all right" rang in my ears like a novena. I repeated it over and over. It was the first time in the last three weeks that *anyone* had said this to me, and the person who'd said it now was in a position to know, was someone whose advice I felt I could trust. I didn't know how it was going to be "all right," but I was sure Marilyn would make it "all right."

For the rest of the day I felt almost like my old normal self. The clouds had lifted; the waves of fear had subsided. I finally felt I had something to pin my hopes on, because *everything was going to be all right!* Maybe it truly meant that the Health Department did not have a case against me because Stadol is not a controlled drug. Maybe Marilyn knows that but wants to meet with me just to get all the facts. How else would she know that *everything is going to be all right*?

EARLY THE FOLLOWING WEEK, I met with Marilyn in her husband's law office. Despite the encouraging words she'd spoken on the phone, the anticipation of meeting her and hearing what she had to say had kept me awake all night. On top of that, I had to walk about three blocks from where I'd parked on this hot July day, so by the time I climbed the stairs to the second-floor office and was seated in front of her at a conference room table, my sore foot was throbbing, I was sweating like a pig, my eyes were puffy from lack of sleep, and my asthma had kicked in. Sweaty, puffy eyed, wheezing, and staggering, I was supposed to convince this lawyer that I was clean and sober.

She looked straight at me. She was about five foot four, light brown short curly hair wearing a tailored blue suit with a small pin comprised of two crisscrossed golf clubs on the collar. Her face was serious, but friendly. Her smile was warm and genuine.

"First, let me tell you a little about myself," she began. "I am also a nurse, as well as a lawyer. I used to work for the Department of Health as a prosecutor from 1985 to 1992, so I know how they operate. I opened up my own practice about four years ago, and began defending nurses before the board of nursing."

Wow! This lady must really know her stuff, I thought to myself as she continued to inform me of her credentials.

Her demeanor was more like that of a nurse than a lawyer. It was the empathetic "bedside manner" that nurses cultivate during their careers. I began to relax, but only a little. I was too fearful of what she was going to tell me, nice bedside manner or not.

She continued, "So that is a little of who I am. Now I need to find out more about you. Did they fire you?"

"Yes, well, not at first. The director of nurses told me that their board had to meet and decide, so they suspended me, but the following week they gave me the final word."

Marilyn sat back and sighed and then sat forward again, "I'm so disappointed that they did that. That really is too bad. Not every place fires nurses. I guess they figure if they fire the nurse then they have eliminated the problem. However, unless the nurse who's addicted gets help, she will just go to another place to work, putting herself and her patients in jeopardy all over again. By the time they are caught and reported to Drug Control, who knows how much harm they've done in the meantime. I truly wish that I could help you with that particular hospital, but I don't think I can. Connecticut is a 'terminate at will' state, so they can fire you and be well within their rights to do so.

"Anyway, I did talk to the two Drug Control agents who confronted you. They were able to tell me the facts they had, which in a nutshell is that they got a call from the pharmacy at your hospital to investigate a large amount of Stadol that couldn't be accounted for. Through the Pyxis records they discovered your name." She was flipping through some of the papers she had in front of her. "They also said that there were some Percocets missing under your name, too."

Those damn Percocets again! I'd never diverted the Percocet. Sometimes when a nurse removes a controlled substance from the Pyxis, and then the patient decides they don't want it, for whatever reason, it's supposed to be disposed of in front of a witness. Sometimes, during a very busy shift or some type of emergency that diverts the nurses' attention, that step is neglected. The medication is therefore signed out under the patient's name in the Pyxis but not accounted for in the patient's chart. This is definitely a mistake on the part of the nurse; however, normally when it is found out, the nurse is merely asked to rectify the record.

Another way a medication may go missing is that one nurse may take it out for a second nurse simply as a favor to her or if the second nurse cannot leave the patient's bedside to get it. Though the medication is removed under Nurse A, if Nurse B administers it to a patient but neglects to enter this information on the patient's chart, the medication is considered missing under Nurse A's name. Normally, again, if the mistake is discovered, the nurse in question is asked to correct the records. Now, with this investigation of me going on, every possible instance of medication gone missing was being thrown in to the mix.

"I didn't divert the Percocet," I told Marilyn. I explained to her what I thought the scenario might have been. "Do you think they are trying to make a big deal about this because Stadol isn't controlled and Percocet is?"

"They might be trying to use that, but in the big picture, it's not going to matter if they throw in a few Percocet. You *did* divert the Stadol, so whether it is controlled or not, it is a mind-altering substance. It's bad, Patty. It's really bad stuff. More and more people are becoming addicted to it, and the best thing the FDA could do is control it. But that is a whole other discussion. What I really need to know, in your own words, is what happened."

I began telling her about my caring for my dad, about the lack of sleep, about the double shifts and overtime, and about how I seemed to have found the answer in Stadol. The tears started flowing freely as I once again related the recent unfortunate events. I was frustrated with myself for crying, but I *still* felt so guilty and afraid. Marilyn very patiently let me tell my story as I needed to tell it. She took notes and occasionally asked a question to clarify a particular point.

"My understanding is that you did not provide the Drug Control agents with a statement."

"No," I replied. "Should I have?"

"No, not necessarily. I can draft one for you to agree with and sign, and then we can send it to them. It's actually good that you didn't, because generally when someone is confronted, they're so vulnerable they might provide more information than the agents already have." She looked at her notes and then said, "Did you ever substitute?"

"What do you mean?"

"Did you ever replace a dose of Stadol with normal saline and administer that to the patient, or replace what was in the vial with normal saline?"

"No." The thought of what she was suggesting horrified me.

"Did you ever use at work?"

"No."

"Did you ever use close enough to the time you went to work that you might have been impaired?"

"Um...Maybe. After a while, it's hard to tell when you're high and when you're not."

When she thought she had enough information, she started explaining what the Department of Health and the board of nursing might do, placing pieces of paper in front of me with relevant legal words and phrases on them.

"After Drug Control gets your statement, they'll send a report over to the Department of Health with the same facts they presented to you, the evidence, and what took place during their confrontation with you that morning. That report in turn is sent over to the legal department, and they decide if there is enough evidence to prosecute. Remember that these people, the Health Department, are the prosecutors. At this point they have several options.

"One of their choices is to offer an 'interim consent order,' which simply means that they will ask you to surrender your license to them for a certain length of time, usually one hundred and twenty days. The purpose, in their minds, is to give you enough time to work on your recovery. However, that doesn't guarantee that your license will be returned in that amount of time. Also, an interim consent order doesn't do anything to move the case forward, or to resolve it. I *never* recommend an interim consent order to any of my clients."

She moved on to the next choice on the page. "What I think they will do initially is try a summary suspension. This is a process where they suspend your license pending a hearing on all the facts. You see, a summary suspension really is an emergency procedure to keep you from practicing nursing because you are an immediate danger to the public. In your case, this isn't so because you're going through treatment and you're 'choosing' not to work right now. If DPH, the Department of Public Health, moves for a motion for summary suspension, we will then put forth an 'objection to the motion for summary suspension.' There isn't any way to know when they might do this, especially since we haven't even submitted your statement to Drug Control yet, but my guess is that they'll move rather quickly."

The waves of fear began to wash over me as she continued with the explanation of the options.

"There are two ways at this point that the case can be resolved. The first one is a consent order. This is an agreement between DPH and the nurse that the board of nursing then approves. They really haven't been offering consent orders lately, so I'm sure the next step will be a hearing before the Board of Examiners for Nursing. It takes several months for them to get to your case for a hearing, but this works to your advantage because in the meantime, you'll be building a solid recovery. DPH will present their side, and we will demonstrate to the board all of the things you're doing for your recovery. Hopefully, the board will then render a decision that will outline terms of probation for anywhere from two to five years. We can talk about the terms at another time. I know that this is a lot to absorb."

She stopped speaking for a moment, to let the information sink in. I slumped back in the chair and stared straight ahead as the tears ran freely down my cheeks. I'm sure my "just shoot me" expression was not the first she'd witnessed in a client.

"Patty," Marilyn gently said, "you can get through this, and you *will* be all right. I know it all seems so overwhelming, but I think I can help you."

Everything she'd told me scared me. I couldn't even keep all of the facts straight. My earlier expectation that she would say the Health Department case was bogus based on Stadol's not being a controlled substance was totally gone. Reality was this lawyer sitting across from me and the documents splayed out in front of me.

"So do you know if you want to hire me, or do you need some time to think about it?" she asked.

I couldn't see how *anybody* could do this all by herself. I knew *I* wouldn't be able to handle it. I didn't know anything about how to maneuver through the procedures Marilyn had just outlined. She knew all of the right people to talk to, and how to get things done. Besides, my emotional state was too fragile for me to try to handle anything like this by myself. How could I focus on my recovery, which was using up most of my energy and much of my time, if I had to counter all the moves the Department of Health or the board of nursing might make? The very idea was too scary to contemplate: from what Marilyn had just told me, they could both be manipulative and unpredictable.

I did not need any time to think about it. "Yes, I'll hire you," I replied, wiping the tears from my face. "I really don't see that I have any other choice. All of this is way too overwhelming for me."

"Good," she replied with a gentle smile and a genuinely sincere expression. "Now, the first thing we have to do is prepare a statement for Drug Control. I'll draft one, and then you can look it over and see if it's what you want to say. I'll have to think about how we'll present the Percocet issue." I took a deep breath to try to control my emotions, but when I exhaled, more tears poured out.

"You've now entered Marilyn's 'boot camp of recovery,'" she said, smiling. "You have to do your part, Patty, meaning your recovery has to be the most important thing in the world to you. No matter whether you have your license or not, unless you continue to do the work of *your recovery,* you'll lose everything. Have you been to any Nurses for Nurses meetings or any AA or NA meetings?"

"No," I replied sheepishly.

Marilyn leaned forward, perhaps trying to penetrate the wall of panic I was trapped behind. "I know that doing treatment every day is tiring, but you have to start going to meetings, as many as you can. Then you can start to feel better about all of this. The nurses who attend Nurses for Nurses meetings are wonderful. They can truly help you."

After a short pause, and not getting much of a response from me, she continued, "I want you to start a 'recovery calendar.' Get a big calendar, and in the boxes write down what you did for your recovery that day: Nurses for Nurses, NA, AA meetings, church, whatever. The other thing you have to do is get a therapist. You have to get established with a therapist because we will need him or her to write a report of your treatment to the board of nursing later on, when you have a hearing. Also, the board is going to require that you to see a therapist regularly during your probation. I know this is a lot right now, so if you have any questions, please call me. Is it okay for me to call you? Does your family or your husband know?"

"No. My husband doesn't know yet. I'm afraid of how he will react. He just won't understand." I started to cry again.

"Is he abusive to you, Patty?"

"No. I just need to feel that things are 'normal' at home. I can't tell him yet. And I don't want to upset my kids. I'll tell my husband as soon as I feel I can." I knew I wouldn't be able to explain it to her so she'd understand. Explaining to her the dynamics of my relationship with Fred would have been futile; I couldn't even explain them to myself. There were times when I felt so confused, like right at that moment, that there didn't seem to be any point in trying to explain it all to someone else.

"You have to find a way to tell him. He'll find out eventually."

"I know. I will. I have to. I just don't know when."

"When it comes time for a hearing, Patty, it would be nice if we could have a letter of support from him. So the sooner you tell him, the sooner he'll be able to begin to understand. Otherwise you'll never know how he really feels about it."

I knew she spoke the truth, but it did not decrease my fear.

She leaned forward, put her hand on my arm, and said, "If you have any questions, please call me, or just call me to let me know how you're doing. I know, it's *so hard* in the beginning, and that you feel ashamed, but you have the *disease* of addiction, and that is really nothing to be ashamed about. Everything *is* going to be okay if you do all the right things to treat your disease. I'll call you to see how you're doing, and I'll let you know if I hear anything from the Health Department. Are you okay?"

I nodded and wiped my eyes.

Walking slowly back to my car, I tried to remember all that Marilyn had told me. The content of the information was staggering. How could any nurse possibly know how this disciplinary system worked? At least when you're arrested for a crime and are facing a trial, you *know* you need legal representation. Since I wasn't arrested, the Drug Control officials had not had to inform me of my rights, to Mirandize me. I was extremely lucky, then, that I *just happened* to be placed in contact with the right people, people who had strongly encouraged me to talk to a lawyer. If not, I would have remained absolutely clueless about how complicated the whole thing was, and how *important* it was to hire a lawyer.

Suddenly I began to feel resentful and angry. It shouldn't have to depend on luck. I was furious at my profession for the total lack of guidance I had received over the last few weeks. *No nurse has any clue as to what statutes apply, or how to even look them up. Nurses don't know anything about the process. We have no fucking idea what it takes to go before the board of nursing,* I angrily mumbled to myself.

It was like some big family secret that no one talked about, but that desperately needed to be discussed. Just like diabetes, addiction is progressive and fatal. And just like diabetes, it is a disease, a treatable disease. If I had exhibited symptoms that my diabetes was getting worse, symptoms that I might have been ignoring, if I had been suffering from hypo- or hyperglycemia, I could conceivably have been functioning "impaired," because my thinking would have been muddled. Had this happened, I would have had all kinds of help and advice from the people I worked with. I could have taken the time off to get well. I certainly would not have been fired from my job!

As I slowly and painfully limped to my car, I found myself becoming increasingly angry at the nursing profession, the profession I loved, the profession that prided itself in caring and compassion. This caring and compassionate profession treated its own like criminals and outcasts.

Still, I had a glimmer of hope within me. My preconceived notion of Marilyn's "lawyerlyness" had been totally dispelled. I had just spoken with someone who really cared, and who understood addiction. I finally had some idea as to how things would proceed with the case that threatened my nursing license. All this gave me a sense of relief. True, I also had new sources of anxiety, what with all the legalese to sort through, but I knew I had someone who would go to bat for me if I did all of the right things, someone who really would know the answers to my questions, or who at least had the resources to find out. Now I could do what I had to do about getting well, and not spend so much time obsessing about what the board of nursing was going to do.

The way I usually let go of something is by leaving my fingernail marks all over it.

CHAPTER 10

Walls and Secrets

THE SUMMER OF 1996 was cool and gray. On a few days some sunlight tried to penetrate the drab, colorless interior of the Braceland Building at IOL, but my environment was not about climate, it was about circumstance. I had acknowledged and even accepted that I was an addict, but a depression born of this reality was now taking hold. However, I didn't recognize what I was feeling as depression. After all, I didn't feel sad all the time or even hopeless. I wasn't lost in abject desperation and I wasn't necessarily pessimistic about my future. Still, I had intervals of despondency, especially when the waves of fear washed over me, but I had no thoughts of suicide. No, it was more like an indistinct vagueness, dimness, a coolness, a place where light and warmth had a hard time penetrating. Even when I got enough sleep the night before, I experienced a lack of energy. If I were to have drawn a picture of myself at the time, my coloring would have been ashen and my hair and clothes would have been hanging heavily, weighted down by inertia.

Braceland had thick sturdy walls that were a protection from the outside elements, but also from reality. I felt safe there. But when I stepped outside at two o'clock every day, leaving the protection and support of the walls of Braceland, the walls surrounding IOL, my senses would be blinded by the light and temperature, whether it was sunny or cloudy, hot or cold, of reality. At that point I would surround myself with my own invisible, self-protective wall of secrecy, the illusion of normalcy. Whereas IOL's walls were real, mine were a manipulation of reality, a distortion of protection. They were built of the dimness of depression, the blackness of concealment: a thick, sturdy wall of surreptitiousness and secrecy.

I knew that I had to start being honest with the people I loved and who loved me, but whenever I thought about telling Fred, I would find some excuse not to: it wasn't the right time; he wasn't in the right mood; I wasn't in the right mood; it was Tuesday. I used anything and everything to rationalize my failure to speak up.

I really needed the support of someone I loved, but then I'd visualize Fred's shocked, hurt, and then angry expression. If I told him, I'd have to endure the questions of how and why, questions that I didn't know the answers to myself yet. I'd have to live the experience all over again. I'd have to suffer through not only my own emotions but his, too: his anger being the most obvious, followed very shortly by fear, for my health, for our children, our finances, our relationship. And anyway, I preferred surrounding myself with recovering people only, people who already understood, people with whom I felt safe.

Besides, it was a relief to be the "healthy" Patty at home, the Patty who didn't have the "disease" of addiction. When I was not at the Institute of Living, I could deny to myself that the other Patty existed.

I don't know why Fred didn't suspect something was wrong. I paid all the bills, so for a while I could hide the fact that I wasn't receiving a paycheck. Maybe he didn't guess because he was preoccupied with taking a position with his company in Buffalo, New York. The new job was a great opportunity for him to advance in the company. It would mean more money and validation for him that he was really good at what he did. The negotiations for the position occupied much of his time and attention. The plan was for him to move to Buffalo at the end of the summer. We would join him after our son Ricky graduated from high school the following June. He would be able to come home every other weekend, and whenever else time allowed.

I suppose this made it easier for me to decide not to tell him. I clung to the belief that keeping the truth from him was the smart thing to do. I could get a non-nursing job, and with him far away in Buffalo, he would be none the wiser. Still, I lived in perpetual fear that he would find out.

We weren't fighting and arguing all the time now, but there was constant tension between us. For so very long we had both worn masks, masks that indicated to the world that we were okay. We wanted our children to have an intact family. We went places together as a family and generally enjoyed memorable, good times with our friends and our children. We loved our boys so much, and always wanted the best for them. But we avoided talking about what was really important; I guess we were afraid any discussion would lead to a fight, which would only upset the kids. So, when the day was over and things were pleasant or even just uneventful, we were content, afraid if we began facing all of the buried hurt and anger, the consequences would be disastrous.

So Fred's going to Buffalo became, in a strange way, a gift from God. Sadly, we needed the distance between us. I had an inexplicable sense of peace about it.

ALL DURING THIS PERIOD, I was living "one day at a time"; things were all right, but in a perverse, upside-down way. I was always figuring out how to orchestrate the day, how to keep my secret. If I was able to keep the secret until the end of the day, then I considered that a success. What I didn't grasp was that carrying out this charade was increasing, not decreasing, my stress. Maybe I wasn't physically hiding my drug, but I was hiding other things: my activities, my thoughts, feelings, the truth. In this, I realized I still had an obsession: figuring out how I was going to conceal my activities from my family occupied all of my waking hours, just as thinking about obtaining my drug had once done. I was drug-free but I was still in an addictive behavior pattern.

AT A CERTAIN POINT it became apparent that my son Michael's coughing was more than just a summer cold. By the end of the second week of my treatment he was starting to run a high fever, and his lungs became more congested. I brought him to our pediatrician's office and he confirmed that Michael had pneumonia; he placed him on antibiotics.

Because of this, I was unable to attend treatment for the next week. The counselors at IOL indicated that in their view any interruption in treatment was just an excuse to leave the program. I assured them that I really did need to take care of my son. My husband worked about ten hours a day and I just couldn't leave Michael all day, every day, in his present condition. When I was able to convince them of this, they said I could resume where I left off the next week; all they would need would be a urine sample on whatever day they called me during that week. I had to complete the twenty days, or my participation in the program would be recorded as incomplete.

While taking care of Michael, and taking time off from the program, it was nice to be just a mom again and to reconnect with my kids by being there, at home, for them. I got caught up on housework, which is always satisfying, even though with three boys, the results last less than the adult life span of a mayfly.

My son recovered from his pneumonia rather quickly. By the end of the week he was starting to have more energy and was going outside to play. I don't think he would have recovered quite as well if I hadn't been able to be with him and care for him. At least I wasn't a failure as a mother that week.

Sleep was still very elusive. The fear still awakened me, leaving me gasping for breath. My body had to learn how to sleep without the effects of Stadol, and it was a slow learner. But now I had my mantra: *Everything's going to be all right.* If I kept repeating that to myself, the anxiety would ease up and I could lull myself back to sleep.

Marilyn called frequently to see how I was doing. She knew that I hadn't told my husband yet, so when she left a message on the answering machine, she'd never say anything that would reveal her true identity. When Fred asked who Marilyn was, I would just say she was someone I worked with. But I suspected she was becoming annoyed with this secrecy when she asked me, "How cryptic do I have to be when I call your house?" Sometimes the cloak-and-dagger thing can get tiring.

It is a strange place to be when your life becomes mostly secrets. The secrets become their own reality and the truth becomes blurred. Still, every day I said my prayer, "Please point me in the right direction," so when I couldn't follow in the direction God's finger was pointing, He would give me a shove. Meanwhile, I sustained the illusion of normalcy and kept it alive for as long as I could.

Each friend represents a world in us; a world possibly not born until they arrive, and it is only by this meeting that a new world is born. —Anaïs Nin

CHAPTER 11

Kindred

I RETURNED TO TREATMENT at IOL the following week. By now I had developed some attachments to the other people attending the program. There was Kathy, whom I looked forward to seeing every day. She had a genuine concern for everyone, like a housemother. She was such a gentle soul, and she struggled with this disease every day in a quiet, courageous way. There was Jon, the trucker who was attending the program due to an addiction to marijuana. He had a tough exterior but a gentle heart, as evidenced by the time he brought in a birthday cake for one of the girls from the halfway house, who had been crying the day before about not having anyone in her life who cared enough to celebrate her birthday with her. There was Karina, who had had a baby just a few weeks before. She was on a methadone maintenance program due to an addiction to heroin and was trying to recover to "do right by her kids."

Together we were learning what had brought us to this place at this time, and we found that we had more in common than we had differences. It really didn't matter what our backgrounds were; we became supportive of one another because of the feelings and experiences that linked all of us in this disease.

However, I still felt slightly isolated because I was a nurse. That was the one perspective the rest of the people in the group didn't understand. It was time, I decided, for me to attend a Nurses for Nurses meeting; there was a group in Hartford that met every Monday night. Charlie had been encouraging me to attend it. Every Tuesday morning he'd ask me if I had gone, and I'd have to admit that I hadn't. Finally, one Monday, when I announced that I would be going that evening, he said he was going to hold me to it, and he made me promise the group that I would. Later I tried to think of excuses not to go, but that night, in spite of myself, I attended my first Nurses for Nurses meeting.

THE MEETINGS WERE HELD in a State of Connecticut–owned drug treatment facility, Blue Hills Hospital, in the north end of Hartford. The building looked like an institution run by the state. Its exterior was faux stucco — actually, cinderblocks covered with some cement painted a sickly yellowish tan — with dark brown trim around the doors and windows, which added to the institutional appearance. A chain-link fence surrounded the entire property. On one side was the main entrance, with a small parking lot adjacent to it. When I pulled into the parking lot that first Monday evening and nervously got out of my car, I peered over at the back of the building: some men were hanging around smoking, and others were playing volleyball. I held tightly to my purse and walked quickly to the institutional brown doors that were the main entrance.

Once inside, I asked the guard behind the desk in the small, cluttered, dingy entranceway where the Nurses for Nurses meeting was and if he knew what time it started. He responded that he thought it started at seven (it was now six-thirty), and then he directed me to which hallways to take to get to the conference room it was held in. Eventually, I found myself at the opposite end of the building in a small, but much less dingy lobby. The conference room, which was right off of the lobby the guard had referred to, was locked.

Oh well, nobody's here. I guess I should just go home. I started walking back down the hall. Then I turned around.

No. I'm going to stay. I'm early. Someone will show up when it's time. I sat down on one of the lobby couches.

Then I got up from the couch. *No. I don't want to be here. Maybe I'll come back next week.*

Suddenly I felt incredibly tired and I slumped down onto the couch. I couldn't move; when I tried to rise back up, it was as if I were being held down by the shoulders. *No. I'll stay and see if someone shows up. I hope nobody shows up.*

All of the feelings and regrets that I had had on that first day of treatment at IOL—that this was what my life was all about now, drug rehab and support group meetings—came back to me. But I stayed. I wasn't going to chicken out and have to face the group at IOL in the morning. The waves of anxiety continued to build until the Nurses for Nurses meeting finally began at 7:30.

The first person to arrive was a man. He introduced himself and asked if I was new; he hadn't been there in a while. Two women arrived together, followed soon after by yet a couple more women. Surprisingly, they didn't look like the stereotypical drug addict, like some of the ones in my group at IOL. They all looked like any staff on any floor of any hospital.

"Are you here for Nurses for Nurses?" one of the women asked.

"Yes, I am," I replied.

"Well, welcome. We meet in this conference room, right over here." The heavy feeling left as I nervously rose from the couch and followed the women into the conference room. This room was less dingy than the rest of the facility, with a big dark brown conference table, comfortable chairs, and pale blue walls. I sat in a chair closest to the door (for a quick getaway; it's true what they say about fear: it stands for *f*alse *e*vidence *a*ppearing *r*eal...or *f*uck *e*verything *a*nd *r*un), and the others sat in chairs around the same end of the table.

The meeting was very informal. No one really was the leader. A woman sitting across from me began by asking me my name and how I was doing.

"I'm scared" was all I could manage to say as the tears welled up again.

"We're all here for the same reason," the woman said. "We're nurses who happen to be addicts, or addicts who happen to be nurses. I can't quite figure out which way it is; probably either way is all right, because no matter how you look at it, we're both of those things. But what is important is that we've been right where you are now, and have felt as bewildered and ashamed as you probably do now. We'd like to hear your story, if you want to tell us."

I was so flipping tired of telling my story, but I was able to tell most of it without crying. They listened for as long as I talked, then asked me questions that only they, having been through it, knew to ask. They knew of the special kind of shame a nurse feels. Nurses are more knowledgeable about drugs, so how could we allow ourselves to become addicted? They reminded me that the amount of knowledge we may have doesn't protect us from any disease, addiction included.

They also offered me practical advice about appearing before the board of nursing. They were very happy I had hired Marilyn, and shared how she was the one who'd helped many of them get through that terrible ordeal, not just as a legal counsel, but also as someone who genuinely cared, and advised, almost like a 12-step sponsor.

Suddenly I realized I was with a group of nurses just like me, of addicts just like me. They gave me their phone numbers and encouraged me to call them for any reason, good or bad, happy or sad.

By the end of the meeting, I was exhausted. The fear that was there before I'd attended the meeting was now gone, and I was finally able to relax. Best of all, I knew I'd found a haven, a refuge, a port in the storm. I'd found acceptance. I'd met my future friends, who would help me through the hard times and rejoice with me in the good times. Through their addictions, I'd learn about my addiction; through their recoveries, I'd learn about my own recovery.

THE NEXT MORNING I reported to Charlie and my group that I had attended my first Nurses for Nurses meeting. They clapped. Charlie was genuinely happy that it had been a good experience for me.

That day the director of the program informed me that there was someone she wanted me to meet. She led me to her office, where a woman was seated.

"This is another nurse, Patty," the director said. "She'll be joining our program."

"Hi. My name is Patty," I extended my hand to her.

"Mine is Erin. I am so glad to meet another nurse," the woman said. And so was I.

THE NEXT DAY DURING the lunch break, Erin and I sat in the waiting area and shared our recent lives and our respective drifts into substance abuse. Erin had been abusing opiates. She and her husband were infertile because of Erin's severe endometriosis. She'd stopped taking birth control pills to become pregnant, so now she was ovulating and her endometriosis became active again, which had caused her to develop painful ovarian cysts. She'd had many surgeries, and her doctor had prescribed Percocet for the pain. Eventually, Erin began diverting Percocet, plus Demerol and Morphine, from work.

To my surprise, she had not been confronted by Drug Control but had come to the conclusion that she was addicted all on her own and gotten herself into treatment! I could not imagine myself having had the courage to do that on my own. If I hadn't been caught, I probably would have stayed in my own little stoned world until I'd lost everything.

Erin worked in the ER, and she hadn't told anyone there the real reason she was out, only that she was in the hospital for depression.

"The people at work would never understand," she said. "We see alcoholics and addicts coming through the door all time. The staff hates them. I could never tell them that I'm one of them!" I understood. This attitude was pervasive in the healthcare community.

Erin had had a prolonged and painful inpatient detox at a different facility. Now she was determined *never* to feel that bad again.

"That's what will keep me from ever picking up a drug again. I still have diarrhea and hot and cold sweats. It was the most awful experience of my life."

I told her that I'd gone to my first Nurse for Nurses meeting.

"You know where they are?" she said, looking surprised. "My counselor said it was like a secret society. He asked me to ask around. Ask around? Can you imagine asking other nurses about a support group for those who should be shot?"

I thought about how fortunate I was to have I found out about Nurses for Nurses meetings from the Drug Control agents the day I was confronted. Unlike many other nurses, I had had the benefit of possessing this information from day one. Treatment centers were apparently clueless about this resource, as evidenced by Erin's counselor referring to them as akin to a secret society where you knocked on a back door and whispered, "Guido sent me."

At later Nurses for Nurses meetings, some nurses shared that even when they'd figured out they were addicted, they didn't know that a nurses' substance abuse support group even existed, not until they were confronted by Drug Control and were in serious trouble. And even after they received treatment for their disease, it was impossible to find out information about Nurses for Nurses. They knew they were in trouble, and probably addicted, but didn't know where to turn.

"Anyway," Erin said. "I really want to go to one of their meetings next week. Can I join you?"

Finally there was a nurse with whom I could share my thoughts, feelings, and fears, and she hers with me. We each knew the other's big, deep dark secret that had brought us together. Together, there was nothing we needed to be ashamed of.

To know the road ahead, ask those coming back.

CHAPTER 12

Turmoil

THE NIGHT I WAS TO meet Erin at her first Nurses for Nurses meeting, I went to visit my father at the hospital and discovered that he wasn't in his room. The charge nurse informed me that he had been transferred to Surgical ICU the previous night; she seemed embarrassed that no one in the family had been called. Neither my siblings nor I had been notified of my father's deteriorating condition. I was furious, and scared. This was not the first time this had happened. We were not notified the *last* time he was transferred to ICU, when he had respiratory arrest after his surgery.

When I finally saw him, I found him confused and heavily medicated. Two of my brothers were at his bedside. The sudden change in him was a shock to all of us. He was disoriented, but had never been confused a day in his life. Not only that, his kidneys were failing and he needed dialysis, and he was facing more surgery as the circulation in his legs deteriorated. He would eventually need to have first one and then the other leg amputated.

One of my brothers had already had strong words with the nurse in charge. I did not have the energy to get involved in an argument with a staff member. I had an unrelenting, raw ache in my heart because I could not fight for my dad now. I had barely enough energy to fight for myself and to take care of my boys.

After visiting Dad for a while, I could see that, in spite of everything, the care he was getting was adequate. I told my sister and brothers that I had to be someplace very important, and promised them I'd call the hospital complaint department in the morning.

I felt so conflicted and helpless. My brothers and my sister looked so worried. Because I was the nurse in the family—a blessing and a curse—they'd turn to me for answers and direction in times like these. But I couldn't focus my energies on anything but getting well again. What made it worse was that they had no idea what I was going through. I couldn't share any of my recent experiences with them—or rather, I didn't want to. They were so troubled and upset over our dad's condition, I didn't want them to worry about me, too. Then again, maybe I was more afraid for myself, afraid to reveal that I'd been a drug addict while he was in my care. What would they think of me then? I was afraid they wouldn't understand, that they'd never forgive me.

I was alone as I rode the elevator back down to the lobby. My feelings were all jumbled up, and the ache in my heart was a pounding torture. I looked at the ceiling of the elevator with tears streaming down my face. This was too much to handle. I was supposed to know what to do. Wasn't I supposed to "fix things"? But I couldn't fix things. Not now. My sister and brothers wanted to know why, how, what to do. But I didn't have any answers for them right now. Silently I asked my father to forgive me for abandoning him and my family. By the time I left the building, I was crying so hard I thought I would throw up. Again, I wanted time to speed up to get past all of these wretched feelings of guilt and helplessness. I walked across the parking lot, sobbing, oblivious to the heavy rain and the thunder and lightning. Once in the van, I stopped crying, but the heavy, sad, horrible feeling remained.

I WAS NEARLY LATE for Erin's first Nurses for Nurses meeting. When I arrived, the discussion was centered on Erin and another woman sitting across from her. Apparently, Erin knew her from the ER. At first I thought, *How nice. Someone Erin knows!* This was immediately replaced with *Oh, no! This was what Erin was most afraid of: that someone from work would find out.* When I joined the group that day, Erin's coworker, and others in the room, were trying to convince Erin that (a) the woman wasn't a spy; and (b) she was there for the same reason Erin was. It looked like Erin was getting over her anxiety and was digesting the fact that she truly was safe in the meeting.

They were also discussing how to return to work in a safe way. What did they mean by safe? Weren't we safe now that we'd been through treatment? One of the founding members of the group, Joan, said that she thought it was great that Erin hadn't gotten fired, but it wasn't good that her nurse-manager didn't know the true nature of her illness.

"Returning to work without telling anyone would be very foolish and would practically guarantee a relapse," Joan said. "That Pyxis is going to be calling your name: 'Erin, come get some Demerol. No one will ever know.'" Joan emphasized: "You are only as sick as your secrets."

Does being safe mean having to tell your boss? That would be professional suicide. To me, that was the opposite of safe.

I could tell by the expression on Erin's face that she was thinking the same thing.

"We're addicts. We love secrets," Joan continued. "We thrive on secrets. Our whole lives became a secret. That's how we survived using drugs."

After the meeting, Erin and I talked before heading home. "I am not going to tell anyone at work," she said. "I had the detox from hell. That is my safety net." I was in full agreement with her. Wasn't that why they called it Narcotics Anonymous? Weren't all support groups anonymous to protect the identities of their members? Wasn't that why Nurses for Nurses was a group of anonymous nurse-addicts? Wasn't that why we were there for each other anonymously?

In the middle of August, Erin returned to work.

Religion is for people who are afraid they are going to hell.

Spirituality is for people who have already been there.

CHAPTER 13

Religion

As I continued on with the last two weeks of treatment, and as I surrounded myself with recovering people, the guilt and shame began to lift. I began attending NA and AA meetings, which was a huge step for me. Walking into an NA meeting for the first time was the hardest thing I had done since I went into treatment. It was even harder than Nurses for Nurses. I have always felt insecure and shy when I've found myself in front of a group of people I don't know.

At some meetings I was welcomed with open arms. The sharing of experiences would be unreserved and sincere. There would be enthusiasm for the program and how it had changed their lives. At other meetings, it seemed like the room was full of old, bored, apathetic people who were there against their will. At a few meetings, I felt as if I'd crashed some private party, where everyone knew everyone else and I was an outsider. Of course, some of the negative perceptions were only in my head. That little voice was still talking to me, saying, "You aren't really like these people, these *addicts*."

The more meetings I went to, however, the more I could relate to the others' feelings when they told their stories. I didn't necessarily identify with the facts of their particular lives, but just like at IOL, I saw in them the same compulsion to seek out and use their drug that I had experienced. Some of their stories were so sad, laced with so much abuse, neglect, and despair, that I would be moved to tears. As they related their triumphs in the face of such odds, I would sit there amazed at their accomplishment, and the serenity they now enjoyed.

They spoke of finding their "Higher Power," which could be anything from the Higher Power of NA to whatever their concept of God needed to be at the time. It wasn't important who they chose as their Higher Power, as long as it wasn't themselves, that it was higher than them or their addiction. Having been brought up in the Catholic faith, it was hard for me to accept the idea of a Higher Power being anything but God, Jesus, the Holy Spirit. To me it was heretical even to entertain the notion of the group as a Higher Power. How could it be higher if they were all just people? But as I attended more meetings, I learned that the reason was so simple: acceptance.

So many of the people in the meetings had grown up believing that God was a vengeful, punishing God; and some never had a Higher Power. Now, for the first time in their lives, they were finding unconditional acceptance no matter who they were. At first, they may have needed a Higher Power to be the nonthreatening and loving presence of NA, where they could be honest in their humanness and be accepted with their imperfections. They didn't feel as if they had sinned and needed to be punished, but rather that they needed directions and a map to help them continue with their lives. People's concept of a Higher Power changed and grew as they became stronger in their recovery; and maybe for the first time, some allowed themselves to believe in God, and that He had the power to change their lives if they allowed Him to.

And in the true application of acceptance, they were always welcomed back with open arms, no matter how many times they relapsed. They came to discover that they were not doomed to eternal failure, but rather, they could start their lives over at any time.

As I wrestled with my own religious conflict, I came to realize that this was exactly what Jesus was all about. In His time on earth, He'd demonstrated acceptance of the people He chose to be His closest friends, many of them the outcasts of society. He also said that the kingdom of God was in all of us, which doesn't make us God, but its power allows us to be instruments for Him. God works through people. "Do unto others as you would have others do unto you," and "Love your neighbor as yourself" were really what Jesus was all about. Maybe Jesus was using the Higher Power of the group to bring us all closer to Him. This rang true with my beliefs, because what God really desires is us, and He will use us all to that end.

I experienced more honest spirituality at these meetings than I had ever experienced at church. This was true witnessing of how a Higher Power changed people's lives. After having their will usurped by the power of their addiction, and sometimes in utter desperation, they'd decided to turn their will over to God *as they understood Him,* not from dogma or religion, and not for anybody else. They'd made this decision for themselves, using the free will that God had bestowed on us all.

When I went to meetings, I had to remember that we were all there for the same reason. I was reminded that this disease crosses all levels and conditions of humanness. I concentrated on being more open-minded as I listened to the others, and my *belief* in God gradually grew to be more *trust* in God "to restore me to sanity."

I remembered the first time I asked God to point me in the right direction, and the first day of treatment, when I went to church and looked into those eyes. The stories I'd heard in the group meetings had reinforced the simple principles of humility, and also the simple willingness to "Turn my will and my life over to the care of God as I understood Him." I was beginning to feel the relief of "Let go and let God," but I had to remind myself every day to turn my will over to Him. In my heart I knew that God was pointing the way, but in my head I wanted to know it all now. But he wasn't going to show me too far into the future. He was going to show me through baby steps, so that I could learn *all* that I needed to know to continue on with my life in the fullest way possible.

What I began to experience in short, and then longer, bursts, and then in a more consistent, steady way, was a level of peace and joy so penetrating and intimate it surprised me, and then began to sustain me. One day, while driving, I experienced a near panic attack. Then I had a clear, in fact audible, message from God. It became part of His answer to my plea to please point me in the right direction. *Stay clean and sober and I will show you how wonderful it can be.*

It was this definitive advisement from my Higher Power that would carry me through the difficult times, and would keep me going in the right direction. I wanted to see "how wonderful it can be."

Face life on life's terms.

CHAPTER 14

Legalese Part Deux

"THEY ARE GOING FOR A summary suspension," Marilyn said when she called me one day in the middle of August. "But this is what we expected them to do."

So, my case was under way. I had signed the statement Marilyn drafted for Drug Control, the one that started the process that would determine the fate of my license. I was done with the intensive phase of my treatment at IOL and was attending their aftercare program, a commitment of two afternoons a week, to talk about relapse prevention. It was also a way to ease the newly recovering addict out of the intensity of everyday treatment — basically more group therapy with people who'd been through the program and were at the same stage of recovery.

At the Institute of Living, behind that big protective wall, my concept of *them* and *us* had changed. Just like any hospital, IOL was a place of healing. The people on this side of the wall were no different than those on the other side of the wall. Those of us inside the wall were learning how to adjust and transform our lives. We were learning how to develop healthier responses to the events that produced stress in our lives, so that we wouldn't revert to old patterns of drug or alcohol abuse, depression and isolation, anger and violence.

I was lucky because I had health insurance that had allowed me to attend IOL for quite a long time. Some insurance companies, such as Erin's, decide when you have had enough treatment, and can cut you off right when you're beginning to comprehend your recovery, and thus leave you floundering.

Outside the wall, I had to face the possibility of having my nursing license suspended. I was still holding on to the irrational hope that all this would go away. It was still so unreal to me, the notion that my first love, my nursing career, might be taken away.

"We need to meet so I can tell you what we have to do now," Marilyn said. "How about tomorrow?" Since I was attending aftercare only two afternoons a week, I had a lot of spare time.

"Sure, tomorrow sounds fine," I reluctantly responded. No amount of wishful thinking was going to get the job done or make it go away.

THE NEXT DAY MARILYN outlined what my job was and what we could expect. "You have to write a statement about yourself to the nursing board briefly outlining your nursing career, why you became a nurse, what you love about nursing, and also a little about your family. The most important thing to convey is how important your recovery is to you and what you've learned so far. I'm pretty sure we'll have a good outcome, Patty. Now, some of the board members may be on vacation, so I hope we'll have enough for a quorum."

"What does that mean?" I asked.

"If there aren't at least six members there, they won't be able to vote on your case. And we won't know until that morning."

I was dumbfounded! "You mean we get all of this stuff together, get gussied up and go there, and they might not even have enough people to vote on it? They can just say, 'Oh well, too bad, you'll have to come back when we have enough people.' They don't have the least understanding of how awful this is, do they?"

"That may happen. I don't think it will, but it might." She sighed. "I probably shouldn't even have mentioned it now." She refocused herself and me: "You need to just concentrate on the job you have to do: namely, writing your letter and, most important, continuing to do all the right things for your recovery. I'll need the letter by the end of the week, or at the very latest, right after the weekend."

BEFORE JUNE 28, 1996, I had never given the Connecticut Board of Examiners for Nursing much thought. I had had no clue what kind of people, or how many, sat on the board. The image I had was of a group of dour, wizened geezers sitting around a conference table deciding things about nurses and nursing. To me, and to most other nurses I knew, the board was merely a very distant entity, like the Supreme Court, something you only hear or read about, not something you ever encounter firsthand.

I began to compose my letter that night: "In recovery, we are encouraged to speak from the heart, not from the head." *Yeah, that sounds like a good beginning,* I thought to myself. I described my nursing life in the most abbreviated way I could, trying to convey how important a nursing career was to me. Then I explained what my recovery meant to me, what my recovery plan was, and how important my faith was in the whole scheme of things.

The day before I was to give the letter to Marilyn, I went to church. One of the readings struck me with such clarity and force that I read it over and over, almost forgetting that I was still attending Mass. This was definitely another direct message from God to me, no question about it. It was from the twelfth chapter of Hebrews:

> Since we have such a huge crowd of men of faith watching us from the grandstands, let us strip off anything that slows us down or holds us back, and especially those sins that wrap themselves so tightly around our feet and trip us up; and let us run

> with patience the particular race that God has set before us... So take a new grip with your tired hands, and stand firm on your shaky legs; and mark out a straight, smooth path for your feet so that those who follow you, though weak and lame, will not fall and hurt themselves, but become strong.

This was an expression of renewed faith I could place at the close of my letter to the board.

To complete the packet, I also had to get a letter from Charlie stating that I had finished the Intensive Outpatient Program between July 8 and August 15, and that I was now enrolled in the aftercare program as a willing and active participant. He also had to confirm that all of my urine screens had been negative. Joan wrote a short note for me on Nurses for Nurses letterhead, and Marilyn had to compose her "objection to motion for summary suspension," a three-page document stating the reasons why I was not a threat to the public health of the State of Connecticut, and that this emergency procedure was not necessary. Oh my God, this was such an involved process!

The date set for my summary suspension hearing was August 28. In the week leading up to then, the waves of fear were relentless and powerful. I was so tired of that punched-in-the-stomach feeling. Through the numbing effects of Stadol, I had lost some of my ability to tackle emotions; now my brain had to relearn which stimuli to permit and which to inhibit. I am thoroughly convinced that my brain allowed every fearful stimulus right on through. I also had tremendous cravings, something I hadn't experienced in weeks.

The *only* things I could do was stay in contact with my support system, and attend as many meetings as possible. With all this meeting attendance, I discovered that there was a cause-and-effect relationship between going to a meeting—whether it was Nurses for Nurses, NA, or AA— and my emotional state. At a meeting, my cravings would diminish as I listened and shared about how scared I was. It was really simple: don't use and do go to meetings. With this program, the waves of fear did not completely go away, but they were made more tolerable.

THE MORNING OF AUGUST 28, 1996, was appropriately gray and damp. The Legislative Office Building is a beautiful structure. The room where the nursing board was to meet was on the second floor. On three sides of the room were theater chairs about three rows deep, with each row higher than the one in front of it. The walls, the carpet, and chairs were decorated in various shades of mauve. *I hate mauve.* There was a large, dark-wood dais, which took up much of the room. It curved completely around like an oval corral, with an opening in the front to enter the center of the corral if need be. The board sat facing the room on the backstretch of the corral, while the people with business with the board faced them on the front stretch. Around the perimeter of the room were seats facing the whole corral. Marilyn directed me to sit in the seats on the left side of the room. The board members were all at their places at the far end of the dais. From my perspective, all I could see were their heads. Anyway, I tried not to look at them all that much. I felt like a disgrace to the nursing profession. I just wanted to get their decision and get the hell out of there. Most of them were women around my age, and I think maybe two men, one of whom was quite elderly.

"Are you okay?" Marilyn whispered to me. I couldn't talk: I didn't have an ounce of saliva in my mouth, and my stomach was in knots. I gave Marilyn an indication that I was okay by the slightest of nods. Any increased bodily motion stimulated a wave of nausea.

A tall man came over to us. Marilyn introduced him as the attorney for the Department of Health.

"Hi. Nice to meet you," was all I could manage to say. But it wasn't at all nice to meet him. I felt stupid for even saying that, but at least I was polite.

The board began discussing the agenda for the day, and as we had hoped, I was first on the list. They called my name, and Marilyn and I proceeded to the part of the dais on the left side of the opening. I sat down in the nice cushy chair, and she sat right next to me. The prosecutor was at his place to the right. He stood up and announced for the record who he was, and then passed out to the board members copies of the packet of information outlining the charges against me.

At the appropriate time Marilyn stood up and announced to the board who she was, that she was representing me, and that we were presenting an "objection to the motion for summary suspension." She then passed around copies of our defense packet; she'd had to make fifteen copies of it. The members started reading. Less than five minutes had passed when most of the members indicated that they were finished reading everything. I couldn't believe it! It should have taken them longer than five minutes to read just my statement, let alone all of the rest of the stuff.

"I make a motion not to accept the suspension, to accept the objection," one of the board members said. I was confused. It all sounded like a bunch of double negatives.

"I second it," another said

"All those in favor?" the chairperson said, and with that, several hands went up.

"Opposed?" she asked. With that, two hands went up.

Marilyn was keeping a tally sheet with the members' names on it. Very seriously, she thanked the board, and then told me to go out in the hallway.

I wasn't sure what they accepted and didn't accept or if my license was suspended or not! I was so tense and drained; I was unable to comprehend what happened. Marilyn and I went out into the hallway.

"Did we win?" I asked her.

Her seriousness gave way to a wide grin and she replied, while chuckling, "Yes!" She extended her arms and gave me a big hug.

My license was not being suspended, and I could look for a new job. The relief I felt was overwhelming. I didn't know how to respond, except by saying, "Thank you."

"Do you want to stay and see the next case?" Marilyn asked.

Do I want hot tar dripped in my nose? I didn't want to spend any more time in that room with those people than I had to.

"It may help for you to see what the process is like," she continued. After all, the nightmare wasn't over. The next step was a hearing before the board, where they could still revoke my license, but that wouldn't be until January.

"No, no. I just want to go home."

I wanted to get out of that building as fast as I could. I felt dazed, and very alone. Marilyn told me that she would call me at home later that day. I cried tears of relief mixed with regret the whole thirty minutes it took to get home.

At home, I tried a few times to call Erin, but I got no answer. I suddenly felt overwhelmingly exhausted. I flopped down on the bed and fell asleep.

I WOKE UP TO the telephone ringing. It was Erin, crying and telling me that she was in IOL again, this time in detox. She had relapsed. She had not been able to stay away from her drug for even one night at work. All of the triggers—the sights, sounds, and smells of the ER—had been right there waiting for her addiction to reawaken. She was sobbing and apologizing. She had also been discovered by Drug Control.

"I guess I'm going to need Marilyn's number," she said. "They didn't fire me. My boss said she wants me well and she wants me back. I'm going to use my short-term disability and stay out of work for as long as I can. The fact that they didn't fire me is a freaking miracle." I could hear her blowing her nose. "Patty, I thought that I wasn't going to be one of those relapsers! But it was like a switch went off in my head, and I went from a rational person to an irrational person. I was on auto pilot. I was using as much or more of what I'd stopped using back in July. It's true what they say: you pick up right where you left off." Her voice drifted off into soft sobs.

I had a mixture of emotions about her relapse: shock, fear, and then anger. I felt like she hadn't even tried, that she'd gone through so much for nothing. Was relapsing as easy as that? If I ever went back to labor and delivery, would I be just as high a risk for relapse?

Joan at Nurses for Nurses had been right. Willpower alone was not going to keep Erin or me from our drugs. We had to learn what it meant to practice our profession safely. We had a lot to learn about addiction. We had a lot to learn about this powerful, cunning, and baffling disease. We had to learn to listen to those who'd been there and who'd experienced this disease over time.

When the horse dies, dismount.

CHAPTER 15

Deliverance

I WAS NOT PREPARED FOR what happened. How could God have used the U.S. Postal Service to "deliver" the news. The envelope had a return address in some obscure midwestern town, so I'd left it on the kitchen table and continued cleaning up the supper dishes. We'd been very busy all day, packing up Fred's stuff for his move to Buffalo, and had eaten late.

I finished cleaning up the kitchen and walked into the bedroom. My husband was looking over at me with the strangest expression on his face. "Why is our insurance telling us they've paid two thousand dollars to the Institute of Living?" he asked.

OH MY GOD! I was immobilized with acute, startling panic. Calmly I denied that I knew anything about it, and that it must be some mistake. *I needed to prepare! I had to plan what I was going to say!* I knew that I'd had many chances to prepare what I wanted to say to him, but this was just too soon! Quickly, and as nonchalantly as possible, but with my stomach churning, I headed for the bathroom, as if I were going to get ready for bed.

Oh my God. Oh my God. Oh my God. Do I have to leave this bathroom? What am I going to do? The answer was clear: nothing. I would do nothing! I left the bathroom without losing my supper and walked calmly back into the bedroom and lay down without saying anything.

"Are you sure you don't know anything about this?" Fred asked again. He was still examining the insurance document.

"Yes, I'm sure," I answered, trying to sound annoyed. Right then, I knew that I couldn't deny the whole damn thing anymore. But I couldn't tell him face-to-face, either.

FOR HOURS, THE WAVES of fear would not allow me to sleep. When I did fall asleep, I woke up with that near-drowning feeling. I wished I had access to a drug, any drug. When daylight was just breaking, I left Fred lying asleep in bed, made myself a cup of coffee, sat at the kitchen table, and wrote him a letter explaining everything.

So, that's how I "told" my husband. A letter allowed me to express myself in a less confused, less defensive way. For me, it was the only way.

I needed this shield. I truly believed that my mental health was at risk, and I was afraid that a confrontation or fight with Fred would bring me to a dangerous point. With a face-to-face confrontation, the emotional pain would have been intolerable. With a letter, I could tell him what happened and what I was now doing about it, and how sorry I was — mostly for having kept it all from him. With a letter, there would be no interruptions, no outbursts, no body language that would make me react with hysterical fear and guilt. I left the letter in his suitcase with the clothes he would be wearing for the next couple of days.

AFTER HE READ MY letter up in Buffalo, Fred called me. As expected, he was confused, hurt, and angry. I was scared and apologetic, and crying hysterically, as I tried to explain it all. In that long telephone conversation that day, I tried to reassure him that I was getting better. I had been too ashamed to tell him, I explained, but also too afraid.

He understood the ashamed part, but couldn't understand the afraid part. "What did you think I would do to you?" he asked.

"Just what you're doing now: acting angry and hurt," I replied. "It would have been too much for me to take, having to come home to questions I couldn't answer, because I didn't know the answers myself."

It was a long, tearful, difficult phone call. I tried to convey to him in that one talk, all that had transpired in the last several months. I wanted him to understand it, to accept it right then and there. I could only hope that he would be able to see I was trying as hard as I could. I could only hope that he could keep loving me long enough to see the results. For him, too, it would be a long and agonizing process.

WHEN FRED CAME HOME a few days later, we told the kids what had happened. I didn't want to face them, but I knew it was necessary. Fred and I explained that I had an illness. We tried to reassure them that I was getting all the help I was supposed to, and doing what I was supposed to be doing. I told them that my new friend Marilyn was going to help me keep my nursing license. Most important, we reassured them that we all would be okay, and that we would be together as a family just as soon as we could. Fred reminded them that since he wouldn't be living with us at home for a while, they would have to help me out.

Telling the boys was so difficult. I was crying so hard, and felt like such a failure as a mother—until all three hugged me and told me they loved me and believed in me, and just wanted me to get better. It was a relief not to have to carry that secret burden around any longer. I have the best boys in the world.

Each day, somewhere in the world, recovery begins when one addict talks with another addict, sharing experience, strength, and hope.

CHAPTER 16

Sponsor-Angel

TO THOROUGHLY ASSIMILATE and incorporate addiction into my identity was still a painful struggle for me. No one would have known from watching me. To others, I looked compliant, but in truth I was not fully ready to commit myself to the total responsibility of my recovery. Much of my motivation, in spite of all I was learning, was still keeping my nursing license, and therefore doing whatever I thought would look good to the board of nursing. If it were left up to me, I would have tailored involvement in recovery to my own comfort zone.

I was attending the aftercare program three afternoons a week, NA or AA meetings two or three times a week for the 12-step support, and Nurses for Nurses once a week. The rest of the time I spent sleeping, watching TV, doing housework, or talking on the phone with Erin or Marilyn. This was all I had energy for. I didn't have time or energy for anyone outside my recovery group.

Everyone — from the counselors at IOL, to my friends at Nurses for Nurses, to Marilyn — had stressed to me that I needed to get myself a sponsor. But how did one go about this? Did I just ask someone? Were there people with specific qualifications whom I should look for? Did it have to be someone from an NA group, or could it be someone from Nurses for Nurses? Afraid of being rejected and embarrassed, I had not yet asked anyone. The fear of losing my license, however, kept me moving forward, forced me to do the right things. So, I would get a sponsor.

In many ways, Marilyn was my first sponsor. She was acutely aware that this was going to be a very difficult process to endure from a legal perspective and she knew that most of my motivation was the preservation of my nursing license. But she also wanted me to recover, she wanted me to "get" recovery, to understand it and embrace it. She knew that my license wouldn't mean anything if I didn't develop a meaningful recovery. For someone who wasn't an addict, or a drug and alcohol counselor, she was remarkably wise about this disease. The nurses at Nurses for Nurses whom Marilyn had represented frequently mentioned how they "couldn't have done it without her." We agreed that, in the beginning, our recoveries would have been quickly off-track it if it hadn't been for Marilyn's "boot camp of recovery."

I prayed to God for a sponsor. I didn't ask for someone with specific qualities, because I figured God knew what I needed. There were a few qualities that NA thought important, however: sponsors should be of the same sex; they should have at least one year of clean time; and they should have worked the 12 steps with their own sponsors.

Then there were the qualities that I wanted: I wanted someone who was wise, whom I could talk to, who would be more of a guide than a boss. I wanted someone who had a good sense of humor, and who was not afraid to laugh at herself. I wanted someone who would be available to me if I found myself in a crisis, or if I just needed to talk. She had to have a solid faith and trust in her Higher Power. I didn't sit down and compose a list of these qualities, but God knew what I needed, and once again pointed me in the right direction. After attending Nurses for Nurses for several weeks, it became clear that one of the women there was what I needed and wanted in a sponsor. God pointed me to Sue.

SUE WASN'T ONE OF the more talkative members, but whenever she shared, the group would pay very close attention. To me, whatever she said made sense. Often she was able to refocus an intense discussion and boil it down to a simple principle, such as "Do the right things for the right reasons," or "Think it through, think it through." She had all of the other qualities I wanted in a sponsor, plus the requirements NA recommended.

Sue's story really helped me comprehend what a powerful illness addiction is. If the definition of insanity is "doing the same thing over and over again and expecting different results," then her story perfectly illustrated the insanity of this disease.

Sue was an ER nurse, wife, and the mother of two teenagers when she was confronted by Drug Control. Like me, she'd been caring for her father while trying to do everything else, and be perfect at the same time. While she was on probation with the nursing board, she continued to use drugs. She turned in urine samples that were not her own. She forged prescriptions. She was arrested. She finally reached her bottom in a jail cell where she had what recovery literature calls "a transforming spiritual experience," and surrendered to the power of her illness. Still, her nursing license was revoked.

Her recovery became her priority. She fought the long uphill battle, one day at a time. Without recovery, she knew she wouldn't have her life. Sue was forthcoming with her story to addicts new to the program. When I met her she had been clean and recovering for five years.

Sue believes that the answers lie in the 12 Steps of Recovery, which she believes are the foundation of a good recovery. She is aware how all-consuming and stressful it is to prepare to go before the nursing board. Considering that the board action tends to fall right at the most vulnerable time for a recovering nurse-addict, Sue becomes a listening ear, an encouraging presence to those who feel like their world is falling down around them.

Sue said, "In the beginning, it's so hard. The nurse has to get through treatment; deal with her employment; start going to meetings; find a therapist; hire a lawyer; face the board; her whole family is in turmoil; her whole life has been turned upside down. She is depressed, guilty, and anxious, and she has to try to do it all without using any of the drugs that she needed to help her cope in the first place! This disciplinary system is such a *huge* hindrance to a nurse trying so hard to find her recovery."

Sue and I would meet for coffee after the meetings. She made me feel at ease. I was still shy being forthcoming about myself in the group, but with Sue, I knew I could share intimacies with her that I could not share with anyone else. I knew I had her full attention during our sponsor sessions. She always gave me homework; usually recovery literature to read that would help me through the particular issue I had that week. As my sponsor, Sue has played one of the most important roles in my recovery. I love her now as a friend and have come to cherish her humor, common sense, and support. She helped me embrace recovery, and incorporate that recovery into my identity. She has shown me how to live my recovery.

Honesty is the first chapter in the Book of Wisdom.

CHAPTER 17

Emerging

THE SUMMER THAT HAD been so depressing, gray, and damp was giving way to the golden and gentle radiance of late summer. I could hardly believe that summer was almost over. There was a hint of crispness in the evening air during Labor Day weekend. I have always loved the fall. The fatigue and sluggishness I usually experienced at summer's end gradually gave way to enthusiasm and renewed energy and hope. Soon, the changing season would so visibly alter the landscape, and by winter it would be almost unrecognizable.

I, too, was changing in an immeasurable way, in a way I couldn't even have conceived of just a few short weeks ago. I was not the same person at the end of this season that I was in the beginning. I felt as if I had lived an entire lifetime in two months. The depression was slowly fading. I was sleeping better.

I had become so accustomed to feeling scared, depressed, and ashamed that I was surprised by these positive feelings. *How could I possibly be happy? I am a cash-poor, unemployed, diabetic, drug-addicted nurse with three teenagers, a distant husband, and a dying father.* It didn't make any sense, but that penetrating peace I had already begun to experience way down deep inside of me was surfacing. *Was this the "peace that surpasses all understanding" that you hear about in church?*

I had to take an active role in my recovery. Every morning I would read my recovery books and pray. If I needed her, I'd call Sue, and the waves of fear would be calmed. I found that my recovery was waking up my happiness. I started counting my blessings: I had a roof over my head, enough food to feed my family, children who were healthy, and clothes to keep us warm. And I had wonderful new people in my life whom I could call whenever I felt fearful about the future.

My trust in my Higher Power was increasing. I knew that He was absolutely and positively pointing me in the right direction. I was trying to live the way He wanted me to, in honesty. All this was breaking down the walls around my secret world, the prison I had built for myself.

I was also trying to be honest with my husband and share with him some of the things I'd been learning about addiction, about *my* addiction, and to convey to him what my recovery meant to me. His reactions were unpredictable at times. Sometimes he would be distant, sometimes angry. Sometimes he would be suspicious that I was trying to hide something from him again. I couldn't help his reactions; if I was going to continue to get healthy, I could only do what was right for me. I needed to remember that it was a learning process for him, too, but I had difficulty being patient with him. I resented having to educate him when I had so much work to do for myself. And of course my need for instant gratification dictated that he understand everything as soon as the words left my mouth.

It was scary for him. Being in Buffalo, away from home, he couldn't observe what was happening every day. He was worried about the welfare of the kids. Did he feel helpless because he couldn't do anything to help me? Probably. He was a bystander, watching me change. It was hard for him to believe, and even harder for him to acknowledge, that his wife of more than twenty years, the person he shared his life with, the woman with whom he'd had his children, the one he thought he knew and could trust, was a drug addict.

It was hard for me to admit that I wasn't trusted, especially by my own husband. But I was determined to earn back his trust. I wanted our marriage to work, and the only way it would was if I was honest.

Through the lessons that recovery teaches, I was evolving. And I wouldn't move on to the next stage until I'd learned whatever given lesson was facing me in the present. One of the lessons for me had been Erin's relapse. Another was trying, as best I could, to honestly explain to Fred what I was going through, regardless of his reaction. I could not let *my* secrets keep me sick.

AT THE NEXT NURSES FOR NURSES meeting, the discussion centered on our relationships and how well or not our spouses or partners were coping with and responding to our recovery. Sue said that we were the lucky ones. "We have all sorts of help, but our spouses don't. Patty, Fred isn't even home to see how you're doing. It sounds like he's really scared. Usually the anger is there because of their fear. *You* just keep doing the right things for *yourself* and your recovery, and everything else will fall into place."

Erin had decided that she was going to divorce her husband. "I only married him for his sperm, and that hasn't worked out. No matter how much marriage counseling we've done, it doesn't change the fact that I am married to an asshole. He's still smoking pot and drinking even though I explained to him that I can't be around that stuff anymore. He says I'm always at meetings, so how are we supposed to have a marriage? I know we aren't supposed to make big relationship decisions in the first year, but if I stay married to him, I can't stay sober."

Sue said, "We won't judge you here. We're here to support you in the decisions you make for a life that make sense."

A few weeks later, I met Erin for lunch. She told me that she'd met someone at IOL, when she was in outpatient for the second time. His name was Paul. "I've never felt this way about anyone, Patty. He kissed me and my knees buckled. We promised each other that if one of us relapsed, we would step back from the relationship."

I was dumbfounded. She wasn't even divorced yet. This didn't make sense, but still, I wanted my friend to be happy.

Erin's summary suspension hearing took place in November. She did not get suspended. Paul was there with her.

"Who was *that*?" Marilyn asked when she called me after the hearing.

"Erin's friend. She met him at IOL. She said that if either one of them relapses they'll end the relationship."

"It just sounds like addictive behavior to me," Marilyn replied.

Erin must have sensed this, too. For a long time, she didn't tell Nurses for Nurses about Paul.

But enough about me, what do you *think of me?*

CHAPTER 18

Quack

I HAD TO GET ESTABLISHED with a therapist, another one of those things I wouldn't have done if it hadn't been a requirement of the boot camp. I was told that a therapist could help me coordinate obtaining urine toxicologies, and would be the one to tell me when to report to the lab. To me, it was just another friggin' person to whom I would have to relate my story.

I found a group of therapists through the network caregiver-provider booklet that came with our health insurance plan. They were listed under "Substance Abuse Specialists." I selected one, a woman, from the list. After I told her some of my story on the phone, she referred me to one of her associates, stating that he was more familiar with drugs and professionals. She assured me that he had clients that were in my situation. I called the number she gave me and made an appointment with him.

A WEEK LATER, I was seated in a comfortable chair in a small room, across from Dr. Martin. He tipped his hand to me as if to say, "Tell me about yourself." So I told him my story. I talked and talked and talked. He sat and sat and sat. I told my story in chronological order, right up until the minute I'd walked into his office that day. I tried to be as honest as possible, with my emotions as well as my story.

All through my account, he displayed no reaction; he only sat and stared at me, as if I were a lab rat. Occasionally he wrote something on the pad in his lap.

I felt uneasy, very self-conscious, and baffled as to what I should do next, so I just stopped talking. It was like a chess game, but I didn't know if it was my move or not.

"Is that it?" he asked dryly.

"Yes," I replied.

"It seems like you're doing all the right things, Pat," he remarked. "Just continue to do what you're doing, and you'll be fine. Our time is up. Shall we schedule an appointment for next week?" I tried to ask him about the urine testing, but he said that we could take care of those details at the next session.

I left the office and returned home not knowing if I'd had a good session or a bad one. I didn't feel any better, but I figured that he'd just needed to get the initial information from me, and get to know me a little. I figured our next session would be more productive.

Marilyn called me that afternoon to ask me how the session had gone, and I related what had happened.

"I don't trust him," she said.

"What do you mean you don't trust him?" I asked

"I don't have a good feeling about him. We need someone who can testify before the board, someone whom we can trust to give good supportive testimony. From what you have told me so far, I don't trust him."

"Well, I have an appointment for next week. Maybe we'll know better at that time," I said.

"Maybe," Marilyn replied. "Please don't misunderstand me, Patty. If this is the therapist that you connect with then that's great. That's what's most important, and you certainly won't know that until at least one more session. But just because he calls himself a therapist doesn't automatically mean he's any good. Please let me know how it's going, okay?"

THE NEXT WEEK I met with him again, at which time he seemed more concerned about my insurance coverage — taking up more than half the time to see if I'd been preapproved for therapy — than my mental health. He asked me how my week had gone.

"I have to give urine toxicologies, and I need to have you help me arrange them so that we can have a bunch before I go for my hearing."

"I really don't know anything about that, or how to do that," he curtly replied.

I was surprised. I had thought that that was one of the things we were going to take care of in this session. I felt intimidated by his attitude, and even embarrassed that I'd asked. In our previous session, while I was telling him all about the nursing board and what I was facing, he'd kept nodding his head, as if he understood, but now he was blowing me off and acting as if he didn't care or wasn't willing to help. I spent the rest of the session providing him with more details about my childhood, adolescence, and young adulthood.

"Wow, you really don't have anything in your background that would indicate you'd end up a drug addict, do you?" he said.

"I guess not. I'm still confused as to how this happened."

"Didn't you learn anything in treatment?"

I didn't know if this was a question or criticism. I just shrugged my shoulders. I was feeling guilty about being confused and, alternately confused about feeling guilty.

"By the way," he said abruptly. "I really like your shoes, where did you get them? I'd like to get those for my wife."

I am pouring my heart out here, and all he's been thinking about are my shoes*?*

I never went back to him after that.

I DID FINALLY FIND out that I could arrange to get my urine toxicologies done through IOL. I told Charlie I needed clean urine samples for my case, so he called the Medical Services Unit to make the arrangements. They said that everything was set, and they would be in touch with me. About two weeks went by and I didn't hear from them. When Charlie called them again, they apologized. Somehow no one had followed up on my request. Again they said that they would be in touch with me.

Now, since this was supposed to be a random specimen, and I was not supposed to know when they'd call me, I didn't attempt to contact them. I didn't want it to look like I was trying to control when I had to give a urine sample. Still, another two weeks went by without my hearing from them, so after one of my aftercare sessions, I marched to the Medical Services Unit and stayed there until the all the *i*'s were dotted and *t*'s crossed. We arranged that I would give them a specimen once a week, and they would send it to a forensics lab in New York.

With these tests, the "chain of custody"—that is, the method for ensuring that a specimen is protected from contamination or alteration—had to be maintained. Someone would have to observe me producing the urine sample, preventing me from altering it in any way. The specimen would then be carefully sealed in a container, and the container signed by the collection monitor and me. Then some very involved paperwork would accompany the specimen to the lab in New York, to ensure that the urine leaving the collection site was in fact mine. At the lab, technicians would have to carry out more chain-of-custody procedures to prevent the specimen from being contaminated in any way. Then the report would be placed in a specially sealed envelope, again designed to continue and preserve the chain of custody, and mailed to the psychiatrist in charge of Addiction Recovery Services at the Institute. I never knew when I'd be called to go. If I was called by 8:00 A.M., I'd have to travel the 20 miles up to Hartford by 3:00 P.M.

THE PAST FEW WEEKS had been really frustrating. I was glad to have finally gotten the urine testing straightened out, but there was quite a large block of time between my first urine tests, performed during my treatment, and those being done now. Marilyn was concerned that the prosecution would make this gap in tests look like I hadn't gotten tested because I was using, and that the nursing board would also see this as the only viable explanation. She did reassure me, though, that it was good I was getting weekly urines now, and that we should have plenty of them by the time of the hearing.

There was no doubt, however, that I needed to get a different therapist, but it was not a good time to be switching therapists, that is, only five or six weeks prior to the hearing; the nursing board might see this as "therapist jumping." Switching therapists may be a sign that a person is still using drugs. The suspecting therapist may ask for a urine drug test, so instead of being found out, the individual starts all over with a new therapist. But, here I was advocating for my own health, my recovery, and I might be screwed for it. How twisted was that?

However, I needed a therapist who was actually going to help me recover, and one who could write a positive report to the nursing board. Marilyn gave me the names of a few therapists some of her other clients were happy with.

I was feeling pretty sorry for myself. My life was not my own and I was being jerked around like a puppet. At times like this, I would be so disgusted with myself and what I'd gotten myself into that I didn't want to face anyone, any group, or anything to do with addiction or recovery or pee. I had other things to do. I wanted to start looking for a job. I wanted a normal life again. I wanted what I wanted when I wanted it. Nothing was going smoothly. I was just fucking pissed off.

Once again it struck me that there was no system, no direction, no one to tell me the rules. At Nurses for Nurses, we frequently discussed just this problem. One of the members voiced her anger at the situation:

"How are we supposed to know how to do all of this stuff that the board wants? No one from there or DPH tells us what to do. But we're fucked if we don't do it, right? If it weren't for Marilyn and her 'boot camp,' we'd be so screwed, and so revoked!"

Sue acknowledged that the system was terribly broken, damaging, and prejudicial, but she reminded me to put first things first, and to do the right things for the right reasons. She reassured me that I had done a good job in pursuing the urine toxicologies, and now I had to use that same determination to find a therapist who was right *for me*, and who'd help me recover, because I deserved it. She reminded me that whenever I resisted, things usually got worse; and when I accepted whatever was happening, things got better. I needed to "accept the things I could not change." She reminded me that I had to do the footwork and let God do the rest.

When the student is ready, the teacher appears.

CHAPTER 19

The Great Oak

THE WAITING ROOM WAS empty when I first arrived at the office of Dr. Adam Jaffe, the doctor I'd chosen from Marilyn's list. The doors to the three offices off the waiting area were closed. Each had a different person's name and qualifying initials on it. The place was very quiet, no muffled voices or any other signs of life. I sat on one of the two couches available and hoped that I had the right time and the right day. There was no receptionist there to confirm my appointment time. After about ten minutes, a nice looking man in his mid-thirties with curly brown hair, glasses, and a beard entered the waiting room.

"Hello. Are you Patricia?" he asked.

"Yes," I acknowledged.

"I'm Adam Jaffe. Please come in," he said and extended his hand for me to shake. I followed him into a small office with a blue striped couch on one side of the room and a desk positioned up against the wall. I sat on the couch, and Dr. Jaffe behind his desk. Dr. Jaffe readied himself with a pad of paper and a pen.

"How are you doing, Patricia?"

I gave a flat and guarded response of "I'm okay." I wondered how he was interpreting my noncommittal reply. I guess I was leery of baring my soul again, especially after the experience I'd had with the first therapist. We began the session talking about my experience with that other therapist.

"I don't feel like he helped me at all," I explained. "I was led to think that he was an addiction specialist and knew about the issues with the nursing board. But he didn't know anything! I did *not* feel comfortable or in any way restored." I related how the first doctor had had a judgmental, impatient, and patronizing attitude toward me and my addiction. I also told Dr. Jaffe about the first therapist's "shoe" comment, which he got quite a chuckle out of.

Dr. Jaffe agreed that the first therapist was not right for me, that it just hadn't been a good match, but that that doctor might be the right match for someone else. Then he said, "Why don't you tell me what's happened and where you are now in terms of your recovery, your nursing license, or whatever else you feel is important at this time. I may interrupt you at some points if I need clarification. Or if there is somewhere else that you'd like to start with, something more pressing you'd like to discuss, then feel free. Does that work for you?"

I looked out of the tall window to my right. Dominating my view was a large oak tree. We were on the second floor, so the canopy of the tree was in my line of vision. It being winter, there were no leaves on the branches, so the tree was laid open to anything the cold wind blew its way. I suddenly felt as bereft and exposed as that old tree.

"I think that my substance abuse is as logical a place to start as any," I replied. "I've never had anything like this happen to me before. I've never been in any trouble with my nursing career or my life until now," I said as I looked downward and self-consciously shrugged my shoulders as the urge to cry arose from deep within me again.

I was trying so hard not to cry, but as soon as I mentioned my father, the dam broke. God, I wished that I could get through this just once without crying. *He's going to think I'm pathetic. He's going to think that these last six months of recovery haven't helped me at all.*

"I can see that it is still very painful to talk about. His tone was reassuring, even comforting. "Take as long as you need. Crying is very healing, Patty, even though it may feel unbearable at the time."

"If that's the case, I should be cured by now," I responded with a hint of a grin through the tears. I was able to divulge the rest of the events with relative composure, with the occasional tear sneaking through. I told him about my impending nursing board action, and how scared I was.

Dr. Jaffe occasionally interrupted, but his interruptions were not intrusive. He instinctively knew when I needed time to contemplate or reflect for a moment. Before I knew it, the session was half over. The time had gone by so fast. Never once did I feel like a lab rat. Dr. Jaffe was professional yet compassionate. I began to relax as a sense of trust infiltrated my guarded bearing.

"What you've told me so far has been very helpful, Patty. You're still experiencing so much, so the feelings of being overwhelmed and depressed are just as I would expect in a normally functioning individual facing this much stress. We can't forget that you may not be functioning completely normally yet as a result of your drug use. I don't know if that's true, but it might be. Your brain is still healing itself. That's not to say that I think you're crazy or anything like that. Quite the contrary. I think you're doing remarkably well. I admire your courage and determination, and it's clear to me you've come a long way in the last six months. You've established a solid support system for your recovery, and that is no small task.

"As I mentioned before, the relationship between a therapist and a client has to be a good match. You have already experienced a bad match for you. Now I'd like to tell you a little of my beliefs and my philosophy so we can determine if this will be a good and therapeutic relationship. You've told me what your spiritual background is and how it has been such a great source of strength in your recovery. I'd like to tell you what I believe, and then we can determine if this will still be a good match."

He put the paper and pen down and, tenting his hands, continued. "You're familiar with metaphors, right?"

I indicated that I was.

He continued: "I think they're a wonderful way to help us illustrate a point, or help us understand a situation. I'd like to use a metaphor to illustrate what I believe. I believe that all of the religions of the world can teach us something. I believe that God has sent many teachers and that He wants us to gain from the wisdom of each and every one. I believe what Buddha said, and that is that we are all on our own spiritual journey, and one of the ways he illustrated this was to imagine that we were all in vessels or boats traveling down a river.

"The boats are all different colors, shapes, and sizes, and each one represents all of the different religions of the world. The people in the boats are all individuals with their own lives; however, they have the same religious philosophy as all of the other people in their boat. The river that all of the boats are in is going in only one direction, and that direction is to the ocean. I see the ocean as a metaphor for heaven, or God. To me it doesn't matter what boat we're in, only that we're in it, and heading for the same destination. In fact, many of the religions of the world extol exactly the same virtues, and have expressions that are very similar. If you read the teachings of Buddha, and of Jesus, they're very much the same. Does that make any sense to you?"

It made perfect sense to me! I often wondered why there were so many religions in the world. Why did God allow that? The religious teaching I experienced as a child had taught me that there was only "one true church," and a nun once told me that even Protestants were going to hell because they no longer belonged to the "one true church." It didn't make any sense to me even then — that God, who is all-knowing, loving, and *who made all of us* in His image and likeness, would disregard millions of His children because they weren't born into the Catholic faith. I had felt for a long time that *all* religions help people uphold the qualities of peace and brotherhood, and guide us in issues of morality, honor, and ethics; but most important give us knowledge of a Higher Power and our spirituality.

I loved Dr. Jaffe's metaphor. However, what he said next made even a more powerful impression on me.

"What I truly believe — and I came to this assurance by study, meditation, and through a crisis in my own life — is that *we are spiritual beings having a human experience,* not just that we are humans imbued with a spirit. The spirit is who we really are, and our time here on earth is but a very, very small part of our whole experience."

I sat up straighter on the couch. There was an excitement within me, and I was feeling an authentic connection. I knew that Dr. Jaffe was the therapist I needed to have. The spirituality he talked of touched my heart and soul. Moreover, I felt that I was in the presence of a sagacious, insightful teacher.

"I think that we would be a good match," I said as I looked out at the oak tree again. "I need someone with some spiritual wisdom, because as much as I believe, I don't feel very strong right now. Facing the nursing board in a few weeks is something I shudder to think about, and I don't feel ready. I know that I'm doing all the right stuff, but the only way I can cope with it is to not think about it. I'm really scared." I was crying again. "I don't want to lose my license."

Dr. Jaffe replied, "First of all, I'm happy that you think I can help you, Patty, because I think I can also. The way I like to begin to approach all of this is to imagine that we have a toolbox. In this toolbox are different tools you can use to help you in your recovery and as you face the nursing board. Some of the tools are ones that you're already using, such as Nurses for Nurses, NA and AA, your sponsor, and so on. Another tool is our sessions here. But also in this toolbox are methods that may help with stressful situations, your anxiety level, and your cravings, should you have any. Visualization and meditation are two of the methods I'm thinking of. Visualization is the easier of the two. You can employ it anywhere you are or in any situation. Meditation requires some training and a quiet space. We'll have that in our toolbox if we need it. If these aren't effective, there may be a more biochemical problem, which will need to be addressed with antidepressants and anxiolytic agents.

"We have a lot to talk about Patty," he continued. "But the most important thing I have to do, what my job is right now, is to help prepare you to face the nursing board, with *grace and ease*."

"'Grace and ease'! That phrase and the nursing board don't belong in the same breath," I retorted.

"You can face them with grace and ease if we use visualization to call upon your higher self to communicate with their higher selves. The people on the nursing board are not any different from you or me. They are human beings with good days and bad days; their own personal problems, joys, and fears. So what I want you do to, Patty, between now and the next time we meet, is to practice visualizing your higher self speaking to their higher selves, and I believe that at that level they won't see you as just an addict—which is what you're afraid of. So, let's practice this exercise right here. Close your eyes..."

I closed my eyes.

Dr. Jaffe's voice became softer and the cadence slower but deliberate. "Now take one or two deep breaths and relax. Imagine that you're filling yourself up with light and that light is pure love. It is the love you have for yourself; it is the love of God. Love and fear cannot reside in the same place, so as the light of love becomes brighter and fills you up, the fear begins to recede and you have a feeling of relaxation and peace. Now that you're in touch with your higher self, convey this to the "higher selves" of the board. You have the advantage of already having seen what they look like, so you'll be able to visualize each one of them."

When I opened my eyes, I found I had not been able to suppress the fear very well, but I did feel better.

Dr. Jaffe continued: "Always remember that we are all spiritual beings having a human experience. They have no real power over you. No matter what they do or say, if they revoke your nursing license, or even if one of them takes a gun out and shoots you — I realize that is not a reality, but I just want to make a point — they cannot hurt or harm you. You will still be Patty. That will not, nor will it ever, change. You can surround yourself with the light of love and create a shell, a shell of light and love, around yourself, so that whatever they say that may be negative, it cannot penetrate."

I sat on the couch for a few moments, staring out the window at the oak tree. I was *still* afraid of the power the nursing board had over my nursing license. Being a nurse was so integral to who I was, and so precious to me, but what Dr. Jaffe had said was a reality I had not considered. In order for them to see that I was deserving of my nursing license in spite of my disease of addiction, and in order for me to convince them that my recovery was the priority in my life, I would have to discover, nourish, and sustain the qualities of grace and ease. In the process of preparing me to go before the nursing board, Dr. Jaffe would help me rediscover my self-worth and value.

"What are you thinking, Patty?" Dr. Jaffe's voice was soft, almost inaudible, as it tried to gently become part of my thoughts, not an interruption.

"I've been staring at that oak tree."

"Is that tree a metaphor for how you're feeling?"

"Yeah, I guess so," I said as I continued staring at the tree.

Dr. Jaffe continued: "The strength of that tree comes from within. It has strong roots that anchor it deep into the earth, that no one can see, but it knows they're there. It is an illusion of itself. Do you understand what I'm saying?"

"I understood the first part, about the roots, but not the illusion part."

"The illusion is the appearance of the tree, which is not what it really is. It looks dead, but it is full of life. When the time is right, God will allow the tree to show its life and beauty. When the time is right, God will supply the tree with the warmth, light, and water it needs, and the tree will use just what it needs to sustain itself or to grow."

"Yeah. I guess I'll have to trust God to give me exactly what I need when I need it."

Our time was up for this session, but I could have spent the rest of the day there. I would have to pay out of pocket for Dr. Jaffe, and at the time I could barely afford him. But I knew that I couldn't afford *not* to have him. God was still pointing me in the right direction. Like my new friends at Nurses for Nurses, like Erin, like Sue, and like Marilyn, Dr. Jaffe was another wonderful person who'd been added to my life. At the next session, I was able to drop the formality of calling him Dr. Jaffe when he invited me to address him as Adam.

Pain is inevitable... suffering is optional.

CHAPTER 20

Losing It

THE CHRISTMAS SEASON was in evidence everywhere I went. I usually love this time of year, but during this particular Christmas, I wasn't able to savor all of the "warm and fuzzy" feelings. For me it was more "cold and itchy." Fred and I shopped for the kids as best we could, considering that our finances were pretty strained. As a couple, we were doing all right. Fred told me he was proud of me, and it was good to have him home for Christmas.

I decorated the house, listened to seasonal music, and lit pine-scented candles. But no matter what I did, it didn't change the fact that I just wanted the whole season to be over. I was slipping back into the gray depression. I tried to remember the fact that this holiday was the celebration of Christ's birth, the event that had changed the world forever.

Although I was grateful for the event, and prayed for my serenity to return, prayed to be delivered from the vacuous grayness, it seemed to be sucking me in once again, and the waves of fear were back in full force. I hadn't expected this. Was I losing whatever peace and serenity I'd found? Was I losing my recovery? If I was, I wanted it back. The obsession about my hearing, which was looming ever closer, took on a life of its own. As much as I tried, I could not keep grace and ease in the forefront. I felt like I was losing my mind.

"I am afraid I'm going crazy," I told Adam in one of our sessions. "I feel like I'm close to losing control of my sanity. Sometimes I feel like at the very next moment I'm going to totally lose touch with all reality and curl up in a ball in the corner of the room."

Forcefully, Adam said, "You're not crazy, and you're not close to going crazy." It was a good tactic, because instantly I felt reassured, redirected. "When you feel like you're going to lose it, call me, or someone else you trust, to help you organize your thoughts and take some of that fear away. You'll have to accept that you'll feel some fear, but remember, Patty, you *can* face the next few weeks with grace and ease."

I was still reading my recovery books, and going to my meetings. And I talked to my friends in Nurses for Nurses, especially Sue. They reminded me that facing the nursing board was truly one of the most exhausting and distressing experiences any nurse could have, so what I was feeling was appropriate. They reminded me that Christmas can be a very depressing time for many people, especially if they're going through a particularly hard period.

Sue advised me that it was okay to experience all these emotions, and that I didn't have to feel guilty about them. In fact, she said that she would be more worried if I weren't feeling bad, or if I were denying what I was truly feeling. She reminded me that I wasn't in danger of losing my recovery just because I had fear or depression. I would be in danger of losing it if I weren't honest or didn't share what I was feeling—or numbed those feelings with drugs. Just because I was having a good recovery didn't mean I was never going to experience adverse or painful events in my life. It might seem scary to feel bad; and as addicts, we don't know how to "feel emotional pain" very well, because we're so used to numbing out the bad feelings. It was all part of living life on life's terms.

"This will pass. It won't be forever," she said.

The fear and depression didn't totally leave, but the load, no matter how heavy, was lightened, made more bearable, every time I was willing to be honest and share, so that the people who supported me could help.

I was so blessed to have Adam as my therapist. Others were not as lucky. Like Erin, some of the other members of Nurses for Nurses had already been in therapy for other reasons, and their therapists usually had no idea there was a substance abuse problem until they were informed by their client after a confrontation by Drug Control. I was truly surprised by the reaction of some of these therapists. Erin's therapist commented that "it was stupid thing to do. Why didn't you have more control?" Erin was in group therapy with three other women. The therapist leading the group was very controlling, and Erin usually felt even guiltier after her therapy. Marilyn called that therapist the "cult mother": "God help them if they disobey!"

Another therapist, when she heard her client's tearful description of what had happened to her, of how ashamed she was and how sorry she'd kept her drug abuse from her, asked her client to stop whining. Yet another told a nurse in our group that she talked too much.

With Adam, I knew I could be as emotional as I needed to be, and could talk as much as I wanted. I never felt intimidated, and I wasn't worried he'd be angry if I couldn't concentrate well enough to have one thought flow into the next thought, or if my talk was disjointed and rambling or it disintegrated into flights of ideas. Actually, these sessions were the most productive because I would be speaking from an inner need, trying to articulate and make sense of pure emotion that heretofore had had no outlet or voice. I would be amazed as Adam ferreted out information from me and organized it. He would be able to locate the theme and focus on it. He didn't just hear the words; he heard the *need*, and responded to it.

In the few weeks leading up to my hearing, under Adam's tutelage, and with his talent for pacing, I began regaining that sense of hope and enthusiasm I had had at summer's end. Although most of my conscious moments were consumed with thoughts of facing the nursing board, we were able to excavate the wellspring of strength and spirit that had been buried so deep inside me for so long. I couldn't possibly face the nursing board with an attitude of one who was damned, one deserving to be punished. I couldn't live in a well of unworthiness. The hope and enthusiasm Adam helped me rediscover were gifts—a portal back to my true self. Adam was the key to the door, and the guide on the pilgrimage.

God speaks through others.

CHAPTER 21

Willingness

FROM THE BEGINNING of the New Year, my hearing before the nursing board was all I could think about. The hearing was set for January 22. Until then the fear resurfaced every morning, and I would spend most of my day trying to regain my serenity. At times, no matter how much I prayed, or how frequently I visualized, or how deeply I meditated, I could not escape the fear that I might not be allowed to work as a nurse again. I was consumed with *What if...what if?*

All through this my addiction lay in wait, hidden in the crevices of my perception, ever ready to attack again, gathering energy like a coiled snake ready to spring, so present, so unpredictable. It was waiting for that first misstep, the slightest hint of vulnerability. And I knew it was powerful enough to overcome rational thought. *You don't have to feel all this pain. I can help you feel better. You aren't sleeping? Let me help you sleep. No one will find out. You're smart. You can fool them.* It was times like these, when my cravings spoke to me, that were the most difficult. And those were the times I had to use my recovery tools.

Sue helped me see that this was what addiction was: the irrational, compulsive craving that overwhelmed all rational motivation. "It comes from the primitive part of our brains that initially taught humans how to survive. It is the pleasure-reward circuit. The purpose of recovery is to retrain the higher parts of our brains to take over when the cravings creep up on us. That rational part teaches us to do the things we need to do to live, like going to a meeting or calling your sponsor or someone else in recovery." It was simple, but it was not easy.

Through reports from others who had been through the disciplinary process, I had come to learn that not only could the Department of Health be manipulative and downright sneaky, but also the Connecticut Board of Nurse Examiners had a reputation for being unpredictable with their decisions. By some accounts, their findings seemed to have little basis in fact, but seemed instead to reflect the prevailing mood of the board that day.

Despite this knowledge, I reminded myself "to accept the things I cannot change." Events were going to move forward and unfold how they would in spite of my attitude or how much apprehension I was experiencing. I was powerless. When I feel threatened and scared like this, I tend to crawl inside my shell. If it weren't for the people and support I had in my life at the time, I honestly don't know if I would have been able to cope with, or prepare for, this hugely stressful episode in my life.

ADAM ENCOURAGED ME TO continue to use the visualization technique that would make the board members seem less threatening, and I asked my higher self, my spiritual self, to convey me to the board as more than just a drug-addicted nurse.

"Have a passion for the process and not for the outcome, Patty," he said at one of our sessions.

"But, Adam, this isn't just some term paper I simply want to get a good grade on. I am heavily invested in this particular outcome. And this process sucks."

"I know the outcome is immensely important to you. In no way am I trying to diminish that, but I am convinced that if we change our focus to the process, and have a passion for it, we do a better job. We're more focused, then, on the task we're doing, and I believe that when we have a passion for the process the outcome is always positive, because then it becomes what it's supposed to be. The outcome is God's. How does that feel to you, Patty?"

"I don't know. I never thought about it that way. I think that I'm too scared right now."

"All I am asking is that you consider this approach."

Although I couldn't connect the principle with my emotions, this one aphorism stuck in my brain like the song that refuses to leave. I prayed for God to take from me this obsession with the outcome. I had no choice about "doing" the process. I wasn't passionate; I was terrified.

At another session we talked about synchronicity. "Have you ever heard the saying that there are no coincidences?" Adam asked me. I said that I had. "When you start to see the synchronicity of different events of your life, well, then you can't help but notice it more and more. I find that it's really fun to notice synchronicity between seemingly unrelated events, because it helps in our understanding of the whole picture of life, and that all of the events in our lives are very synchronistic. Life happens. We are constantly interacting with each other whether we are aware of it or not. Look for the synchronicity and it will amaze you."

He continued, "One of the clearest synchronicities I see for you is that your husband had the *opportunity* and then *chose* to go to Buffalo exactly at the time you needed to recover and recapture who you were, on your own, by yourself. I know that he was not aware of your addiction at that time, or maybe he was, on some level. It is possible that he needed to have his own lesson in all of this."

I looked out at the oak tree outside his office window. "It's God working in our lives, isn't it? Maybe the only way to save our marriage was to separate, but we didn't know it. It just happened. It's a whole different perspective when you try to see it that way," I said.

When it's clear to Adam that I understand a given lesson, or have some insight into a situation, he closes his eyes for a second, leans back in his chair, and brings his hands together, raising them to his face. He then smiles like Mona Lisa, and nods. I feel a great deal of joy at these times and I imagine that he does, too, as we both savor the moment.

My sessions with Adam always left me feeling that a burden had been lifted. I felt transcended to some degree for the rest of the day. Though I wasn't able to carry that feeling for the rest of the week, until the next session—I wasn't emotionally healthy enough to do that—I knew I could get another much-needed dose of encouragement and support at the next session.

AT NURSES FOR NURSES, I was enfolded in understanding and love. This was the kind of understanding that could only have come from people who'd "been there," who knew the particular agony of the disciplinary process. They were the voice of encouragement because they knew that I would get through it as long as I paid attention, stayed connected, and, most important, stayed clean and sober.

The program. The steps. The basics. This is when it works. This was the medicine that would keep me well, keep my disease at bay. "It works if you work it, so work it; you're worth it" or "You'll die if you don't" is how many meetings end.

Sue, my sponsor, was a constant and faithful source of encouragement and support. "You'll get through this, Patty. Just do the right things for the right reasons. Do the footwork and let God do the rest. Start really working on the first three steps—the basics. Read step one: 'We admitted that we were powerless over our addiction, that our lives had become unmanageable.' This one is all about surrendering our reservations about recovery. It is very personal. Think about where you are in this step."

Sue continued, "Step two, 'We came to believe that a Power greater than ourselves could restore us to sanity.' I know that you have a very deep faith, but we need to apply the three principles of honesty, open-mindedness and willingness so that we don't defeat ourselves.

"Take real time with step three. 'We made a decision to turn our will and our lives over to the care of God as we understand Him.' This step helps us move away from self-will."

"We'll work on them formally after this is all over. You can call me anytime. It's your job to call me."

I could call her anytime, even if I just needed to empty myself of anxiety with rambling monologues of regret or self-pity. She made me laugh at myself and helped me gain perspective.

"I pray to see signs of God's will. Sometimes they aren't easy to recognize because they conflict with what I want to do, but if I look for God's will every morning when I wake up, I have a much better day, and a lot more peace. All we have to do is be *willing*, and then God will help us with the rest."

Adam also focused on will. "Having free will also means *we can ask* for what we want. God gave us free will—*such a gift*—the free will *to ask*! 'Ask and you shall receive.'" To me, free will had meant only the action. I had the free will to *do* whatever I wanted. Grasping the notion that I had the free will to *ask* for what I wanted took me to a whole new level of understanding. Realizing I had the free will to *ask* made God more tangible for me.

I had the free will to ask for a good outcome. I could pray to see signs of His will. I could be willing to carry them out, and trust God to do the rest.

Step three: Make a decision to turn my will and my life over to the care of God as I understand Him. Let Him have the investment of this outcome.

Have a good day, unless of course you have other plans.

CHAPTER 22

The Passionate Process

AS FAR AS FACING the nursing board, Marilyn was indispensible. The vulnerability that comes with lost self-esteem makes us susceptible, and even willing, to accept any punishment imposed, even those that are unfair. I knew I didn't have the knowledge, experience, or emotional capacity to defend myself effectively. Since the Department of Health had assigned a lawyer to work to the best of his ability to prosecute me, I had a right and a responsibility to defend myself the best way possible.

Three weeks before the hearing, Marilyn and I met to prepare ourselves. Her office is in her home, and since we don't live very far from each other, she invited me over. I woke up experiencing the type of migraine that would normally have kept me from going anywhere. The strobe effect of the sun shining through the barren trees as I drove to Marilyn's house enhanced the nausea and pain I was already experiencing. By the time I arrived at her house, I wished that I had elected to stay at home in my own bed with my heating pad on and the shades drawn.

"Are you sick? You look sick," Marilyn said.

"I have a bad headache," I replied. "Can I use your bathroom, please?" I thought I would be sick, but after I splashed some cold water on my face, the nausea began to subside. I rejoined Marilyn, sitting at her kitchen table with my head in one hand and paper and pencil in the other.

"We're going to use the documentation from the summary suspension packet, but we need a lot more for the hearing. You need to ask your counselor at IOL for a discharge summary from when you were in the day program. And we need to obtain all of the urine reports from when you were in treatment, and those since then. How often are you getting them done?"

"Once a week."

"These are all random, right? You never know when they're going to call you; there's no prearrangement of any kind?"

"No. If they don't call me by eight in the morning, then I don't have to go that day."

"Good, then they should have several of those reports. All of your urines from treatment were negative, right?"

"Charlie said they were in the report he turned in for the summary suspension."

Marilyn continued: "Well, you have to get those reports, not a statement, but the actual lab reports. I'd also like to have as many letters of support you can get. Who can you get letters from?"

I knew I could get letters from Erin and Sue, and there was a member of my aftercare group at IOL with whom I'd become friendly, a former priest recovering from alcoholism. I was fairly certain he would give me a letter. The only adult member of my family who knew about my addiction was my husband, and I was sure he would compose a letter as well.

Marilyn told me that she'd need all of this documentation in about a week and a half.

Ooooh, boy!

"We need to have Adam testify at the hearing, but I don't know if he can on such short notice. At the very least, we need a letter from him. I hope he'll be able to give the board a prognosis. I'm not worried, because he does write a great letter."

Marilyn then proceeded to scroll through the questions she would ask me on the day of the hearing. Some of them were basically about some of my history as a nurse. She asked if I had ever had a problem before with substance abuse. Then she asked me to describe what it was like on the day I was confronted, what my treatment had consisted of, and what I'd learned in treatment and if I thought it had been helpful. Then there were more questions about what my recovery consisted of now, and how I felt about that.

I'd have to explain why I'd needed to switch therapists when I had, and how I thought my therapy was going now. At the end she wanted me to tell the board what my recovery meant to me personally. "It means everything to me" seemed contrived. I told Marilyn I would have to think about that one.

She informed me that we would meet again the day before the hearing, but that we'd be in touch frequently until then.

My head was now pounding more than ever.

"Oh, Patty, you look like you feel just terrible," she said. "Let me fix you some lunch. I have some turkey soup I made. Let me heat it up for you."

The warmth of the turkey soup and the cup of tea accompanied it soothed my nausea, and the aching in my head lessened. We talked about our kids, and laughed about some other things not related to my addiction, recovery, or the hearing. I saw again that Marilyn genuinely cared, and willingly extended herself beyond the role of lawyer.

I SPENT THE NEXT two weeks gathering the reports and letters I would need. I saw Charlie the very next day and told him what I needed. He said that he would provide me with a summary of my treatment, and he would make it a priority, but a week later I still did not have the document from him, and I was a nervous wreck. When I reminded him, he said, "Oh, my God! You need it that soon? I'm so sorry! I'll have it for you by the next session." I continued to be a nervous wreck until I had it in my hand.

Marilyn was happy with the summary. It outlined my treatment and explained that I was engaged in my recovery, and that the prognosis for me was extremely favorable. I asked Charlie for my reports on the urine drug toxicologies that had been done when I was in the day treatment program, as well as the reports from the New York lab doing the chain-of-custody urines now. Since the reports were going to the psychiatrist at IOL, Charlie was going to have to get them from him, but he assured me he would take care of it. Time was getting short. I was now a colossal nervous wreck of a woman.

I got a wonderfully supportive letter from Bob, the former priest; a sponsor letter from Sue that outlined how we had been working on the foundation of my recovery with the first three of the twelve steps; and Erin composed her letter. Even Paul wrote a letter to attest to the fact that I was attending my support group meetings. I would frequently see Erin and Paul at the same meetings.

Whether I was embracing the passion for the process or not, the process was proceeding.

Marriage is the glue that keeps you together until you fall back in love again.

CHAPTER 23

Hurting

THE WEEKEND BEFORE my hearing, most of the country was gripped in a huge cold wave. The Midwest had been locked in ice and below-zero temperatures for weeks. We did not have much precipitation in Connecticut, but the wind was so cold it was painful to endure.

My husband decided it would be a good time to come home, since he had a three-day weekend due to Martin Luther King Day. He'd been home for two weeks over the Christmas holiday, but the kids really missed him and were looking forward to having him home again. I, on the other hand, had very mixed feelings.

My anxiety level was right back up to that of six months ago, when Drug Control confronted me. I couldn't eat unless I forced myself, and I had to constantly make adjustments with my insulin to accommodate this lack of appetite. I couldn't sleep, and when I was able to fall asleep, the drowning fear would awaken me over and over. I was exhausted. I felt like I was trudging through mud in an effort to carry out the simple activities of daily living.

I had not yet composed my statement to the board. I had tried several times, but the words were not there. I knew how important my recovery was to me; it did mean everything to me. It was changing me. It was awesome. It was too deep and intimate for simple definition or narration. How could I possibly make them understand something that was changing me from the inside out? I was afraid that the nursing board would misinterpret my words as shallow and trite, or that, without intending to, I would somehow incriminate myself.

The waves of fear were once again paralyzing me. In our telephone conversations, I tried to explain to my husband that this was the most frightening experience I had ever had to face, and that I was finding my statement hard and painful to compose. I'd need some time alone to do that.

"I just need some peace and quiet, so it would be great if you did things with the kids that would take them out of the house," I told him during one conversation.

"It just sounds like you just don't want me around," he said. I felt guilty and then angry. It wasn't just him. I didn't want *anyone* around. I needed to be alone! I needed him to take care of the boys, and the boys needed to see him. He did not, or could not, realize how utterly terrified I was.

He decided to take the train home instead of renting a car and driving. Michael and I met him at the Springfield train station. He looked very tired. Michael leaped across the room and gave him a big hug and kiss. He gave me a light kiss and then we went to the car. As I drove us home, we had a strained conversation about my preparations for the hearing, and then, when we were about halfway home, he said, "What if I don't write a letter?"

"*What?* What do you mean? You won't write a letter?" I was so stunned, so hurt by his question, that I ached to the very center of my being. "Why don't you think you can write a letter?" I asked.

"I didn't say I wouldn't. Just tell me what it would mean if I didn't. Is it so important to your case?"

Shocked, confused, and with the ache increasing, I could barely catch my breath. I replied, "It's *just* the only letter I'll be able to get from *any* member of my family, since I haven't been able to tell any of them because Dad is so sick right now. If you feel you can't do it then *just don't*!" Now I was furiously sobbing. "This is the worst thing I've ever been through. I really need your help right now. I don't know what kind of an impact it will have on the nursing board's decision if there isn't a letter from you, but if you can't, then don't!" I tried to calm myself, but fury had overtaken me. "So why don't you think you can write a letter? Why can't you support me?"

"How do I know if you're doing okay? I'm stuck up in Buffalo. I have no one to talk to. I don't know what's going on."

"You talk to me every day on the phone; you were just home for two weeks. You told me you were proud of me. What was that all about? You know that I'm doing all the things I'm supposed to be doing. I know it's hard for you to understand all of this. *Ugh.* Just forget it!"

Even in my confused and enraged state of mind, I knew I could not be a support person for him, and keep myself sane. I was too physically exhausted, and mentally and emotionally depleted, to try to convince him that I was getting better. He needed a place to share his feelings and be with people who had been through a similar predicament.

After a few tense silent minutes, I said with forced calmness, "Go to an Al-Anon or Nar-Anon meeting. All you have to do is call the number in the phone book and they'll tell you where the meetings are. You need to talk to people who are experiencing the same emotions you are. I just can't have this now! I can't deal with all of your anger now, not with what I have to do and what I have to face in the next few days. Please try to understand that this is hell for me." I cried all the way home. There was silence from Fred. Michael was in the farthest backseat in the van. It looked like he was sleeping.

THE NEXT DAY, SATURDAY, I was no closer to composing my statement, and my husband was no closer to understanding my terror. We had a huge argument. He told me that I had brought all this on myself, and that maybe I shouldn't be a nurse anymore. The tension was so bad that I knew I couldn't write my statement in that house.

I had a longtime friend named Judy, an attorney. I'd contacted her after I was terminated from the first hospital. That morning, I called her, weeping, "I don't know what I am going to do! I have to compose my statement by Monday, but I can't do it here. Can I come to your house?" She said she had to go to the office the next day, but that I could spend the day there and compose it.

When I walked into the bedroom, I found Fred staring out the window. I took a deep breath and sucked in all of the courage that might be in the air.

"Judy is going to pick me up tomorrow morning and take me to her office. I have to write my statement for the nursing board so Marilyn can have it on Monday. I can't write it here. There's too much tension. I'm not getting what I asked for, and that is some space, peace, and quiet."

Against my determination not to, I began to cry. "Fred, please, this is so hard for me . . . " My words hung in the air, waiting for a place to land, but then dissipated in the intensity of silence that was as thick and disorienting as pea soup fog. I stopped striving to make him understand.

The grim realization took hold that no matter what I said, I couldn't *make* him understand. I wanted him to hold me, comfort me, and say, "Don't worry, we'll get through this together." I wanted him to console me by reminding me that I was the same woman, wife, mother, and nurse whom he had shared his life with for more than twenty-two years.

I needed the same unconditional support I had had from him when he was encouraging me through the labor and birth of our three boys. He couldn't take away the pain then, either, but he was just there, helping me cope, letting me cling to and squeeze his hand when the pain was unbearable. As he had then, I now wanted to hear him whisper in my ear, "Come on, Patty! I know you can do this! Not too much longer. We're almost there."

Only there was no such response, just silence, a silence that made me sink back into the black hole of guilt and shame and regret. After a few moments, he turned from the window with an expression of anger mixed with the most intense sadness I'd ever seen. He walked past me and through the door without saying a word. I had never felt so lonely.

I didn't want to leave—but I had to. I was filled with too much confusion and self-doubt even to think straight, let alone compose any definitive statement about myself.

The rest of Saturday and on into Sunday, until Judy picked me up, Fred and I didn't say a word to each other. I was relieved just to get in Judy's car and leave. I had no regrets about this decision. I had some nagging regrets about leaving the kids, but Fred was a great dad, so I knew the boys would be okay.

At 10:00 A.M., Judy went into her office, and I went into the front conference room with some recovery books and a notebook. With silence and concentration, considerable prayer and tears, and many rewrites, by 5:00 P.M., I had composed a handwritten rough draft of a statement I was satisfied with. During that afternoon, Judy periodically asked me if I needed any help, and when she heard me crying, she would made sure I was okay just by letting me know she was there. Mostly she gave me what I needed the most—the solitude that allowed me the mental clarity to do what I had to do.

We committed the final copy to print. Judy then composed her letter of support. The only thing left to do was to fax the two to Marilyn for approval. It was about 7:00 P.M. when we finally left her office and headed home. Needless to say, I was emotionally wrung out and physically exhausted.

THE IMPORTANT FOURTH STEP in the twelve steps is to make a "fearless and moral inventory of ourselves." This can be a very painful and forbidding task. Feeling ready to work on this particular step is a very personal thing; some people are ready sooner than others. But it shouldn't be rushed. The recovering addict has to be in the right frame of mind, and in the right place in her recovery. And she has to be "fearless," in the sense of free from fear, as well as courageous. If the step is attempted too soon, or completed too fast, recovery is not enhanced, and may even be hindered.

Composing my statement for the nursing board was like working on the fourth step before I was ready. I had too much fear to be courageous. Writing the statement was more traumatic for me than healing. The disciplinary process was actually interfering with the timing of my recovery, because for several weeks after my hearing, writing about the fourth step was something I couldn't bring myself to do. With the help and support of my sponsor, however, I concentrated on the first three steps, which restored me to sanity again after the insanity of the hearing.

WHEN I CAME HOME, I found my husband staring out of the bedroom window again. He stated that he was very hurt that we only had these few days together; how could I have left him for the whole day?

"What about your children? Aren't they reason enough to come home?" I asked. "*Please* try to understand that this is the most horrendous, most terrifying situation I have ever been in. I asked just for some peace and quiet, or for you to at least hold off any arguments until after all of this was over—but you couldn't. You just couldn't put some of your anger—or whatever you're feeling—aside long enough to see what I needed. That's why I went to Judy's office. I didn't want to leave, but you gave me no other choice."

I was too tired for all of this. I needed to crawl into bed and sleep. He seemed so closed off and distant. Angry? Sad? Scared? I didn't know anymore, and right then I didn't care. I just knew that I had absolutely nothing left to give. I could barely form a sentence because of the profound fatigue I was feeling. I went out to the living room to sleep on the couch. At first, I slept very deeply, but the rest of the night I tossed and turned, and endured more waves of fear.

I FELL DEEPLY ASLEEP again somewhere around six o'clock. Then, at around nine, soft tapping coming from the kitchen awakened me. I took a few moments to wake up and then walked in to the kitchen. The soft tapping was coming from the keyboard of my husband's laptop. He looked up at me briefly, then looked back down at the computer screen. Tears were streaming down his face.

"Can you read this to see if it's okay?" he said through a sob. "I don't know exactly what Marilyn or the board wants in my letter. I tried the best I could to give them a picture of how tough it was for you with your father here. I think that's important for them to know."

"Just speak from your heart" was all I could say through my own tears. I sat down at the table next to him, and he turned the computer screen my way. It was difficult to focus on the screen, but I read a letter that was filled with love and support, and also hints of bitterness about the time that Dad was in my care—but that was okay because he was speaking from his heart. The two of us sat next to each other crying.

"It's a great letter. Thank you," I said.

I truly was grateful for that letter, and I knew how difficult it had been for him to write it, but I was too wounded and exhausted to allow this letter to be a vehicle for forgiveness. As we sat there crying, I started to feel strange, disconnected. It seemed like my senses were filtering stimuli from the outside world. Colors became muted, and sounds became muffled. I got up from the table and tried to concentrate on my surroundings, but to no avail. It was not a conscious act, it was just happening. I didn't feel lightheaded or anything like that; nor was I afraid of this feeling. It was like I was in a "brown-out." After I took a shower, the sensation left. But during the rest of that day, I vacillated between the brown-out and normalcy.

"I HAVE TO GO up to IOL and get my urine toxicology reports this morning," I told Fred. "Then I have to bring your letter and the reports over to Marilyn's house." I was looking forward to being alone for a couple of hours — in the car, playing the music I enjoyed. No statement left to prepare, nobody talking to me. I needed some solitude, a chance to reflect and try to use one of my tools, meditation or visualization.

"Do you want me to come with you?" Fred asked.

"Okay." I don't know if he heard the reluctance in my voice.

He added, "Since the boys are off today, and I have to go back to Buffalo, I'd really like to do something relaxing, like taking them to play pool. We should do something as a family, so why don't we do what you have to do, and then we can come back and pick up the boys."

"What time do you have to be at the train station?" I asked

"By six."

Six o'clock couldn't come fast enough. At another time in my life, I would have enjoyed the prospect of doing something as a family. But on this day my entire being was consumed with my appearance before the nursing board.

Fred and I went to IOL for Charlie's reports, and then took that, Fred's statement, and a copy of my own statement to Marilyn's. Although I had completed everything that was required of me to that point, it did not dispel my feelings of acute apprehension and dread. They just wouldn't leave.

We picked up the boys and went to play pool. I was crawling out of my skin with anxiety.

Having to face the board of nursing could make you want to use drugs whether you're an addict or not!

IT WAS FINALLY TIME to bring Fred back to Springfield so that he could catch the train to Buffalo.

"Good luck tomorrow," he said as he boarded the train. "You know I'll be thinking about you all day. I love you."

I was filled with so many conflicting emotions saying goodbye to him. On the one hand, I felt so betrayed and hurt by his behavior over the past three days that I couldn't wait for him to leave. On the other hand, I was grateful for his letter, and worried about his well-being so far away in Buffalo. Once the train left, however, complete exhaustion took over, outweighing everything else. I was functioning on pure willpower just to put one foot in front of the other. I was too weary even to care.

I know now that Fred was mad at my disease rather than at me, and he didn't know what to do with all of his fear and anger. He had held his emotions in for so long because he didn't know what to say. This was his crisis, too. He also loved my nursing career, and he felt helpless and afraid that there was nothing concrete he could do to help, or to fix it or me.

I met Erin at her house and we went to Nurses for Nurses. The timing for this meeting was a gift from God. I wanted and needed to be surrounded by the unconditional support of this group. I shared all of what happened over the last few days, which helped me process some of my conflicting emotions. Sue reminded me that I just needed to do the necessary things to get thorough the next few days, and through the hearing. I needed to get back to basics — eat sensibly and try to get some sleep.

"Even if it as basic as washing your face and brushing your teeth, keep it simple," she said. "Do what Marilyn says to do, because, remember, you aren't going through this alone: she is there; we are there. You can't look to your husband for support right now; he's just not ready. Acceptance means accepting what *is* right now, not what you want it to be. Accept that Fred is really scared for you, and himself, and he doesn't know how to process that yet. Hopefully, he'll come around, but in the meantime, do what you have to do for yourself.

"Patty, you have a good, solid recovery and you have so much spirituality. You've done all of the right things for your recovery *and* for the board. If you can stay focused on that, then the board will see that you're sincere about your recovery."

Once again, I found myself so thankful to be in the company of the people in this group. I felt enfolded and uplifted enough to get through the next few days. I left that meeting with more peace than I'd entered it with, and even a little serenity. I knew I wouldn't be able to feel any undiminished serenity until the excruciating ordeal of the hearing was over.

As much as I wanted his complete and unmitigated support, I had to accept that Fred needed to deal with his own fears, doubts, and mistrust of me. Still, I couldn't accept the stinging reality that I had created many of those fears, doubts, and mistrusts in our relationship with my drug abuse, and by my keeping it a secret for so long, even after I had been confronted. It would take me a long time to forgive Fred for his unmerciful attitude and his refusal even to try to console me in my anguish and fear. I did not expect him to understand it, just to recognize that I needed him now more than ever. True, he had his own timetable for acceptance, but I didn't know if our marriage would survive the wait.

Face your deficiencies and acknowledge them, but do not let them master you. Let them teach you patience, sweetness, insight. When we do the best that we can, we never know what miracle is wrought in our life, or in the life of another. —Helen Keller

CHAPTER 24

Laboring

IT WAS THE DAY BEFORE my hearing. I had to meet with Marilyn to finish preparing my testimony, and gather the information to prove that I was in fact in recovery. After my boys kissed me goodbye before leaving for school, I dragged myself out of bed. As I heard them laughing and kidding around on their way out the door, I was somewhat reassured that all I was going through didn't seem to be adversely affecting them.

Generally I answered their questions when they had any. I told them that I had learned to ask for help when I needed it and not to stuff all my bad feelings inside. I left out a lot of the details about my drug use, though. I was afraid I would destroy in their minds the image of the mommy who could make everything better. I don't know if this was a good choice, but it was the one I made at the time. Mostly, I depended on my prayers to God to be answered—to please take care of the boys, protect them, and keep them happy, until I could again be the mother I desired to be for them.

I HARDLY SLEPT AGAIN that night. My sleep deprivation was now at a critical level. In the shower, my head cleared somewhat, but any physical movement required a lot of effort. *How am I going to do this? How much more can I take? How long can a person go without sleep?* I wished I could be left alone for a week—with no one to talk to, nothing to prepare for, no responsibilities for myself, my kids, or my home. I needed to stare at nothing, sleep, and vegetate.

When I arrived at Marilyn's house for the final phase of preparation, she asked me about my weekend with Fred, and I told her how things had gone.

"He sounds like he's really scared and, like a man, wants to fix it, but I have to tell you, Patty, I'm furious with him for this. This whole thing is stressful enough without..." She took a deep breath. "I need you to be able to testify on your behalf and show the board of nursing that you're serious about your recovery. You can't look like an emotional basket case. You need to focus on *yourself* now, Patty, and not this past weekend. Try to put this in the back of your mind at least until the hearing is over; then you can deal with your marriage."

After a short pause she continued gently, "He did write a really great letter, though. He sounds like he's really struggling with his own emotions, but he does love you. Just try to think of that."

I glanced sideways at her. "I'll try, but I really can't go there right now. I can't think of him at all if I want to get through this."

We walked downstairs to her office, and I sat down in front of her desk. Marilyn sat down next to me. I noticed that her whole expression had changed—she was clearly worried about something.

"Did you see any of the urine reports they gave you from IOL?" she asked, looking directly at me from a distance of about ten inches.

"No," I replied. "I just brought the envelope over here. I never opened it. Why?" I was starting to have a panicky feeling in the middle of my chest. I couldn't imagine what could be wrong. Marilyn handed me a report dated July 24.

"I have to tell you, Patty, that I hardly got any sleep last night because of this," she said, handing me the report. My eyes tried to take in all the information on that page. On the left side of the page were the classifications of drugs they tested me for, the normal ranges and so on, and on the far right side of the page, a column listing the results. One word stood out. Right in the middle of the page was the word *POSITIVE*. I looked over to the class of drug it indicated: barbiturate. At the bottom of the page was the specific drug: butalbital. I wasn't familiar with this particular generic name. I didn't even know how to pronounce it, so I sounded it out phonetically.

"What is bu-tal-bit-al?" I asked, giving the same weight to each syllable.

"It's but-AL-bit-al," Marilyn said, correcting my pronunciation, "and I think it's Fiorinal."

"Fiorinal?" I exclaimed. Fiorinal is another type of pain medication. I couldn't take my eyes off of the piece of paper in my shaking hand. First numbness and then disbelief and then alarm took hold as I stared at the lab result. This could be disastrous for my case because it would appear that I was keeping secrets, that I had used drugs during my treatment at IOL. I felt faint, and my heart was beating so fast I was finding it hard to breathe. A huge wave of panic and fear washed over me.

Marilyn probably thinks I've been lying to her. Everybody is going to think I've been lying. People are always going to think the drug addict is lying, not that the lab made a mistake. I was in a state of complete shock.

Marilyn picked up the phone. "Let me call Drug Control to see if it really is Fiorinal." Her voice sounded far away. The Drug Control agent confirmed that it was indeed what Marilyn thought it was. She put the phone down and then turned directly to me.

"I have to ask you this, Patty, and you have to be completely honest with me. Have you taken any drugs, in particular Fiorinal, or anything containing butalbital, since you entered treatment?"

"No," I replied. "I don't and didn't have any access to Fiorinal. I didn't get any prescriptions for Fiorinal, nor was I around anyone whom I knew had Fiorinal."

Marilyn stared right at me for a second to assure herself that I was telling the truth, and then she relaxed a little. When I was reassured that she trusted my answer, the panic subsided a little, but I felt like someone had just pulled the switch on my ability to react, and all that was left was an expressionless façade, a mask to hide the terror I felt.

"Did anyone at the Institute of Living ever tell you that any of your urine samples was positive?"

"No!"

"Are you sure?"

"Yes!"

She sighed. "Okay. Well, that isn't the only problem we have."

"Oh my God! What now?"

"There were only five urine reports in the envelope you gave me, two of which were from the lab in New York. Where are the rest of the reports? Didn't you give urines every week in treatment?"

"Yes, of course I did: every week from the week of July eighth to the week of August fifteenth. The urines they did at IOL were not chain-of-custody, though. We would pee in a cup and put our cup on a tray with twenty or so other cups. They had our names on them, but they were all together, very close." I explained. "Then I was in aftercare two days a week. They didn't do urines as a requirement of that phase. I didn't know that right away, so it was into September before I finally asked Charlie to help me set up the chain-of-custody urines. I thought everything was all set, but it wasn't—but I didn't know that, and Charlie didn't know that, and I didn't want to call them because I was afraid it would look like I was trying to control the situation! We had to call them again—the Medical Services Unit—so it wasn't set up until the end of October. Those reports go to Dr. Jacobs, the psychiatric director of IOL's addiction unit. I thought everything was in that envelope! And, then in the middle of all of that, there was the screw-up with that first therapist."

"And you go to Adam every week?"

"Yes!"

I couldn't believe this was happening *the day before* my hearing. I was beginning to experience that brown-out sensation I'd had the day before, except this time it was gray. My senses could not absorb any more stimuli. My demeanor became utterly flat, emotionless; my voice, monotone.

"We have to call Dr. Jacobs and get him to write a letter of explanation for this, and we have to have it today," Marilyn said angrily.

Suddenly I remembered that in the letter he'd provided us for the summary suspension, Charlie had reported all of my urines as negative. That letter was dated July 28, after he would have gotten the urine toxocology report. Also, he stated in his last letter he wrote, just a couple of days ago, that all of my urines were negative. I wondered why he'd never told me that one urine was positive. I was baffled, and Marilyn was pissed off.

"We *still* need that letter from Dr. Jacobs, and we have to have the rest of your reports." She got on the phone with Dr. Jacobs and explained the situation to him. He agreed to write a letter and investigate where the missing reports were. I had no energy left even to feel relieved at this. Although we had an explanation for the positive toxicology report — that is, my urine sample could have been contaminated with someone else's, or it wasn't even my urine at all — Marilyn wasn't sure the board of nursing would be able to see past it. Unless we got negative chain-of-custody reports from the New York lab, that positive report would be seen as even more credible by the board.

"Well, I wasn't planning on having to do this," Marilyn said, "because we have so much work to do today to prepare you, but we have to go up to the institute and get the letter and hopefully the reports from Dr. Jacobs."

We got in her car and headed up to Hartford. To this day I couldn't tell you if the day was brightly sunny or completely overcast. The grayness of my mood was all I noticed; it was making me nauseated. In my state of anxiety it felt like every beat of my heart issued forth a panicky feeling in my chest. I felt like a puppy Marilyn was telling to "come here," "go there," "do this now," and I had to follow obediently.

But I was also angry. I had done all the right things! I had been a good soldier in Marilyn's boot camp. Nevertheless, I was at the mercy of other people's blunders. Sometimes that happens in life, but with this, the consequences of another person's actions could be disastrous. It could cost me my nursing license.

DR. JACOBS DID WRITE a letter stating that he had no explanation for the positive urine test because it did not fit in with my behavior and demeanor in treatment. He also stated that it was most likely a false positive, a lab error due to the fact that it was not a chain-of-custody test. What we really needed, however, and what he did not have, were the rest of the specimens from the New York lab. Marilyn asked Dr. Jacobs to please call that lab and have them fax the results. She stressed that this was critical and that she needed them by the end of the day because I was to go before the board of nursing tomorrow. He said that he would try his best, and if he got the results, he would fax them directly to Marilyn.

Everything was getting grayer and grayer. I wanted it all to be over. We took a trip to Office Max and had them make fifteen copies of all the documents we had, and then went back to Marilyn's house.

As soon as we got there, Adam called. He was checking in to see how I was doing on this stressful day. He told Marilyn he would have his report to her by the end of the day. Then he talked to me for about twenty minutes — a mini-session. I don't think I told him about the grayness, but I told him I was not feeling very good, that I was stressed way beyond my limits, and what had happened with the urine reports. He reminded me that no matter *what* they said, they could not destroy me.

He encouraged me to visualize the board and to communicate to their higher selves.

"Just remember, Patty, you're doing very well in your recovery, and the board of nursing will see that if you want them to. I have confidence in you, and intuitively I think that everything will go well." His calming reassurances felt like a dip in cool water, not enough to make it all better, but just refreshing enough to get me through for now.

IT WAS TIME TO go over the questions Marilyn would be asking me at the hearing. We sat across from each other in her dining room, with me facing the windows. Everything was totally gray now—the dining room walls, the furniture, the view outside the window. Marilyn went to the kitchen to make tea for the two of us. As I waited for her to join me, I mindlessly stared out of the window and became aware of a brown-and-white basset hound walking by. For some reason, the brown-and-white fur of the dog was the only color I was able to see. Marilyn placed the cup of tea in front of me. Although it was very hot, I wrapped my hands around it, welcoming the heat on my skin. I put the cup close to my face to feel the steam. The strong sensations counterbalanced the blank grayness.

Marilyn sat down across from me. "Is the tea okay, too hot?"

"No. It's just right. It's just what I needed."

"Okay. Let's go over the questions again, Patty. I don't know yet how we're going to approach the problem with these urines, or lack of them, though."

I was in a no-man's-land of indifference and listlessness holding onto my mug of tea. Marilyn started asking me questions, and I tried to answer. Some of the answers came easy, like "What's your full name?" But for the rest of them, I just could not answer. I was beyond the ability to think. Marilyn became increasingly frustrated as she tried to prompt answers from me. Suddenly, we heard the unmistakable sound of her fax machine coming to life.

"Let's just hope..." she said as she rose from her chair and went down to her office. After what seemed an eternity, I heard her coming back up the stairs. Was the fax from Charlie or Dr. Jacobs? Had they been able to get any more urine reports? Could we put part of this nightmare to rest?

When she came upstairs and sat down across from me, she had several pages fanned out in her hand. "I have a cover letter from Charlie that says, 'Here are seven clean chain-of-custody toxicologies from the New York lab!' I had to wait for all of them to come through, but here they are. I don't know if any of these are ones we already have, but I'll check that later."

I felt a wash of relief from my head to my toes. Marilyn looked relieved, too, but still had serious concerns as to how this would play out in the light of the positive urine test.

"This is good, this is very good. I think it'll help." She rifled through the reports and then put them aside. "Okay, let's just go over the questions just once more, Patty."

As we continued, I tried to focus on what she was saying, but I could barely hear her voice. The feeling of relief did not bring with it any renewed energy. I was as limp and lifeless as a rag doll. I tried to grip the cup of tea, hoping it would give the same comfort it had before, or some magical powers, but now it wasn't helping.

Marilyn asked the last question, "What does your recovery mean to you?"

I stared back at her. My mouth opened and closed once or twice, and then I just dropped my arms, palms up, onto the table. I couldn't see right, I couldn't hear properly, and now I couldn't speak. I was scared. I wanted to continue. I wanted to know that we were all set. I wanted Marilyn to say, "Good job Patty! We're ready to face the board of nursing. See you tomorrow." Marilyn looked at me across that table and seemed to realize that all she had across from her was a blank stare from a rag doll.

"Okay. You've had enough, Patty. You're exhausted." She rose from the table. "Go home. Get some sleep. Call me to let me know that you arrived home all right. You need to be at the Health Department, Conference Room C, by nine o'clock tomorrow."

I was free to go, but neither one of us was happy with how it was ending. I knew that Marilyn was concerned about my ability to face the board. She still had an evening's worth of work to do, completing the packets of documents for the board, which still needed to include Adam's letter, which had not arrived yet.

THAT NIGHT, I COULDN'T sleep. I was craving my drug so badly. The clock ticked away the hours and the minutes as I tossed and turned and got more and more restless. The panicky feeling was making me break into a cold sweat. Around 2:00 A.M. I started to cry and pray, "Please, please..." I didn't even know what to pray for as I lay there crying in choking sobs. I tried telling God how sorry I was, and even though I was sure He knew this, I just kept repeating it over and over. Then I went from repentance to anger, pronouncing, "This is too painful. What do you want from me? I can*not* take anymore. You took me away from my moms and my babies! Please don't take away my nursing license, too! Give me a chance to be a nurse again."

I cried until I absolutely couldn't cry another tear, and then lay there in the dark in that strange calmness that follows such crying. As I stared at the ceiling, I started remembering some of the things Sue had said to me, such as "I pray to see signs of His will" and "The answers are in the steps." My mind drifted and floated in that semi-alert, pre-sleep state, and I started to reflect on these two things.

Make a decision to turn my will and my life over to the care of God as I understand Him. Step three again. I realized that I had not ever *fully* made that decision yet. I would take my portion of what I needed to control, and then I'd dole out the rest to God. And things began to feel different. I began to see the subtle secret of step three—*deciding* to let go, *deciding* to be willing, the *conscious* decision to turn my whole life over to God.

"Help me trust You," I whispered. Gradually, I felt the resentment, the anger, and the fear lifting away from me like someone was actually taking it off my chest. I seemed to be releasing myself from the struggle of trying to control how the hearing would turn out, or even how my husband should feel. I asked God once again to point me in the right direction.

My mind wandered to the day I'd been confronted. I remembered the last patient I took care of, the delivery of her baby, and how that might be the last delivery I would ever attend. I thought about how my life had changed profoundly and forever on that day.

I remembered a pregnant teenager who hadn't told her parents she was pregnant, not until she went into labor. She must have been so scared, must have tried to deny the pregnancy for so long. As with my addiction, initially she was unaware of what had begun to grow, but her suspicions surfaced as the subtle clues suggested that something was changing her. She was afraid of the truth. Denial insulated and severed her from the reality she needed to face. Her efforts to conceal the pregnancy became the primary focus of her life. It preoccupied most of her thoughts, and increasingly dictated her daily conduct.

The enduring denial was suddenly jarred loose with the first labor pang. What followed was the excruciating pain, and the exhausting and grueling work of having a baby. The baby was born, and she was grateful that the acute agony was over—but now what? Her body did do its job, and she healed physically, a miracle in its own right. But now the newly recovering mother wondered, "How do I take care of, nurture, and help foster another human to be a healthy adult?" The task seemed too overwhelming in its scope as she faced the fear of the future, and the unknown.

But something else was at work here—the new life she'd ushered into the world demanded that it be loved. In the very basics of nurturing it and meeting its needs, she discovered the love that overpowered the fear. Some days it's easy and some days very hard, but the unconditional love she has for her child keeps her going, keeps the child growing. She learns to reach out for help, and it is there; she just has to ask.

The result is a beautiful new life, healthy in mind, body, and spirit.

Addiction, too, is a secret that cannot be kept due to its very nature. The addict is at first unaware of her condition, until it grows beyond her ability to control or diminish its progression. It occupies most of her thoughts and increasingly dictates her daily conduct. The enduring denial is ripped away with the first searing pain of the revelation "I am an ADDICT!"

Once the pain of withdrawal is over, the physical self heals, but the newly recovering addict wonders, "What now?" She slips into the anger, bargaining, and depression that eventually give way to acceptance. The miracle of recovery cannot be understated or obscured in any way *because a new life is truly ushered forth.* I demanded to be loved, to be nurtured, one day at a time, by discovering that long-buried part of myself that knew how to do that. I learned to reach out for help, and that I only had to ask. In the last six months, some days were hard and some were easy.

The past several days had been extremely hard. But as I lay there in the darkness staring at the ceiling, I remembered that I did not have to be perfect, and that I was unconditionally loved and cared for. I would continue to grow in mind, body, and spirit, continue to love God, so that I could go forward and contribute to the world the best of myself. Now I could face the board of nursing with grace and ease. Now I could sleep.

It is only when we are relieved of our
fear of the results that we have a choice.

— *Denial Is Not a River in Egypt,* by Sandi Bachom

CHAPTER 25

The Morning of January 22

WHEN I SHARED AT Nurses for Nurses that my hearing before the nursing board was one of the most spiritual experiences of my life, some members, especially the ones who had cases pending before the board, looked at me as if my river didn't go all the way to the sea. The obvious and prevailing sentiment was that it was something to suffer through, to endure. How can there be anything positive about exposing the worst part of yourself? How can revealing the most distressing, humiliating, bewildering, and shameful time in your life, to people who are going to judge your behavior and who have control over your future, be positive or uplifting in any way? However, when I tell them how my Higher Power was in control, and that He was giving me clear synchronistic signs that He was with me throughout the day, they began to understand. Of course, Adam was not at all surprised.

THE ALARM AWAKENED me with its rude and persistent EH-EH-EH at 5:00 A.M.

"Wow. A whole three hours of sleep," I glumly thought to myself. Actually, it was more sleep hours in a row than I had had in the last week, so I tried to be grateful for that. I didn't have to be at the Health Department until nine o'clock, but I had so much to do. I had to perform the usual grooming routine, which meant applying enough "natural beauty" so I would present well.

Marilyn stressed that appearances were important. I had to wear something conservative and not revealing or tight. She had already given her stamp of approval for the outfit I had selected. However, I still had to disguise the fact that I had barely slept in a week, so out came the moisturizers, toners, and concealers, quickly followed by the liners, shadows, and mascara. Then I styled my hair and donned my conservative suit.

As I was surveying myself in the mirror, I thought, *Hey! This is January 22, and I am about to face the board of nursing and I don't feel afraid!* I felt nervous, but not terrified. I knew I experienced that serenity before I fell asleep, but *this was January 22!* I had expected to wake up to all of those same feelings again, just like every single morning since the day I was confronted!

Oh well, the waves of fear aren't here now, but they'll show up at some point today. The tide must be out.

I woke up the boys for school. I made coffee but could not drink it, nor could I eat anything. I decided not to take any insulin for that very reason, and because I didn't know when I would be able to eat again that day. I got in my car and drove to Erin's, because she was going to bring me to my hearing. For the entire thirty-minute drive to her house, I kept wondering where the fear had gone—and that frightened me! I knew the tide would come in and that old familiar fear would return at any moment, and I wanted to be ready.

God, grant me the serenity…

I arrived at Erin's and narrowly avoided having my conservative suit ripped to shreds as her dog, Buster, greeted me with his typical exuberance. I gave him the attention he craved, then called Erin's name to let her know I was there.

"I'm up here, doing my hair," she responded from the upstairs bathroom. "I can't decide what to wear. You'll have to tell me if what I'm wearing is okay."

I sat down on the couch, then stood up, sat down again, got up, and walked around. I walked around to the kitchen, through the dining room, and found myself back in the living room, contemplating sitting down again. I didn't want to wait. I wanted to get in the car and get going. I was restless and fidgety. That this was the day that could forever alter my life hit me from time to time, and I'd feel the rise of acute anxiety, but then it would disappear. Erin came downstairs in a nice sweater and matching pants. "Is this too informal?"

"Well..."

"It is, isn't it? I'm going to change. Maybe my suit, my turquoise suit." With that, she quickly retreated up the stairs and, after a few minutes, reappeared in her turquoise suit. "You look great," she said, "but how are you really feeling? Did you get any sleep?"

"Yes. I actually was able to."

"I couldn't sleep at all. I just kept thinking and worrying about how you were doing. Do you want any coffee? I made coffee."

"No. I— " I followed her as she whooshed past me into the kitchen.

"Can I fix you anything to eat?"

"No. I can't— "

"Some toast?" She took a bag of bread out of a drawer, removed two slices, placed them into the toaster, then twisted the bag closed, and returned it to the drawer, all in about six seconds.

"No, thanks, I— "

"I'm going to have some toast. You should eat something. Are you sure? How's your diabetes?"

"Yes, it's okay because I didn't take my insulin this— "

"You have to take care of your diabetes."

"Yeah, I know, but— "

She breezed into the living room and perched on the end of the couch. She snatched up one of her many pocket-size daily meditation books and began rifling through the pages at breakneck speed.

"I don't understand how you can be so calm."

"I don't understand it, either. It just happened last night and it's continuing now. On the way up here I was wondering where the — "

"Here, here we go."

" — fear went."

"This is what I was looking for," she said. She smoothed out the page with her hand as she started to read it aloud.

At that moment, her toast popped up. She placed the open book facedown on the coffee table and dashed into the kitchen. I followed.

"Are you sure that you don't want anything to eat?" she asked as she buttered and then ate most of her toast, then threw the rest to Buster.

"Yes."

"I can't believe how calm you are. How can you be so calm? I'm a nervous wreck!" she said.

I'd found the fear. Erin had it.

Before I knew it, we were back in the living room with Erin on her perch. She took a deep breath and then read a beautiful text about faith and acceptance that brought tears to both of our eyes. We held hands and recited the Serenity Prayer.

"Are you ready?" Erin asked, quietly and softly.

"I am... but are you?" I replied, chuckling.

"No!" she replied, laughing.

"YOU KNOW, PATTY, I have this incredibly good feeling about all of this. This is truly in God's hands."

When the Connecticut General Assembly is in session, there's no room at the Legislative Office Building for the board of nursing to meet. My hearing was during this time, so the board was conducting its meetings at the Department of Public Health, a huge building. Erin and I entered the main door at the far end and followed the signs to "Conference Room C." This involved taking the elevator down to a subterranean level and then walking the equivalent of two city blocks through the long corridors connecting the various sections of buildings.

Out of breath, we finally reached the end of the hallway and Conference Room C. As we approached its open double doors, I gasped.

"Oh my God," I said to Erin, grabbing her sleeve. "We have to walk right past them!" It was not like at the Legislative Office Building, where we could just slip into the back of the room. My legs felt like Jell-O. Panicking, I thought that maybe the board was in the middle of something that we shouldn't interrupt. I looked for Marilyn, but she didn't seem to be there yet. *Should we wait in the hallway until she gets here? Should we just go* in? I had the paralyzing immobility of acute indecision.

"Come on. It'll be all right," Erin said. "We'll just walk in quickly and go sit down." We walked into the conference room attempting to look confident and calm. I was sure that the sound of my pounding heart could be heard by every single board member, and that they were passing judgment on me as we walked directly in front of them to take our seats. The thumping in my ears was like the drum section of a marching band, the kind that causes that scary feeling in the middle of your stomach.

We selected two seats on the right side of the room, about halfway back. I took several deep, slow breaths to try to calm my racing and pounding heart. It was a rather large, auditorium-type room with brick walls and floor-to-ceiling windows with gray see-through shades that the sun was trying to shine through.

Feeling somewhat more relaxed, I recited the Serenity Prayer to myself. Erin and I spoke occasionally about nothing in particular. The acoustics in the room were terrible; it was rather difficult to hear normal conversational tones.

The board of nursing sat at a long table in the front of the room. Erin and I watched them talk and laugh among themselves as they drank their coffee and ate their bagels and pastries. I was able to get a better look at them from this perspective than I had been the last time, when they were behind that big desk. They looked pretty normal. There were more women than men. The age range seemed to be from 35 to 75. One of the members looked very familiar, and another one looked vaguely familiar. I'd been in nursing for a long time, so I could have had some sort of casual association with any one of them.

In front of them were two tables, one on the left, where the respondent (the "bad" nurse) and the attorney were to sit, and one on the right, where the prosecutor sat. There was a small table in the middle whose purpose I was wondering about; my question was soon answered when a court reporter began setting up her audio equipment there.

Suddenly, we were all startled by a loud, disgusting, sucking sound coming from outside the building. A sanitation truck was parked in the alley, its wide hose extended down into a sewer opening. The driver had turned on the sucker and now was nowhere to be seen. With a look of annoyance, the court reporter walked to the back of the room, toward the source of the sound.

"I hope that doesn't last too long," the court reporter said to no one in particular, "because it will make it very hard to adjust my equipment. Everyone is going to have to speak very loudly."

"Where's Marilyn?" Erin asked me.

"I guess she'll be here in a minute," I responded, and with that, Marilyn, in a hot-pink wool suit, came walking in to the conference room pulling her wheelie cart behind her with my case documents contained in two boxes. As soon as she saw us, she smiled that smile. In contrast to the day before, she looked rested and calm. It was reassuring to see the smile that told me "everything's going to be all right." But her smile quickly changed to a scowl as she looked in the direction of the sucking noise.

"How long are they going to keep that up, I wonder?" She walked to the back of the room, to the door that led to the alley. "Maybe we can get them to turn it off." She came back and sat down beside us. "You look much better than yesterday," she said to me. "Did you get any sleep?"

"About three hours," I responded. "But I do feel much better." I was still experiencing some of the strange visual effects from the day before, but not as persistent or severe. Everything looked gray.

"I was worried after yesterday."

"I don't want to even think about yesterday."

"Just concentrate on today. You're going to do just fine. How's your diabetes?"

"I didn't take my insulin this morning because I couldn't eat."

"Are you sure you'll be all right?"

"Yes, I will."

She told me that Adam had faxed over his report from some Quik Mart at seven o'clock the night before, and she had had to run out and copy it after that, but that it was an excellent report. In it, he commented on the positive urine screen, agreeing that it was probably due to lack of chain of custody. We had hoped that he could testify today, but he had a previous commitment, so there was a good chance my case would be continued until the following month, if they decided they needed to hear his live testimony. She was hoping his letter would be accepted by the prosecutor and the board. The thought of having to return for another hearing made me sick to my stomach. I needed this all to be over.

Now I can see it's all coming home, the message rings clear and bright.
Just as He promised, no one ever walks alone; and His love will show the light.
See the light shine! Oh how it shines!
Everything's gonna be alright.

—Fred Carter, Jr.

CHAPTER 26

The Hearing

I WAS TREMENDOUSLY comforted by Marilyn's demeanor. She looked relaxed and composed as she walked around and said hello to various people in the room. When the prosecutor appeared, she handed him the letter from Adam, and had a small conversation with him.

The chair of the board of nursing announced that they were ready to start. As the attention of the people in the room became focused on the nursing board, I felt that familiar, uninvited, and sudden wave of fear. *Here it is. The tide is in,* I thought to myself as the palpitations, the cold sweat, and the desire to run from the room washed over me.

My mind was blank. I was sure I had forgotten everything I'd learned in the last six months. Marilyn would have a mute for a client, looking back at her silently just as I had at her house.

God, please help me, I pleaded. I remembered Adam's suggestion. I closed my eyes, took my two deep breaths, and tried to relax all of my muscles. I visualized myself full of light.

"I can't believe how bright that sun has gotten all of a sudden," Erin said. I looked around the room and noticed that the sun was shining at the section of seats we were in. I felt very warm and I was beginning to feel blinded by the brightness.

"Let's move to those seats," I said, pointing about two rows in front of us. We moved, and Marilyn came and sat down right next to me, on the aisle seat. We could relax for a while because my case was not the first of the day. The first respondent on the schedule stepped up to her place at the defense table. The sun went behind a cloud.

"Raise your right hand…" The court reporter started. The gurgling sucking noise of the sanitation truck continued to invade the proceedings.

"Adam would have some kind of metaphor about that sanitation truck," I remarked to Erin.

"Probably about how shitty this whole thing is."

"And it sucks."

The first respondent, who had been a nurse for only about a year, did not have any legal representation. Her husband sat with her during her testimony. She looked terrified. She didn't have a "packet" like Marilyn and I had, so she didn't have letters of support or a day-by-day account of her recovery activities.

"How could anyone do this without a lawyer?" Erin whispered in my ear.

"I don't even want to think about it!" I responded.

The nurse seemed pretty clueless about recovery and safe practice. Her husband had to be sworn in because he kept interrupting his wife, much to the consternation of the board, who had to remind him whom the questions were being directed to.

"It's my understanding that you're working for the same facility, as a nurse's aide, correct," one of the board members asked the respondent.

"Yes"

"And they're willing to hire you back as a nurse once you have your license?"

The respondent replied that they were, and went on to say she had received a lot of support at her place of work.

"Are you ready to resume your role as a nurse?" the board member asked.

"I feel that I am more than ready," the nurse responded.

"If we give you your license back, you will be working around your drug of choice. Do you feel that you're able to handle narcotics once you return to work?"

"Yes. I know I'll be able to control myself now that I've been through treatment. I know that it was wrong to do that, and I won't do it again." Erin and I looked at each other; I remembered how little self-control Erin had had when she returned to work.

This was the one question to which the board needed to hear the exact opposite answer. The respondent kept repeating that she needed to get back to work to help support her family. Her husband told the board that he would "watch her," and that "she would be a good girl."

"What a jerk," Marilyn whispered to us. "He probably doesn't let her do anything by herself."

When the board of nursing was finished with their questions, they closed the hearing and discussed what they thought the remedy should be. The board member who'd asked the most questions spoke directly to the nurse and told her that she did not show much, if any, evidence that she understood her recovery, or what it meant to practice safely. She seriously doubted the nurse had attended any Nurses for Nurses meetings (she testified that she had) because she seemed to be very misinformed, and that nurses who do attend Nurses for Nurses meetings get a great deal of information and support.

The board of nursing recommended that the woman's nursing license be suspended another six months. After that, she was to come back to the board and show them better evidence of her recovery by clean urine tests and a better understanding of her recovery by attending more meetings and getting a therapist.

The nurse got up from the table and gathered up her things. As she and her husband turned in our direction, it was apparent by the looks on their faces that they were angry with the board's decision. They quickly exited the conference room

The board announced that they were going to take a break before they heard the next case—mine! The skin on the back of my neck was getting taut, like just before I got a migraine. I was still not experiencing any fear, just nervousness, like before you give an oral report in front of a class.

Erin and I were talking to each other when the sun came out in full force, shining on the seats we had moved to. The heat felt good on the back of my neck, but the light was blinding. Marilyn got up to talk to the prosecutor, to see if he'd read Adam's report and would agree to having it included as testimony. When she was finished with her conversation, she went to the front row and beckoned me to join her there. Erin followed me, sitting in the row behind us.

"He didn't have any objections to having Adam's report in lieu of his testimony," Marilyn announced. "So maybe we'll get this done today. At least I hope so,"

"*You* hope so?" I retorted. Marilyn put her hand on my arm for reassurance.

After about ten minutes, the board members returned to their seats, and it looked as if they were ready to begin. I turned around to say something to Erin, and I saw that the sun, which had gone behind the clouds for a few minutes, had come out in full force again. Again, the blinding light and the heat were directed to the chairs we were now sitting in.

"No matter where we sit, we can't seem to get away from this sun, can we?" Erin remarked.

It was time for me to sit at the desk in front of the Connecticut

Board of Examiners for Nursing, the respondent's seat, the defense seat, the hot seat, the guilty seat, the "I'm bad" seat. As I stood, Erin grabbed my hand and encouraged me not to worry; she was going to be praying for me the whole time. As I sat down in "that seat," I again closed my eyes and imagined myself filling with light, and prayed for the serenity to face the board with grace and ease.

The sun got brighter.

This is it, I prayed, *the moment I've been dreading for the last six months. Please let me know that You are here.*

The prosecutor took his place at the other table. I sat up, remembered to smile, to look composed.

Fill with light. Grace and ease, grace and ease. Fill with light. Grace and ease, I kept repeating over and over to myself. I took a slow, deep, cleansing breath.

The sun's rays were now exerting their full authority directly at the defense table where I now was sitting, suddenly igniting the powerful message to me that this was the gift of my Higher Power, shining on me wherever I was and "filling me up with light."

I had Erin behind me with the gift of her loving friendship and her prayers. I had the gifts of the friends who couldn't be here, such as Judy, and the gift of my sponsor, Sue, who'd guided me with her wise advice. I had the gift of Adam, from whom I was learning to use the tools to repair my life. I had the gift of Fred, who did love me and was trying to understand through his own pain and confusion. I had the gift of the unconditional love of my boys, who kept me grounded and in the real world of day-to-day life. I had the gift of the love of my parents, my stepfather and my brothers and sister, even though they didn't know what I was going through. And I had the gift of my Higher Power, who was giving me what I'd asked for, the sign that He was there: the bright, warm, soothing sunlight that was now shining on me, on Marilyn, and on the Connecticut Board of Examiners for Nursing.

"We are ready to proceed," the chairperson announced, as she frowned at the unrelenting sucking noise still coming from the alley. "And the next thing we have on our agenda is the hearing for Patricia Holloran, RN." She nodded at the prosecutor to begin.

Marilyn leaned toward me and said, "Everything's going to be all right." The sun shone directly on Marilyn and me.

The prosecutor stood up and said, "Good morning. I am representing the department in this matter, and the respondent and her counsel are also here."

Marilyn stood, "Good morning. Marilyn Clark Pellett for Patricia Holloran, who is here and who has been advised to speak very loudly so that we all can hear."

The prosecutor elected to defer his opening remarks, and instead to save his comments for closing remarks. First he and then Marilyn passed out their respective packets of documents. Marilyn had to explain to the board about Adam's letter, which she'd received at the "eleventh hour," and where to insert that into their packets. An attorney general, always present at board of nursing hearings, made sure that everyone had the same information, and labeled the exhibits for the respondent or the prosecution. It was as formal as any court.

The members of the nursing board then began reading through the packets. After the standard five minutes, one by one, they closed the pages and looked up. A member of the board sitting directly in front of me smiled as if to say, "It's okay. Don't worry." I weakly smiled back.

The chairperson indicated that Marilyn could now proceed. She stood up and began her opening statement: "Patty Holloran is a forty-five-year-old nurse who is married with three teenage sons. She was confronted at the hospital where she worked in late June of 1996 for diversion of Stadol. She will tell you about her drug history, and you will hear in her testimony that her abuse began around the holidays of 1995.

"When she was confronted, she orally admitted the diversion of those drugs to the Drug Control agents. Shortly thereafter, she was terminated from VMMC, but before she was terminated, she had an opportunity to work with Employee Assistance and her insurance company, to arrange for treatment at the IOL.

"The evidence presented with the objection to the motion for summary suspension and in the package of material today show that she actively participated in the intensive phase of treatment at the Institute of Living, which began on July 8, 1996. That was the first treatment she'd ever had for substance abuse.

"The evidence will show, and the testimony will show, that she completed the intensive phase in August, and was transferred to the aftercare phase, which she still participates in two times a week.

"Throughout this entire treatment course at the Institute of Living, she has had the same counselor, Mr. Wilbur, who has provided documents, which are within the package. He's prepared three letters.

"You will hear Patty testify about the events that led to her abuse of Stadol, and you will hear her testify about the events in her life that have occurred since her recovery began. You will also see evidence of urine screens. You will hear testimony from Patty today that yesterday, when she first saw the urine screen reports, she discovered that there was a positive, despite being told on numerous occasions that all her screens were negative, and as is reflected in Mr. Wilbur's letters to you, in July and January the urine screens were negative.

"You will hear her testify to the fact that this was rather upsetting to her and what she did to find out as much as she could about that positive screen since she found out yesterday. You will hear testimony that she did not abuse any substance in July of 1996. You can also see in Dr. Jacobs's letter that they regard that report as inconsistent with her clinical presentation and progress at that point.

"You will hear about Patty's attempts to get her urine screens arranged in aftercare, and I think from the timing of the facts you can see the difficulty in getting the hard copies of the reports. You will hear about her recovery. You will hear testimony of a strong recovery. You will hear what her program consists of, the aftercare that she attends, meetings she attends, her sponsor, but also in Patty you are going to hear about a recovery program that is spiritually based, that it has been reawakened, and she has rediscovered a relationship with God that somewhere got lost along the way.

"Along with Patty's program that she is working, she sought out individual therapy. She used her insurance company in order to get a therapist who was within her plan. The evidence will show that it wasn't therapeutic from Patty's perspective; that she did not feel she was getting anything out of it, so she sought out a new therapist. Should she have stayed with that therapist just until she got through this just to put on a good show for the board? Actually, there are different theories about that on this side of the fence. My perspective is that any relationship that any nurse in recovery has with a therapist, sponsor, whomever, should be a relationship that maximizes their recovery programs.

"You will see a letter from her current therapist, Dr. Jaffe, who also has assessed, based on his conversations with her, that her prior therapy relationship was not a good match.

"Finally, in terms of work, she is not working. She has not worked since she was terminated from VMMC. She has gone out on interviews, looking for a job, for a position that fits in well with her recovery program, and is safe.

"In brief summary, the evidence that you will hear will show that healing has begun for Patty. Recovery has allowed Patty to begin to care for herself again. And as she has said in her statement to you, it has brought her away from isolation and despair to fellowship, connection, and hope. She has rediscovered loving relationships with family and friends and has developed new and very special relationships within the program that she will tell you about.

"At this time, I'd like Patty to be sworn in so that she can testify. I have asked her to keep up her voice and I will remind her of that again."

Marilyn turned and gave me the gift of her confident, warm, and reassuring smile, and a quick glare toward the offensive noise. I positioned the microphone directly in front of myself, so that I wouldn't have to repeat anything.

Marilyn began the questions with the basics to establish who I was and if I had any other licenses in the state or any credentials that might be pertinent. I listed where I had worked in my career up until I was confronted.

Q: Where were you working on June 28, 1996?

A: At Veterans Memorial Medical Center in Meriden.

Q: Do you remember that date?

A: Yes.

Q: Why do you remember that date?

A: Because that was the day I was confronted by Drug Control.

Q: Okay. Can you tell the board about the confrontation?

A: It was the end of my shift. I was working nights, and the assistant director of our floor, accompanied by an official from the Department of Nursing, accompanied me to the administrative offices, and placed me in a room with two gentlemen. I didn't know who they were.

Q: And then what happened?

A: And then the gentlemen presented evidence that there was more Stadol missing from the Pyxis system that could be accounted for the patients that had actually needed to use it.

Q: Did they introduce themselves as the Drug Control agents?

A: Yes.

Q: And what did you tell them at that point?

A: I admitted orally to the diversion of the Stadol.

Q: Did you provide a written statement at that time?

A: Not at that time; they gave me the option of waiting about a week. I really felt that I needed to consult with a lawyer and that I would get back to them at that time.

Q: Did you ultimately present them with a statement?

A: Yes.

Q: Your statement indicates that you diverted Stadol and Percocet. Is that true?

A: Yes.

Q: Have you diverted any other drug from any other facility?

A: No.

Q: Okay. What is your drug of choice?

A: Stadol.

Q: Is there any doubt about that?

A: No.

Q: Can you tell the board what your drug history is?

A: I never had a problem with abuse with alcohol or drugs, ever in my life. I had been prescribed normal pain-control medications after childbirth and post-operatively, and it wasn't a problem.

Q: What do you mean it wasn't a problem?

A: I didn't abuse the drugs. I used them according to how they were prescribed and then, when I didn't need them, didn't take them anymore.

Each time I responded, I watched Marilyn closely to see if she wanted me to continue with my answer or stop where I was. I was afraid I would say too much. I wished I could have done better the day before, at her house; then maybe I would have had a better sense of the rightness of what I was saying.

Q: Okay. Go ahead.

A: I was prescribed Nasal Stadol for migraine headaches during the previous year and I didn't abuse that.

Q: And when you say, "during the previous year," what year do you mean?

A: 1994 to 1995 [I couldn't remember exactly when it was first prescribed.] I just used it as prescribed until 1995 or just prior to the holidays in 1995. I found myself taking care of my father and not getting any sleep. And I knew how Stadol would make me feel, that it would help me sleep when I got home from work, and he would be... um... and I would be able to attend to his needs and be able to return to sleep, and I seemed to be functioning better.

Q: Okay, let me cut you off there. What was going on in your life in 1995?

A: My father came to live with us in October 1995.

Q: Did he live with you at all before October of 1995?

A: Well, he moved up from Alabama in May of '95, but he was in a nursing home from June to October.

Q: Okay, and then what happened in October?

A: The reason that he was in a nursing home is that he has severe rheumatoid arthritis and he injured his knee severely, and he came home more disabled than when he initially came up in May.

Q: And when you say he came home, he came home to your house?

A: Correct.

Q: What were the kinds of things that you had to do for your father when he was living with you?

A: I had to get him in and out of the bathroom, and on and off of the toilet and help him in and out of his wheelchair, make sure that he ate and had his basic needs provided.

Q: So this was going on between October and December?

A: Yes.

Q: And you weren't abusing Stadol then?

A: Not then, no.

Q: Okay. What happened in December?

A: That's when I just decompensated and I started diverting Stadol to get some sleep.

Q: How would you divert the Stadol?

A: Stadol wasn't a controlled substance at the time and it was in a drawer that also contained Motrin for staff use—Motrin, Pitocin—all of the drugs that we would [use would] be in a general use drawer, and when I had access to that drawer, I would take Stadol out for myself.

Q: And what kind of Stadol was it?

A: Injectable.

Q: Okay. Did you deny any patient?

A: No.

Q: Did you share any doses?

A: No.

Q: Did you substitute any other drug?

A: No.

Q: Where did you use the drug?

A: At home.

Q: Why did you use the drug?

A: So that I could sleep, initially.

Q: Did you ever use it at work?

A: No.

Q: How did you take the drug, through what route?

A: IM and then IV.

Q: Did your use of Stadol change over time?

A: It increased to become more of a coping mechanism rather than something to just help me sleep.

Q: Well, what do you mean by that?

A: Well, at the time I was experiencing a lot of hostility from my husband about my father living with us, and all I had to do with him, and so I used it for that reason, so I could numb out feelings that I was trying not to have.

Q: Did you develop a tolerance to Stadol?

A: No.

Q: Do you know why not?

A: No, it just, I just never developed a tolerance. I always had the same feeling whenever I took the same dose.

Q: Has this issue ever come up in your treatment, whether Stadol is a drug that you build up a tolerance to?

A: Yes, it has come up.

Q: And do people build up a tolerance to it, to the best of your knowledge?

A: To the best of my knowledge, I don't know, because there hasn't been enough exposure to it. [I was the only one I knew who had been in treatment for Stadol.]

Q: It is indicated in the Drug Control report that you told the agents that you were prescribed the Stadol nasally?

A: Yes.

Q: Do you still have a prescription for Stadol?

A: No.

We explored some other areas, such as the dates of my intensive outpatient and aftercare treatment, and some issues that predated my employment at VMMC, to establish that I did not have a history of, or even an inclination toward, drug abuse.

Q: Your physician prescribed that?

A: Yes

Q: Is that physician still your doctor?

A: Yes.

Q: Do you see that physician regularly?

A: Yes.

Q: Why is that?

A: Because I am a diabetic.

Q: And are you currently taking any medications?

A: Just insulin.

Q: When was the first time that you admitted out loud that you were an addict?

A: The first day of the first group therapy session at the Institute of Living, on July eighth.

Q: Okay. What happened that got you into treatment at the Institute of Living?

A: Well, after I had my session with the Drug Control agents, the officials from the Department of Nursing came back in and called a counselor at the Employee Assistance Program and directed me to go over there, where I went, and she arranged through my insurance for admission to the Institute of Living.

Q: Had you ever had drug or alcohol treatment prior to the Institute?

A: No.

Q: Had it ever been recommended to you?

A: No.

Q: Your counselor's letter indicates that you had been seeing a psychiatrist and you were given Prozac and Ativan for depression. Can you tell the board about that?

A: That was at my place that I was previously employed at. I went to see this therapist for depression and that is what she prescribed for me. That was early in 1995.

Q: Did you continue to take the Prozac and Ativan?

A: Not very long.

Q: Why did you stop taking it?

A: I didn't feel it was helpful. I had my new job.

Q: Okay. Did you stop going to treatment?

A: To this therapist, yes.

Q: Why?

A: There was no therapy. It was just—she was just trying to give me medication.

Q: Okay. What is your recovery program right now? Just the nuts and bolts of it.

A: Once a week I go to Nurses for Nurses on Monday nights, and twice a week I go to the institute for aftercare, and three times a week I go to NA and AA meetings.

Q: Do you have a sponsor?

A: Yes.

Q: Why do you attend both NA and AA?

A: The principles are the same as far as recovery goes, and they are meetings that I sought out and went to and felt comfortable with and was accepted.

Q: Do you think that your meetings are significant to your recovery?

A: Absolutely.

Q: Why?

I was starting to feel drowsy from the effects of the sun shining into the room, and Marilyn was having a very difficult time referring to her notes because of the glare. At one point in her questioning, she stood up and moved to stand sort of in front of me, which made it easier for her to read her notes. Beads of perspiration had broken out on her forehead, and her cheeks were flushed. Her hot pink suit, I'm sure, was just that.

I stretched a little to get the blood going and try to overcome the drowsiness.

A: There is such a sense of acceptance and spirituality that I don't think that I've ever found anywhere else. And I've developed some really close relationships, especially with one friend in particular. And it is where I found my sponsor and I consider her to be also one of my close friends. It is an experience that I can't even bring up from my heart to describe very well.

Q: Which meeting does your sponsor go to?

A: Well, I met her through Nurses for Nurses, but she also attends two of the other meetings, the NA meeting and the AA meeting that I attend during the week.

Q: And your sponsor wrote a letter on your behalf. Is that correct?

A: Yes.

Q: Why don't you describe your relationship with your sponsor to the board.

A: It was important for me to obtain a sponsor that was going to be there for me, that had a lot of recovery time, that had walked the road of recovery, because for me, I still consider it a journey and I needed somebody that could point out the right road signs, and tell me when I was following them or when I wasn't. The other important thing to me is that she has a strong sense of spirituality.

Q: Are you working the steps with your sponsor?

A: Yes.

Q: And what step are you on?

A: We're starting to explore step four.

Q: Do you think that there is a difference between abstinence and recovery?

A: There is no recovery with just abstinence. It is a process. You really don't know why you took the drug, and that is important to know.

Marilyn flipped through a couple of pages of notes, then looked directly at me, raised her eyebrows for a moment, and then turned toward the board:

Q: All right. You have urine screens, and the first urine screen in this book is a positive screen. Is that accurate?

A: Yes.

Q: Okay, when did you find out that you had a positive screen?

A: Yesterday.

Q: Okay, were you surprised at that?

A: Very surprised.

Q: What had you been told, if anything, about those urine screens prior to yesterday?

A: I was told that they were all negative.

Q: All right. When you saw this positive... well, first of all, do you know what it was positive for?

A: I didn't know what the medication was. I saw the report yesterday, but I didn't know what it was.

Q: Did you subsequently find out what it was?

A: Yes.

Q: Can you tell the board what it is?

A: Fiorinal compound.

Q: Did you take that drug?

A: No.

Q: What did you do when you found out this report was positive yesterday?

A: I tried to gather myself together emotionally, and that wasn't really easy, but we called Dr. Jacobs at the institute to find out why I was never told about this, why I was told that my reports were—I was informed that my reports were negative, and how could he explain this.

Q: And what did Dr. Jacobs tell you?

A: He said that he couldn't explain it. It didn't go along with my clinical picture.

Q: And did he write a letter to you?

A: Yes.

Q: What was going on in July, besides the fact that you were in treatment at the institute? Did you have any medical problems in July of '96?

A: Actually, the day I was confronted by Drug Control, I went home after I went to the EAP, went downstairs and stepped on a hacksaw blade.

Q: On purpose?

A: No.

Q: What happened?

A: I sustained an injury that required five stitches in my foot.

Q: Were you prescribed any medication?

A: No, other than antibiotics.

Q: So, Fioricet wasn't prescribed?

A: No.

Q: And did you take any Fiorinol or Fioricet...

A: No.

Q: Did you tell Dr. Jaffe about this positive screen?

A: Yes.

Q: And when did you tell him?

A: Yesterday.

Q: Do you go to a therapist?

A: Yes.

Q: And who do you go to?

A: Dr. Jaffe.

Q: Why didn't you start seeing him earlier?

A: I was seeing another therapist from October and—

Q: How did you get Dr.—

A: Through my insurance's physician directory.

Q: Can you describe your relationship with him?

A: I felt that the relationship was solicitous, that he was just having me there for the hour, told me I was doing all of the right things, and sending me home.

Q: Do you think you benefited from these sessions?
A: No.
Q: When did you start seeing Dr. Jaffe?
A: December tenth.
Q: Is there a difference, in your opinion, between therapy sessions with Dr. Jaffe and Dr. Martin?
A: Yes.
Q: What is it?
A: The most important thing that Dr. Jaffe does for me is, he gives me tools from week to week, like meditation, or prayer, or something along those lines, like a tool box that I can reach into whenever I am feeling stress.

She asked me about who, other than the people I had already mentioned—people from the institute in my aftercare—was in my support network. She also explored if I had been looking for a job:

Q: What kind of nursing job are you looking for?
A: The most important thing is that I'm in a safe environment, away from substances that I could abuse.
Q: But Stadol isn't a controlled substance, is it?
A: Well, now I consider Stadol a narcotic.
Q: Why do you consider it a narcotic? The FDA doesn't.
A: Because it is a mind-altering substance.
Q: How many months have you been in recovery?
A: Six.
Q: Is there anything different about your recovery today than there was in July of '96?

A: When I started my recovery, I was really in denial because—and part of that, I think, is because Stadol wasn't a controlled substance, so I could tell myself it's not a drug. After about a week in treatment I started to realize how much denial I was in. When I got myself out of the denial, that's when I started to move forward. And now I'm finding out that I am really happy in my recovery. I find a lot of joy. I'm recovering myself, the better part of myself that I had before I became an addict—a lot of self discovery.

Q: Do you think your recovery program is strong?

A: I feel it is strong.

Q: And why do you think it is strong?

A: Because I am working the program. I am doing whatever my sponsor tells me, as far as what prayer tells me, I am trying very hard to be a whole person again.

Q: Is there anything else that you'd like to tell the board about your case or your recovery that you haven't conveyed to them?

I still didn't know what I was going to say when she asked me this question. I didn't want to just say that "my recovery means everything to me" because I was sure the board had heard that from every nurse addict who'd ever come before them. I reflected on the metaphorical revelation comparing pregnancy and birth to addiction and recovery that I had had the night before. I decided to go for it, and hoped that it didn't sound too hokey. In the end, I didn't say it the way I wanted to, and it *did* sound hokey. Oh well, that *is* the best I can do right now.

Q: I have no further questions.

If you have a sense of impending doom,
it could be that doom is impending.
—*Denial Is Not a River in Egypt,* by Sandi Bachom

CHAPTER 27

The Prosecution

THE SUN WAS VERY bright now, and shining on the whole front of the room. It was time for the prosecutor to begin his cross-examination:

Q: Good morning. When you were initially confronted by Drug Control, it is my understanding that you didn't take any responsibility for diverting any Percocet. Is that correct?
A: Yes.
Q: Okay, and what did you tell them?
A: I told them that I... I don't really remember what I told them. But I think I told them that I didn't remember diverting the Percocet, that it was a... a nursing note error, for lack of better words.
Q: So you told them that you didn't remember, or that you didn't do it?
A: I think I told them it was an error in recording.

I didn't really remember exactly what I told them at this point. That day was a blur. To me the Percocet was a nonissue, because I never abused it, and didn't think about it since the day Marilyn and I discussed it in her husband's office. It seemed really punitive and silly to me that over the course of 6 months there were more than 151 Stadol missing under my name and only 4 Percocets!

Q: Your current sponsor is Susan. Is that correct?
A: Yes.
Q: And when did she start becoming your sponsor?
A: In September.
Q: Okay, so for July and August and at least part of September, you didn't have a sponsor?
A: Right.
Q: Why not?
A: Because getting a sponsor is a real special relationship to me; it's not something you jump into without thinking.
Q: When you speak with Dr. Jaffe, you discuss all the details of your history. Is that accurate?
A: Yes.
Q: Okay and did you tell him about the Percocet?
A: I think so, yes.
Q: Okay, and also Mr. Wilbur?
A: Yes.
Q: Did you tell him about the Percocet?
A: Yes.
Q: And you are sure about that?
A: Yes.
Q: Okay, then can you explain to this board why neither one of them would mention in their reports, regarding your current situation, why Percocet isn't mentioned?
A: I don't know why it wasn't mentioned. If the people that were treating me didn't mention the Percocet, it was because it wasn't important.

I am not responsible for their documentation. I was being treated for my addiction, not for any particular drug.

Q: I mean presumably if he is providing a summary of your treatment to the board of nursing, certainly the abuse of a controlled substance would be something that he would remember, if he was told.

A: I think the overwhelming abuse of the Stadol—and there was plenty of Stadol for me to obtain, to not need the Percocet.

Q: No, I understand that. My question is in none of the records that you have provided to the board do I see Percocet mentioned at all.

He did not want an answer. He moved quickly to his next topic.

Q: Do you currently suffer from depression?

A: I am not being treated for any clinical depression, no. I feel depressed sometimes, but I don't feel that it is clinical depression.

Q: You mentioned in your testimony that you were asked whether or not you had told your close circle of friends regarding your addiction. You mentioned that you told one. Why haven't you told other of your friends regarding your current situation?

A: I was counseled that it was pretty much my timetable and when I can do that, they will be supportive in my life at that time.

Q: And as far as you're concerned, you have no explanation for this positive urine screen?

A: Right.

Q: And none of your physicians or health providers told you about this at the time?

A: No.

Prosecutor: "I have no further questions."

Ms. Clark Pellet: "I have nothing else."

Oh my God. Is it almost over?

Now the nursing board itself got a chance to ask me questions:

Q: Patty, why were you terminated from VMMC?
A: They told me it was for the theft of the Stadol.
Q: But when they first confronted you, they directed you to EAP?
A: Yes.
Q: And then how long were you involved with the EAP?
A: Just that one day. They directed me to the Institute of Living.
Q: And when were you terminated? How long from that period?
A: It was exactly a week from the twenty-eighth of June, when I was confronted; that was a Friday, and it was the following Friday.

Marilyn asked a bunch of questions at this time to clear up for the board of nursing the timeline of when I was terminated. Then the board resumed its questioning.

Q: When you had the positive screen, which was July 1996, how frequently were you having urine screens?
A: Approximately once a week.
Q: Approximately once a week. So, the one before was negative? And they weren't random at that time?
A: Yes, they were random. We didn't know we were giving urines until that morning when we arrived at treatment. So, we went Monday through Friday; it could be any one of those days that we gave a urine.
Q: And there was a chain of custody?
A: No. Not at that time
Q: Not for any of those?
A: Right.
Q: And then there was this one that was positive. So, when this happened in July, you don't remember your counselor sitting down with you...

A: No…

Q: …and asking you what's going on or…

A: No.

Q: You said you found this out yesterday and confronted your therapist. Is that what occurred?

A: I called him. I called my therapist and I called Dr. Jacobs, who is the doctor for the program.

Q: And what was their rationale for not discussing that with you?

A: I'm really not clear on that, what their rationale was. They just said it was not in…they thought it was an aberration and it wasn't in line with my clinical picture.

Q: The drug that was in question on the positive screen, had that ever been discussed by your internist for you to be taking for your migraines?

A: No.

I explained to the board that I had not been prescribed anything for my migraines since the prescription for Stadol ran out. *If I get through* this *without a migraine* that *will be a miracle!*

Now the prosecutor felt his obsessive need to again explore the urine tests.

Q: And you were seeing your internist about migraines?

A: Yes. Not for that—particularly right at that time—you know, that was months before.

Q: What were you using to control your migraines during that time?

A: Nasal Stadol.

Q: You were still using Stadol during that time?

A: Not in July, no. I was not—I wasn't using anything at that time for my migraines; originally the Stadol was prescribed prior to that.

Q: Right, but I was talking about in July. Were you still having migraines during that time?

A: No.

Q: So you were on no medication and there was no discussion of any medication to be used?

A: No.

Q: I have a follow-up on that. You said you were being screened weekly since July. Is that accurate?

A: Yes. [I misunderstood, or didn't hear the "July" part.]

Q: Okay... Can you—I'm having trouble in your packet locating where all these screens are, then. So, there should be four, approximately, four screens for July, four screens for August, four screens for September, October, November... and I see about, you know, six or seven screens here. This is the only one I see for the month of July, which is positive... and then we jump to December, and then we jump back to October... and my question is, where are all the results of the urine screens for all these weekly tests?

Have there been enough questions about the urines? Do you want me to pee in a cup right here? The fear was coming back... the grayness.

The sun was so bright, and coming from where the prosecutor was sitting, so I could not look in his direction. I closed my eyes to stop squinting and to keep them from watering. The board was also being bothered by the bright sunshine. I turned my head to the front of the room and opened my eyes, just in time to see the chairperson put on a pair of sunglasses. I looked for a second, not knowing whether to laugh, but then the board member sitting next to her (the one who had been asking me all of the questions) looked over at her and burst out laughing. The rest of the board members joined in one by one as they looked in her direction. I then felt I had "permission" to chuckle. I thought of what Adam had said, "They are people, just like you…" and I was able to relax, a little. The jocularity didn't last very long, however, as the questions from the prosecutor continued.

A: I submitted weekly urine screens during my four weeks of treatment. When I was put into aftercare; that's when I asked my counselor if they could set up chain-of-custody urines.

Q: Right.

A: And that didn't get done until November, because I thought that they were going to call me once I talked to them, and they didn't call me. So, several weeks went by before I was able to set that up.

Q: Well, more than several weeks between July and November. Right?

A: No. I had screens done in August.

Q: Okay. How many screens, approximately, did you have in August?

A: Two, during the last two weeks I was in the program.

Q: Okay, and then after your screens in August, when were your next screens after that?

A: Not until the beginning of November.

Q: All right. That's my point. So for the second two weeks in August and then all of September and October and part of November there are no screens.

A: Right.

Another board member continued:

Q: You were in the aftercare program in that time frame, September and October?

A: Yes.

Q: And they didn't require urine screens in aftercare?

A: No. I thought that they were going to require screens in aftercare and then I found out that they weren't required.

Q: It's not part of their program to do urine screens?

A: Right.

Q: And then you pursued on your own screens for chain of custody?

A: Yes.

Q: Were you under the jurisdiction of the State of Connecticut, of this board, at any time?

A: I don't understand.

Q: Were you undergoing this treatment by direction of any constitutional authority—the board, the federal government, the State of Connecticut? This was a purely voluntary endeavor on your part to recover…

A: Yes.

Oy. Back to the prosecutor:

Q: How long were you abusing Percocets?

A: I did not abuse any Percocets. I am not really clear as to whether a patient didn't take it and I went home with it or what. It was not a drug that gave me the same results as the Stadol did as far as what I needed it for…for sleep. It made me too hungover.

Q: So you tried it once?

A: Yes. I have been prescribed it…

Q: Were you using the Stadol on the job?

A: No.

Q: But you can't quite remember how you diverted the Percocet?

A: I was not even really aware that there was any records of "diversion" until I was confronted by Drug Control, and they said there were times when I withdrew the Percocet from a Pyxis machine twice that they could not account for, and I remember once taking it home by accident, but that was way before I was diverting the Stadol.

Q: You just kind of forgot that you diverted the Percocet? Or you thought that you wouldn't get caught?

A: I am not sure. I think that a patient refused it and I ended up taking it home. I... I just forgot that I had it with me, that's all.

Q: Were there any other drugs that you were using?

A: No.

Q: So, when you talked about when you were first in recovery, you were feeling that—or reflecting on your denial—and you felt that part of that denial was because you were using noncontrolled medication; that really wasn't true. You were also taking controlled narcotics?

A: My addiction was for Stadol. That's what I required, that what I desired.

Q: Is that part of your concern about being around narcotics in the future; that there might be others you could...

A: I've come to learn that that's a possibility, through the recovery process, that it's really important, especially in early recovery, to stay away from any mind-altering substances.

Back to the nursing board. We covered who in my family knew about my addiction, and then some questions about how my father was doing now and where he was.

A: My father is in a convalescent home up in Torrington.

Q: So you are no longer caring for him directly?

A: No. He spent from June ninth until the middle of last week in Waterbury Hospital because of ongoing problems with his rheumatoid arthritis, and the fact that he was on steroids for many years. He ended up having both of his legs amputated and he's on dialysis.

Q: How do you deal with the stress of your father's illness? Because I am sure that it requires a great deal of your time.

A: It does. Because I am not directly involved with his care, a lot of the stress isn't there...and I have my brothers and sister; they always wanted to help, but because he was at my house, they didn't know what to do to help. Now they are taking an active role in being supportive of him, and my sister was instrumental in what nursing home he was going to be in because they are all living up in Torrington...

Q: Is your father aware of your illness?

A: No.

Q: Are your brothers and sister aware?

A: No, not at this time

Q: Thank you.

Marilyn: We didn't plan on calling any more witnesses today because Dr. Jaffe was not available. We asked Dr. Jaffe to prepare a statement at that time, and we thought we would keep the case open for him to testify, if the board would like to hear from him, although I think that he's pretty much summarized his assessment of the case, and indicated his prognosis, so we would call no more witnesses at this time.

The chairperson of the board indicated that the statement was all that they needed, and she asked that the attorneys move on to their closing remarks.

Prosecutor: In closing, I think that there are several important things that have been identified in this case which raises some questions regarding the nurse's recovery in this particular matter that the board should take into consideration when deciding what remedy is appropriate. A few things—one of the things that Nurse Holloran just recently said that when she diverted the Percocet, that she forgot that she had it with her and just took it home. Well, I don't think that is really plausible given what we know about controlled substances, given what we know about addiction, and given what we know about the controls within a hospital or a nursing facility about controlled substances. You just don't put Percocet in your pocket and walk home with it and forget that you had it in there.

Talk to any nurse who spends her day going in 50 different directions at once...

Prosecutor: Secondly, some very important members of her family and her support group in terms of her friends are unaware of her addiction... and that may also cause concern from the board regarding that. There are a lot of people that don't know about this.

Thirdly, there seems to be a lot of denial surrounding the area of the Percocet. When she was initially confronted, she didn't admit to it, in fact she told them that she had nothing to do with it... and then we have the "circumstances" of "I walked home with it. I didn't know I had it." Those are problematic.

In addition to that, with respect to the Percocet, none of her treaters mention the Percocet at all... and Percocet is a controlled substance. It is a schedule two substance, as you well know, and no one is really mentioning that. These are serious allegations, which are all admitted to by the Respondent.

Stadol: 151, Percocet: 4

Prosecutor: Dr. Jaffe didn't admit it, and her other counselors and therapists have not discussed this at all, which leads me to believe that she did not mention it at all to these people. I mean if we have a report, that he's been asked to prepare a summary—and it's fairly extensive; I mean he goes into the factors and what her history is and what she reported. He said Ms. Holloran's reported substance abuse began approximately in December of '95 and it goes through a history of that. Well, presumably, if Ms. Holloran told him about the Percocet use, he's going to write about that in his report, which is dated two days ago. It's hard to believe that she told him all these things and failed to mention that there was Percocet involved at all. I understand that her drug of choice was Stadol, but it doesn't mean that Percocet is not a serious issue in addition to that.

Finally, we have the positive urine screen. We are in an interesting situation that when the screens are negative, the board is supposed to accept those screens, that there's no problem, and, if the screen is positive, then we have, "Well, there were chain-of-custody problems," in addition which also raises some questions, that we have letters from an MD here saying, "I have no reasonable clinical explanation for this result." Well, maybe the result is that there was a problem and she tested positive. I don't know why there would have to be a separate clinical diagnosis for something when there is a positive screen. The board is expected to accept all the negative urine screens with no problems, but when there is a positive one, we have to make exceptions for it and make excuses for it.

Exceptions? Excuses? How about lab error and contamination? Errors that could mean the end of my career!

Prosecutor: I mean, that it is disgraceful that they didn't tell her about it. I don't know what kind of recovery program it is when someone tests positive and they are not told about this at all. I don't know about a recovery program that has two and a half months with no screens...

So... how many have you been through?

Prosecutor: So I think there are some serious inconsistencies, and I think there's some problems that have been identified which leave one to conclude that the recovery is not as strong as it initially appears.

If the board is inclined to place Nurse Holloran on probation, the Department would certainly recommend, as she's even requested, a safe environment. There could be no keys for a period of at least a year, and there would be weekly urine screens for an extended period of time, especially, when she does gain access to keys again. Thank you for your patience and your time today.

A Higher Power is someone who makes everything turn out the way it is supposed to — whatever that is.

—*Denial Is Not a River in Egypt,* by Sandi Bachom

CHAPTER 28

In Closing

OKAY, SO YOU'VE MADE ME *feel like a scum-sucking bottom feeder.* I turned to Marilyn, whose turn it was to give her closing statement.

Marilyn: In closing, I'd first like to respond to the issue of the Percocet and the Stadol. I think you heard Patty Holloran talk to you a lot about the Stadol because it is her drug of choice. And while Stadol is not a controlled substance, I think the health community is becoming aware that it probably ought to be a controlled substance, that it is no less addictive than Percocet. I don't think that Patty is trying to minimize the Percocet issue. It is the *addiction* and coming to terms with the *addiction* and then moving off of the admission of the *addiction* and on to the other steps in recovery that she has done.

I'd like to point out to you in regard to the treaters that they obviously didn't put much credence in this positive screen, that two days after they got the report, her primary counselor wrote a letter to Patty indicating that she was in good standing and all her random urine screens were negative. He goes on in his letter of January sixteenth to say the same, to also say that the urine screens were negative. Dr Jaffe also indicated in his letter that he sees her prognosis as good and he doesn't see that there is a red flag. There is nothing Patty Holloran can do about the fact that she found out about this yesterday!

In terms of the other urine screen reports, yes, she would like to know where they are, too. We did our best to pull together as many as we were given and we've provided all of these to you when we got them.

In closing, Patty has a strong recovery. She has developed very close and strong bonds with people in the fellowship…Patty is working a good program. She goes to treatment because she gets some benefit out of it. She could have said to her counselor at the beginning of the year, "I don't need this anymore." She changed therapists to have a good match, to get something out of her therapy, not to just have consistency. She wants a good, therapeutic relationship, something that's going to last.

She has a good, solid sponsor who also goes to other meetings with her. She's got people in the fellowship who are very supportive of her. She's got a husband who is extremely supportive of her.

I think Patty Holloran is the person who knows best what the stresses of her family have been over the last six months and who in her family is ready to hear she's addicted. It's not just a one-way street of Patty telling another family member. It is a two-way street, and it will have an impact on them, so it is not that she's hiding this. I think she has to make an assessment…in her words it is the timing in the recovery program.

I think you really ought to take a look at Patty's letters because it comes through what recovery has done for her, and I think you've seen it. This person has a good sense of humor and it's starting to come through. Recovery has given her hope. It's brought her closer

> to God. It's created a chance for her to live a happy life again....and we hope that you will put her on a probationary program that will be consistent with a good fit for continued recovery. Thank you.

The chairperson said, "At this point we will close the hearing and move on to fact finding."

MARILYN SAT DOWN next to me again and all her attention was focused on the people at the front of the room. She had paper and pen in an anticipatory posture, ready to write down anything they might say. There was no reassuring smile or hand on my arm at this point. *All* of her attention was on the board, which made me really nervous, because I thought that my answers to the prosecutor sounded like I was trying to be deceptive. The Percocets...the urines...the Percocets...urines...made me feel like I had done something wrong when I hadn't. But I also felt that I had let Marilyn down in an odd way. I had given her a rough couple of days. I was thinking that she would be glad to get rid of me after this was all over. Shame and guilt came back in full force.

The nursing board reviewed the charges one by one and my answers to those charges, and said they were satisfied that I had answered them satisfactorily. They then began a discussion about what I had testified to. They seemed to have entered their own little world, talking about me as if I weren't in the room and referring to me in the third person; they didn't even look my way.

Neither Marilyn nor the prosecutor was allowed to say anything at this stage. The board member who had asked the most questions seemed to be the one in charge now. I don't remember all of what was said at this time, because there is no official record of this part, but I do remember that her attitude: as far as she was concerned, I was in some denial about the Percocet use; she focused on the fact that it was a "controlled substance," thus a more severe problem than I had tried to present. She mentioned that I must have used Percocet as well as Stadol, because it was her belief that addicts don't begin with injectable medications; that the usual progression is from pills and then to shots.

She acted as if she were the self-appointed expert on recovery, but I knew from going to Nurses for Nurses that nurses frequently start out injecting. After all, we know how, and a liquid is easier to divert.

The board member who appeared to be in charge also commented on my not having shared my addiction with more members of my family. *Yeah, they need this on top of a dying father!* I thought. And she again discussed urine ad nauseam. Some members of the board joined in on the discussion; others just sat there. When all discussion had ceased, the chairperson asked if everyone was ready to render a decision, and they indicated that they were.

The chairperson leaned back in her chair, put her hands on her head, and announced, "I recommend that there be a six-month suspension, a four-year probation, with urines twice a month, a one-year key restriction, and the usual employer and therapist reports."

Panic time. A six-month suspension? What were they basing that on? That isn't even something the prosecution wanted! Isn't that the same sentence they gave the previous nurse, the one who hadn't had a clue about recovery or how to practice her profession safely? Was today the two-for-one sale for suspensions?

Wait and trust. I am with you, my Higher Power told me. I immediately and intuitively knew that I was not going to be suspended as, one by one, I mentally appealed to the board's higher selves.

"Comments?" the chairperson asked the board.

There was a moment of silence. Then one of the members spoke up: "I don't agree with the suspension. I think it is far too punitive. Why should we suspend her now when she was not summarily suspended last August? She has removed herself from the workforce for the last six months; that is like a self-imposed suspension. I will not vote for this decision based on that. The rest of it is fine, but I don't believe she needs to be suspended."

"Good, good," Marilyn said under her breath.

There was a brief moment of silence from the board, and then an elderly gentleman spoke up: "I have to concur with the conclusions that a suspension is unwarranted in this case. I, too, will not vote for this decision."

Very quickly after that, one by one, the rest of the board members agreed with this, expressing the desire that the suspension part be removed from my sentence. The board member "in charge" laughed and said, "I was kind of wondering if that was a good idea or not."

You're laughing? This is funny to you? You feel like you can just screw up my life on a whim?

"So, I am in agreement that we can remove the suspension from the decision, but leave all of the other elements."

The chairperson asked, "Are we ready to vote? All in favor of the amended decision?"

All the hands went up.

"Good luck," the chairperson said to me, and then the other members followed suit.

That was it. It was over. We'd won. I was still a nurse.

Thank you, God. Thank you, Adam. Thank you, Marilyn. Thank you, Erin. Thank you, Judy. Thank you, Sue. And thank you, Fred! I wanted to call him right then, to share this with him. Was he wondering about the verdict? I needed him now. I needed to collapse with his arms around me. Would I ever have that again? Had we destroyed it all?

The total and absolute exhaustion was now taking hold. I did not have to hold it back anymore.

Marilyn and I thanked the board. I looked at the clock: it was 12:57. It had been 10:00 when I sat in that chair. I turned to Erin and hugged her, turned to Marilyn and hugged her. Erin was so relieved. She kept repeating, "Congratulations, you did it," over and over, and I think it was the first time she exhaled in more than two hours.

Marilyn just gave me a look of relief and told me that I'd done a good job, but then followed that with, "That was one of the strangest hearings I've ever seen."

Erin and I started helping Marilyn pack up her wheelie cart when somebody behind me said, "Patty?" I turned around, to see the nursing board member who had objected to the suspension.

She continued: "You don't remember me, do you?" She was also the board member who had looked very familiar to me. I just shook my head slightly as I tried to remember where I knew her from.

"You probably remember me by my maiden name." She told me it, and I did remember her, from almost twenty years before. We had worked together in a Coronary Care Unit. *(They are people just like you…)*. I thanked her for having intervened on my behalf.

"It wasn't just because it was you; that decision was bullshit, and I just could not agree with it, but I'm glad she changed her mind and agreed to amend it. I am happy for you. Good luck."

Marilyn continued to pack up her things next to me while this exchange took place, and when she became aware of what was transpiring, she looked up with an expression of pleased surprise. Erin had gone to the bathroom during this exchange, coming back only for the tail end of it.

I filled her in on my having worked with the woman in the seventies.

"That's probably why she objected to the suspension. Thank God!"

"Who knows what the reason is. I'm just happy she did!" Marilyn piped in.

"What time is it? I'm starving." Erin said.

"Lunch time. Do you two want to go to lunch?" Marilyn asked. We decided that we would help Marilyn out to her car and then go to one of the local restaurants.

I'm feeling better than I think I am.

—*Denial Is Not a River in Egypt,* by Sandi Bachom

CHAPTER 29

Celebration

WE PILED INTO Marilyn's car to go to lunch at Lena's Restaurant. I stared out of the window while it sank in that it *was* finally over. I was totally depleted and unable to express any of the emotions or sensations that wandered into my awareness.

The restaurant, Lena's, was bustling with the lunch crowd. At our table in the middle of the room Erin and Marilyn were talking like magpies about the morning's events and how happy they were for me, and how relieved they were that it was over.

Marilyn leaned toward me and said, "It's over, Patty! Is it still hard to believe?" I just nodded my head. She was overjoyed, and I should have expressed my joy, too, but I had only enough energy for nodding. "After this, go home and relax—nap if you can. Be good to yourself. You deserve it. Patty, you did great. This will be so good for you."

"I thought you were awesome," Erin added. "I hope I'm as composed at my hearing next month."

I felt reassured that I at least *looked* composed.

Marilyn was alternating between sipping her soup and ripping her garlic roll apart and eating it. "This soup is so good. Did you try your garlic roll yet? Wow! This is good food!"

"This pizza is awesome. I love the sauce," Erin chimed in.

I became detached from the conversation and the noise of the restaurant as I luxuriated in the perfection of the excellent soup. Its warmth relaxed my stomach, releasing a tension that I had not been fully aware of until now. The heavenly comfort then spread outward to soothe and relax every cell in my body, making me feel as if I had just lowered myself into a warm bath. It was the replenishment that my body needed, the caress that my soul craved. When I was finished with my soup, I was able to rejoin the conversation.

"Oh my God. This is just what I needed," I said, leaning back in my chair.

"Is your diabetes okay? How are you feeling?" Marilyn asked.

"I'll tell you how I feel: I'm grateful, I'm happy, and I'm exhausted. I feel like I've been shot at and missed and shit at and hit. But coming here has really helped a lot. It feels good to laugh." I then handed Erin and Marilyn the special presents I'd been saving for them, to express my thanks. With the lunch crowd dissipating, the noise level was lessening, so we stayed for about an hour talking and going over the events of the day.

"This was one of the strangest days I've ever had," Marilyn said. "That was *the* most unusual hearing I've been at! That sun! The chairperson and the sunglasses. The board cracking jokes, changing their decision for the remedy. That board member remembering you."

"The sewer truck sucking shit out of the ground," Erin continued. We burst out laughing.

As we left the restaurant, I knew that Lena's would always be special for me. *Thank you, Lena.*

I HEADED HOME in a daze. Before I knew it, I was flopped on my bed, too tired to cry, laugh, or even begin to process the day. I fell deeply asleep.

I awoke a short time later to Ricky calling my name. He and Shaun were standing in the doorway.

"How did everything go, Mom?" Ricky asked

"Everything's gonna be okay. They did not take my license. I'll just have to be on probation for a while"

"I'm so happy for you, Mommy," Shaun said

"That's great!" Ricky added.

They both gave me a big kiss and hug.

A little while later, Michael came home from his friend's. He saw that I was lying in bed. I smiled at him and told him I could still be a nurse.

"Yea!" he responded. As he stretched out at the foot of my bed, he described something that had happened that he was excited about. We decided on pizza delivery for supper. I turned on the television and we watched a silly sitcom. That evening, the boys did whatever they needed to do—homework, or not—and settled into their rooms.

I CALLED BUFFALO to tell Fred how I'd made out at the hearing. I was so tired I just wanted to fall asleep watching TV, but I knew it was important that Fred hear the news as soon as possible.

"We got what we expected. Four years' probation, one year of key restriction, urine drug screens twice a month, therapist reports, and employer reports once a month."

"That's great," Fred said. "I knew you could do it. They had to see what a good nurse you are and a good person."

I told gave him the particulars of the day and asked him if he remembered the nurse who knew me. He had.

"You must be exhausted," he said.

"I am."

"Well, I'm proud of you.Get some sleep, and we'll talk later."

"Okay."

"I love you."

"I love you, too."

I hung up and tried to comprehend all that had happened, but I had no brain cells that would cooperate. At some point, I fell asleep watching TV.

Fred was relieved and happy that it was over for me. He was proud of me. He loved me.

I believe that every single event in our life happens as an opportunity to choose love over fear.

—Oprah Winfrey

CHAPTER 30

Baggage

I FELT LIKE I HAD BEEN on a trip to another planet, and now was returning to earth. Everything was the same and different at the same time. I had thought that after a successful hearing, my anxiety, fear, and guilt would ease, but they'd merely moseyed themselves into the next dilemma. They were like the irritating relatives who never leave.

My father was still in the hospital, weakened by all of the surgeries. His body was failing him, and he was in pain all the time. But he faced this with the faith and trust that God was with him.

"I'm ready to go whenever He wants me, but I'm not in control of that." He was such a powerful example of unyielding faith in spite of all the pain. He had always led by example, and he was doing that now: with courage and faith, trust and acceptance, grace and ease. What a gift I had in this man whom I was blessed with as a father, a teacher.

EVEN THOUGH WE WOULD be moving to Buffalo in a few months, I needed to get a job. Our finances were at the breaking point. I was afraid no one would hire me, but it was reassuring to know that other nurse addicts had gotten jobs while on probation, so mine wasn't a lost cause.

But I was afraid that I might get a job I detested. (There were some areas of nursing I'd never wanted to experience voluntarily.) Sue reminded me that I would get the job my Higher Power wanted me to have. This was hard to accept. I thought I knew what was best for me. People at the Nurses for Nurses meeting reminded me that a job in the same area where I'd diverted Stadol, so early in recovery, might trigger a craving or a compulsion to use the drug again. So, even though I longed for my moms and babies, I applied for jobs I thought I could tolerate for the short haul,

The nursing board's decision, which would start the clock on my probation, would not be in effect for four months. It had to be written up and reviewed by the Attorney General's Office, then signed by the board of nursing's chairperson. So my probation was going to begin a full year after I was confronted by Drug Control! During that whole time, I would have no restrictions on my license. I could have been out there—if I had not had my recovery—working and diverting drugs, impaired, harming myself and maybe others, and no employer could have found out by looking into my license information. I could have been experiencing the "yets" and getting sicker in my disease.

Despite my worries and concerns, I held tight to my recovery. My aftercare at IOL, my Nurses for Nurses meeting every week, and my NA and AA meetings were what kept me grounded in reality. Working my recovery didn't mean that my life was perfect. It meant that I could face whatever life was dealing out in a sane and rational way. Walking through my panic and doing what I needed to do told those irritating relatives who'd come to stay—fear, guilt, and anxiety—that they were not inhabiting my space anymore. I developed a peaceful center. No drug could ever provide this level of serenity.

I CONTINUED TO SEE Adam every week, to help me begin the long journey back to myself.

"Why do you function out of guilt?" he asked during one of our first sessions after the hearing. It was a very provocative question, and it took me by surprise—and made me feel guilty.

"I don't know," I answered. "I don't even know that I do."

"Well, do you feel responsible for other people's feelings?"

"What do you mean?"

"If other people have any negative feelings, such as sadness or anger, do you 'carry' those feelings as your own?"

I stared at the oak tree outside his window for a moment and slowly came to the realization that I did, especially with my husband. If he had a bad day at work and came home crabby, for example, I always felt I had to make it better, and if I couldn't, I felt inadequate and, yeah, guilty. Or if I couldn't take away a patient's pain, I felt guilty. If another nurse was having a bad shift, I felt guilty.

"Do you mean do I feel like I'm supposed to make it all better? Yeah, I think I do. If I can't make it better, then I feel responsible." For the first time, I became aware of how much guilt I carried for things I wasn't able to control.

"How about your father? Do you feel responsible and guilty that you can't make him feel any better, or that you, Patty, the nurse, can't actually make him better?"

"Yes." I began to cry.

"That feels like such a heavy burden—to carry your own feelings and the feelings of everyone else." Adam posed his body as if he were carrying a heavy bag over his shoulder. "I feel so weighed down with this heavy bag, carrying it day after day. It is getting painful. I need to put it down, but I can't. I need something to take away the pain. Does it feel like you've been carrying the burden of everyone else's feelings?"

I couldn't speak. I could only cry.

He was quiet for a moment, then he continued in his calm, soothing voice: "Why are you crying, Patty?"

"I'm feeling that burden. I never thought about it that way before."

"What is in that heavy bag on your shoulder?"

"It's *everything* leading up to my using. It is my father's pain, it is my husband's anger, it's my guilt that I couldn't make everything better, make everyone feel good, couldn't fix it all, to please everyone *else.* I was working so hard, trying so hard, and yet, I was so afraid to be a...like... a..." *What was it? What was it I was so afraid of?* "...a failure!" My body sank into the couch.

Adam's soft voice eased into my awareness. "To lighten your load, you took drugs. You didn't know that then, however. All you felt was the pain, and then the relief. You couldn't carry that heavy burden anymore."

I sat looking out the window at the strong but barren tree as I tried to absorb this metaphor.

"You're responsible only for your own thoughts, feelings, and actions. It's easier for us to take on others' feelings rather than our own. It keeps us from looking at ourselves. Other peoples' thoughts, feelings, and reactions will be their own. I want to leave you with that until next time."

I left his office absorbed in our discussion and this revelation about myself. He was right. I had to separate my own sadness, grief, anger, and fear from that of others. But I suddenly realized that I didn't know where the line was! I didn't know that boundary: where my feelings were separate from someone else's.

I had to own my negative feelings. Not only was I absorbing everyone else's, but my doing so was diverting the attention I should have been paying to myself. I was afraid of seeing me, warts and all. I was so used to presenting the Patty who could handle it all that I had deluded myself into believing that was who I really was. If I didn't suppress or numb or circumvent the fearful events and feelings in my life, I could learn and grow. I needed to accept all of myself, not just the parts I liked. This journey was going to be hard work, but My Higher Power was with me, and my soul was excited about the trip.

The courage to change the things I can…
The perception of what's happening and what's
really happening are two completely different things.
—*Denial Is Not a River in Egypt,* by Sandi Bachom

CHAPTER 31

Judgment

I WAS PRETTY PROUD of the parking spot I found the morning of Erin's hearing, February 19, 1997, on the corner of a side street, right in front of the Department of Public Health! We took this to be a sign of good things to come.

Erin had had a session with her therapist, the "cult mother," a few days before. "She made me lie on the floor and 'feel the pain,' as the other women stood around me to help me feel it."

"You've got to be kidding me," I responded. "Did it help?"

"No! I was hysterical by the time it was over."

Erin informed me that Paul, the new love in her life, had been acting "weird," so last night she'd gone to see him at the sober house where he was living. He told her he had relapsed! He'd gone to see his daughter, who had bronchitis, and had drunk her bottle of Vicodin cough syrup. I suspected that wasn't his only lapse. Erin said she was furious with him, and that she would deal with it after the hearing. I was worried for her. She'd said they would call off their relationship if either one relapsed, and now she seemed to be considering doing otherwise. I hoped that Paul would get the help he needed, but I didn't think Erin should be around him. A character trait for nurses—which can become a defect—is that we are always trying to "fix" people. Erin could fall into that trap and be sucked into something that could jeopardize her recovery. "Helping" Paul would be a co-dependent nightmare for both of them.

Erin and Marilyn were afraid that the relapse she'd had at the end of the summer before she returned to work, would be an excuse for the board to revoke Erin's license. They were planning on portraying Erin's first treatment as abbreviated and not effective enough to have helped her cope with returning to her abusive, dope-smoking husband. They hoped the board would see it that way, but we knew that they tended to see relapse in general as a failure to comply, and that could mean they'd see Erin as unfit to practice nursing at this time.

Erin's hearing was held in a much smaller room than mine had been, one inadequate to accommodate all of the nurses who had hearings scheduled that day. Marilyn was representing three other nurses as well as Erin. The room quickly became crowded.

Erin's nurse-manager was to testify at the hearing, but could not take the entire day off work to attend. When it was time for her to take the stand, I was to call her on Marilyn's cell phone. It would take about twenty minutes for her to arrive.

Sue was there. She reminded Erin that she had already done a great job in preparing for the hearing. She'd done the footwork; now the outcome was up to God.

It was time for Erin's case to begin. I went to the front of the room to sit with Sue.

The lawyer for the Department of Public Health was a small-built man with sharp features. He was new to the department. He made his opening statement, which, of course, made Erin look like the worse nurse in history. Marilyn followed with her opening statement, about how hard Erin has worked on her recovery and how she'd recognized her problem without any prompting from anyone, and had gotten *herself* into treatment. She pointed out that Erin had the support of her hospital and especially of the Emergency Department.

Erin's answers to Marilyn's questions were calm and confident. She didn't seem nervous at all. Marilyn ran through the questions about Erin's work history and her credentials as a nurse. The next series of questions covered Erin's history of infertility. Erin described to the board how much she had wanted a child, and how her failure to become pregnant in spite of numerous procedures and surgeries had led her down the road to opiate addiction.

Marilyn then moved along to the history of Erin's addiction, and when she'd realized that she had, indeed, become addicted to opiates. Erin described the day she had her revelation, which gave her the ability to see the truth. She described how she sought out treatment for herself. Many of Marilyn's questions related to Erin's treatment. Their major focus was on how Erin had felt when she was discharged from her first treatment. She was neither physically healthy nor prepared to return to her emotionally abusive husband at home.

Erin gave her account honestly and courageously to this board that could revoke her license in a heartbeat. It was very clear that her recovery was the most important thing in her life.

"It is not about my license or my job; it is about my life. I know I have to put my recovery first or I'll die," Erin told them.

As Marilyn guided Erin through her testimony, I watched the board's reaction to Erin's answers. Many of them tried to mask their reactions, but I could see empathy in some of their eyes. One or two members' body language suggested that they saw Erin's story as just another line of bullshit from a drug addict. And one member looked as though he were simply preoccupied with other thoughts: he sat there with his eyes closed most of the time.

It was time for the Department of Public Health to have its turn. The prosecutor rose from his chair.

"You mentioned that your physical pain was a trigger for you," he began. "How are you dealing with, or controlling, your pain now?"

"Like I said, I am on birth control pills," Erin responded.

"And how will the birth control pills control your pain? These are not pain pills, right?" The prosecutor looked confused.

"No," Erin replied with deliberateness. "They are birth control pills. They are not pain pills. But by taking them, I won't develop the painful cysts that cause my pain."

"These pills, how do they prevent cysts from forming?"

"The cysts are formed when I ovulate. The birth control pills keep me from ovulating, so no cysts form."

"And you have been assured by your gynecologist that this is so?"

"Um . . . yes," Erin replied, with just a hint of sarcasm in her voice.

"So," the prosecutor said, "is it your plan to be on birth control pills for the rest of your life?"

Sue leaned over and whispered to me, "Yeah, they'll be giving them to her in the nursing home."

"I can't believe that an attorney from the Department of *Health* would ask such stupid questions, especially that last one," I whispered to Sue.

"I don't know what will happen in the future," Erin replied. "I know that I have no plans to go off of them anytime soon, but any other decisions after that will be between my physician and myself. The goal is to have as little pain as possible."

It was now time for the nursing board to ask any question they had. One of their questions was about Erin's relationship with her husband. "I see your husband as a huge part of the problem for you," one board member said, "a big trigger. How are you addressing this in terms of your recovery?"

"We've separated, and I am going to be filing for divorce."

"I, for one, am glad that you are addressing this issue," the board member replied.

"I don't have a question as much as an observation," another member said. "I see your treatment and relapse as one long acute phase of your illness. Your relapse was not really a relapse, because you'd clearly been undertreated. I'm not saying that you didn't benefit from the treatment you received, but it wasn't enough for you to cope with your stressors, and to work around your drug of choice with no safeguards in place." Several other board members nodded in agreement.

Marilyn responded, "That is how we truly see it, too. We presented that episode as a relapse because we thought that you might see it that way, in the true sense of the definition of a relapse. Erin didn't want to minimize it in any way. It was her decision to present it in that way. Thank you for your observation."

This was major! The board was able to grasp the real picture of Erin's addiction. Erin turned around to Sue and me and mouthed, "Yes!"

"Any more questions?" the chairperson asked.

"I just have another comment," another member said. "I'm tired of hearing all of the rhetoric that is passed off as recovery talk. It's the same phrases and words I hear over and over. Anyone can spout off sayings and recite 'steps,' but it doesn't mean anything. It's just rhetorical recitation."

"Does she have a better idea?" Sue whispered to me.

I shook my head in disgust.

"I also have a comment," a board member suddenly said. "I see this young woman as working very hard and very committed to her recovery activities. She is highly respected by the institution that employs her. That is all."

"Have you learned anything in your therapy?" another member asked.

"I have had the same therapist for the last three years," Erin responded. "I don't think she is good for me anymore. I need someone who is an addiction specialist, so I'm going to be changing therapists as soon as I can."

I noticed that Marilyn was staring at Erin with no expression, but her lack of expression spoke volumes. Erin had just violated the *big* rule. Don't give more information than is asked for—and certainly not without your lawyer's advice. Marilyn took a deep breath. We all hoped the board would understand Erin's motivation for wanting a new therapist and that they wouldn't see it as "therapist shopping."

The prosecutor gave his closing statement, trying to make Erin look like an irresponsible, chronically relapsing drug addict. Then came his surprising recommended remedy: a three-year probation. Only three years!

Marilyn gave her closing statement, emphasizing Erin's recovery strength and how she had addressed every issue she'd had to face.

The chairperson announced the hearing closed. All we could do now was wait as the board members discussed Erin in the third person. Sue and I held hands. Marilyn and Erin remained seated at the defense table. Marilyn flashed Erin one of her great smiles.

I know we were all praying. Some, undoubtedly, were praying for acceptance, no matter what the decision was. I was praying for what *I* wanted: for Erin to be able to continue her practice of nursing. I was not ashamed to pray for what I saw as the right decision. Erin's retention of her license represented truth: the truth that Erin had the courage to reveal; the truth of recovery.

"Remedy?" the chairperson asked the board. The word made me jump in my seat. The chairperson assigned one of the board members to speak.

"I think Erin has done much work in her recovery," the board member started, "...*but* she certainly has a long way to go...*but* I feel that she is headed in the right direction...*but* I also think that the ER is going to be a tricky place for her to stay clean and sober...*but*"—*for Christ's sake, woman, make up your damn mind!*—"she has a good support network... *but* I do agree that she has to hook up with a therapist who specializes in addictions, so I recommend..."

I was so tense my bottom was almost off the chair.

"...now I know the department has recommended a three-year probation... *but* three to four years, we have found, is a dangerous time for relapse... and Erin has had a rocky course already..."

Now I was actually levitating.

"I think that a four-year probation with urine screens twice a month, monthly employer reports, and monthly therapist reports are what are called for in this case."

"Any further discussion?" the chairperson asked. No one had anything further to say.

"Let's move on to the vote."

"Vote to accept?" All but one hand went up.

"Deny?" One hand went up from the member who commented on the meaningless rhetoric of recovery.

"Congratulations, Erin," the chairperson said.

I exhaled. The tears flowed. Erin stood up and turned to us. She looked drained, relieved, but happy.

I hugged Sue. Marilyn hugged Erin. Erin hugged me. I hugged Marilyn. Sue hugged Erin. Marilyn hugged Sue.

"I'm starving. Are we going to Lena's?" Erin asked.

"That sounds like a wonderful idea," I said.

THE DELICIOUS AROMA OF Lena's made its presence known even before we walked in the door. We passed the counter, where the pizzas, stuffed pizzas, homemade soups, and incredible dinner rolls brushed with garlic and oil tempted our appetites, and took seats at a table. Since it was two o'clock and past the lunch crowd, we were practically the only patrons in the dining area.

After we sat down, Erin said to me, "I have to tell Marilyn about Paul."

"What do you mean you have to tell me about Paul," Marilyn said. "What about Paul?"

"Paul relapsed," Erin said. "I didn't want to tell you before the hearing. I saw him last night. He'd been avoiding me for a few days, so I went to the halfway house where he lives and..."

Marilyn stopped in mid-chew and looked disbelievingly at Erin. "He what? He relapsed?" She slapped herself on the right cheek, pretending someone had hit her.

"He took his daughter's cough syr—" Erin began.

"He's got kids?" Marilyn slapped her left cheek.

"Yeah, but he's filing for divorce pretty soon—"

"He's married?" Marilyn slapped the cheek she'd slapped at the first question. "I thought you said you'd call off the relationship if either one of you relapsed."

"We're going to have a long talk tonight. I was really angry at him last night for lying to me, but he said he was trying not to upset me before my hearing."

As the three of us continued to talk, it was clear that Marilyn was very concerned for Erin. She tried to advise her to step back from this relationship for a while, until she was sure Paul was "healthy."

Marilyn reminded Erin that she had to take care of herself, that she'd just been through a grueling ordeal that was going to require some of her own healing. She told Erin she was getting in over her head, and that this played right in to her "nurse-caretaker" role. She pointed out that focusing on Paul prevented her from focusing on herself, which was a way to close her eyes to herself, to avoid the things in her own life that needed healing or tending to. It was also a great way to avoid personal pain.

"I am going to make an appointment with Adam as soon as I can," Erin said, as a diversion, and maybe to reassure us that she was going to take care of herself.

"Good. That is very good," Marilyn said.

As for me, I didn't know what to think. I wanted to trust my friend to do the right thing.

I WAS SO THRILLED at the board's decision, because this would give Erin the chance she needed to continue on with her life. Marilyn and I were also happy that Erin now could fire the "cult mother" and get some real therapy with Adam. She made her first appointment the day after her hearing. She had "felt the pain" long and hard enough.

PART TWO

From Acceptance to Transcendence

Courage is reclaiming your life after a devastating event robs you of your confidence and self-esteem. It is facing tomorrow with a firm resolve to reach deep within yourself to find another strength; another talent. It is taking yourself to another level of your own existence where you are once again whole, productive, special.

—Catherine Britton

CHAPTER 32

Disclosure

THE HEARINGS BEFORE the Connecticut State Board of Examiners for Nursing that had so consumed my life for so many months were now over. Now I had to return to my "real" life. But what was my real life? Things were basically the same. I was still married to the same man; I still had the same kids; I still lived in the same house; and I was still a nurse.

All the fear leading up to the nursing board hearing precipitated symptoms of posttraumatic stress disorder, or PTSD. Spending so much energy trying to keep myself from falling apart, and trying to recover from an illness that by its very nature had robbed me of the ability to process my emotions and feelings, had set me up for this "battle fatigue syndrome disorder." My PTSD did not rise to the level of that of a war veteran, but it was a traumatic experience for me nonetheless, and there was going to have to be a period of adjustment. I wanted to feel good, emotionally and physically. Again, I thought that there must be a better way, a healthier way, for nurse-addicts to recover. And I wondered how many nurses relapsed with the humiliation and trauma of the nursing board hearings coming at such a vulnerable time in their recovery and their lives.

SPRING WAS ARRIVING. I stared at the oak tree outside Adam's window. Hints of light green were appearing on the tips of the branches. The tree was thawing, and producing the life-renewing sap that would restore the unambiguous beauty hidden inside. The tree had transcended the winter, and was concentrating on its internal responsibility to itself. Only then could it reveal its magnificence, no longer trapped, no longer an illusion.

"You aren't trapped anymore either, Patty," Adam said. "You are transforming because of your willingness to transcend. You have transcended much of your fear, which we know is an illusion. We always have the choice to transcend or stay stuck. Of course you cannot say, 'Oh, I am going to transcend now,' because it is the *process* that our Higher Power wants us to have the passion for."

The process of returning to reality meant I would have to face the dreaded thought of moving to Buffalo. How could I leave these new people in my life who had become like family to me, who had saved my life? I did not want to go.

I was afraid to tell Fred of my fears. He had given up so much. He missed his family desperately and wanted us to be together. How could I tell him? My recovery was my recovery, which meant that no matter where I was, it would be my responsibility to work my program. If that was where my husband was, then that was where I was supposed to be, too. I would keep these fears to myself. I would be a grown-up about the move. I was going to have to prepare myself mentally to accept this eventuality in my life, but I was a very scared grown-up.

Real life was here. Our finances were strained to the breaking point. I had been trying to prioritize whom to pay and whom not to pay. The not-to-pay list was getting longer and longer. It was a huge source of stress. I began a job search again, going on interview after interview, but as soon as I disclosed my recent past history, and my probation, the tone of the interview changed. I always remained hopeful, but I would eventually get the letter or the phone call that said that another candidate had been selected, but that they would keep my application on file. Yeah, right! After a while, I was ready to apply at local department stores. Still, I held to the belief that I would get the job that God wanted me to get, so I continued to try.

ON MARCH 1, MY husband called me from Buffalo. He had just received the news that his mother, who was only in her sixties, had passed away. She had suffered a stroke in December and seemed to be recovering and progressing in her therapy. But when she and her husband took a trip to Georgia to visit his son, she suffered another stroke, and died down there.

Fred came home for about a week. He helped his family plan the services, and then we all attended the funeral. This was such a painful time for him. He was close to his mother and was going to miss her, and I know that she'd missed him while he was in Buffalo.

While Fred was home that week, we talked about whether our moving to Buffalo was a good idea. I didn't want to go, the kids didn't want to go, and Fred didn't even like it up there. We talked about my support system and how it would not be the safest thing for me to leave. And we decided that Fred would begin making arrangements with his company to move back to Connecticut when his two years were up. I was so relieved and grateful.

Soon he had to return to Buffalo to grieve alone. My heart was breaking for him. I wanted him to stay home. We needed each other. It seemed absurd for him to go back there. He belonged here with us! Not up there alone. We became closer again as we talked on the phone every day. We were confronting the lesson that life is too short and unpredictable to waste time on regrets and fear.

Fred was transforming and transcending as well, though most of the time not as fast as I wanted. Instinctively I knew that we needed this separation so that our marriage could survive, and it would.

With our decision not to move to Buffalo, my need for employment here became even more crucial. For several weeks there had been an advertisement in our local paper for RNs at a long-term care facility. The director of nurses had been my supervisor early in my career. I had a great deal of respect for her and knew her to be a good manager and a good person. She was a dedicated nurse who had more than thirty years of experience. Long-term care, a convalescent home, however, was the last field in which I'd ever wanted to work, however. I love and respect the elderly, but caring for their daily needs was not the kind of nursing I ever desired.

"Just call her. What have you got to lose?" Fred asked.

"Yeah, I guess I will. I can do that for a while, I guess. I'll call her tomorrow."

"She was always good to you and you had a good relationship with her. She might be able to help you." I had seen her at a nursing function about a year before, and at that time she said if I ever needed a job, to contact her. *Talk about synchronicity!*

THE NEXT MORNING, I faced my fear and picked up the phone. I was shaking as much as I did the day I was confronted by Drug Control.

The phone rang and a receptionist with a high-pitched voice answered, "Hello, Cheshire Convalescent Center. How can I help you?"

"Can I speak with Pat Rzewnicki, please?"

"Just a moment." I was put on hold. It was all I could do not to hang up the phone.

"Hi. This is Pat Rzewnicki."

"Um... Hi, Pat. This is Patty Holloran. Remember me?"

"Hi, Patty! Of course I remember you! What can I do for you?"

"Well, I would just like the opportunity to talk to you, and I really don't want to discuss it over the phone."

"Okay. It sounds important. Can you come in tomorrow morning, at about ten?"

YIKES. So soon.

"Um... yeah, that looks okay to me." *Like I had big plans. My calendar being so full and all!*

The next morning, in Pat's office, I explained all that had happened to me in that last year. I told her that I was coming to her for a job, but that I was going to be on probation, and I was not allowed to have any access to narcotics for the first year. I gave her the statement I had prepared for the board, and she quickly read it. I tried very hard to get through this without crying... but was not successful.

After she read through the statement, she looked up at me and said, "Of course I'll hire you. You're one of the best nurses I've ever worked with."

For a few seconds, I sat there in stunned disbelief.

She continued: "I just have to let my administrator know. There shouldn't be any problem, because I am going to tell him that you're an excellent nurse and will be an asset to this facility." She went across the hall to the administrator's office for about five minutes.

They'll find some reason why they can't hire me. They won't like the narcotic restriction. They'll have some rule about hiring nurses on probation... or something. Mentally I prepared myself for rejection.

She returned to the office and said, "No problem. When would you like to start?"

I was absolutely stunned. This seemed to be no big deal for her. We just had to iron out some of the details. She left it up to me as to how I would tell the rest of the staff, which certainly was a necessity, because I could not handle or administer narcotics. We agreed that I would start as soon as she was back from her vacation, March 25.

"We'll help get you through this year with the key restriction. Don't worry," she said compassionately.

She went on to tell me that there was a lab right down the street that would send my urine samples out to the lab in New York. Pat was also familiar with the forms that had to be sent to the monitor at the Department of Public Health, because another nurse there was in the last year of his probation. *Another nurse on probation!* I couldn't believe it was going to be so easy. Everything I needed was right here.

I left Pat's office with such an intense feeling of relief. If this is where God wanted me to be, then this is where I would be!

WHEN I GOT HOME, I called Erin and Marilyn and they both were thrilled. I saved the call to my husband till last. "See! I knew she would give you a chance. You must feel so happy. I am happy for you. You can be a nurse again!"

I know that he was genuine in his happiness for me, and it felt really good to have his unconditional love and support. Only he really knew, from the inside out, what we'd been through these last few years. Maybe we didn't see things the same way much of the time, but there was no one else who had experienced the day-to-day stuff others could never understand. We had memories no one else in the world shared, and that was too precious to let go of. We were together for better or worse. We'd made that commitment, that vow before God, and it would take more than all of this to force us to break it.

THE FIRST WEEK AT my new job, I was getting settled and learning the routine. I dreaded having to tell the staff about my probation and the key restriction, certain they would see me as a burden and that they would have to do some of my work. But the people I told were understanding, empathetic, and supportive. They agreed without hesitation to help me while the key restriction was in force, and to administer to my patients any narcotics that were needed.

To some, I shared the bare minimum; to others, I disclosed more details. I still experienced those old familiar feelings of shame and embarrassment, but they diminished with every telling, and with time. I felt I was accepted by the nurses there. They were amazed at what I had to go through with regard to my disciplinary action.

Yes, this was where God wanted me to be. This was part of my healing process, something that I hadn't thought possible less than a year ago: acceptance from fellow nurses outside of my circle of Nurses for Nurses.

The biggest surprise to me was that I liked working there! It still was not the type of nursing I'd normally gravitate to, but the people I'd found myself working with were some of the best.

I met the other nurse who was on probation, and we became recovery friends. He told me of a woman he knew who was just beginning her recovery and wanted me to meet her. Her name was Faith. I took her to her first Nurses for Nurses meeting, and we became fast friends. She lived in the same town, so now I had a companion to ride to meetings with.

And the truth shall set you free, but not till it's finished with you.

—*Denial Is Not a River in Egypt,* by Sandi Bachom

CHAPTER 33

Confession

I NEEDED TO TELL my mother and stepfather. I never doubted that they would love me and support me, but I couldn't possibly have told them before my hearing. My mom would have been heartbroken enough without having to worry about the outcome of the hearing on top of it. And I would have been worried about her worrying about me. With the hearing behind me, it would be easier to tell them now.

Adam gently challenged me as to when I was going to tell them. He reminded me, again, that my fears were an illusion, and not reality. I had the choice either to live in those fears and that illusion, or to transcend them. I just couldn't let go of the residual shame. I didn't want to let my mother and stepfather down—or was that my pride that was in the way again? Was my pride the front for my fear? Adam reminded me that as long as I didn't tell them, I would remain in the fear.

I shared my dilemma with Sue. She helped me "fourth step" this by taking a fearless and moral inventory of myself. She told me that she saw my having to tell my mother and stepfather about my addiction as a lesson in humility. I had to take myself off of the pedestal of being the nurse. "You can't control everything, especially how they'll react, but you can be humble and honest. Just pray to see signs of His will and have the willingness to carry it out."

"Have a passion for the process," Adam told me. "And don't invest in the outcome. Because even if they took a gun out and shot you, they couldn't destroy you." *Therapy at the OK Corral.*

I was waiting for the fear to go away before I told them, but that was backward thinking. I wanted to face them with confidence, but that would be a false face. The fear wasn't going to go until I made the call, until I told them—a lesson in facing my fear and walking through it.

WITH MY HEART POUNDING, I called my mom and told her that I wanted to talk to her and Jack. The next day, still feeling like the bad daughter, I sat in their living room (crying...again) and told them all the gory details, and how sorry I was that I hadn't been able to tell them sooner. I explained that I hadn't wanted to tell them before the hearing.

They were wonderfully supportive. (*Poof! There goes the illusion.*) They told me they knew I was going through "something," because I hadn't been myself in a very long time. My mom felt bad that I hadn't come to her sooner, but she was glad I'd been able to tell them now. She was shocked that I'd had to go before the nursing board, that my addiction had taken me to that level, but she was glad I'd been able to retain my license, and that I even had a job.

Jack reminded me that nobody is perfect, and that at some point in our lives we go through hard times or make mistakes or are unable to cope and make poor decisions for our lives. They acknowledged that taking care of Dad must have been extremely difficult, and from that perspective they "understood" why I'd taken the Stadol. They'd both been through tough times in their own lives and had wisdom born of experience. Then, graciously, and without hesitation, they loaned us some money to help out until our financial situation stabilized somewhat.

Humility? You bet. It felt good to climb off that pedestal I'd been on in my own mind. I felt loved and grateful. I learned that I could practice being honest and not fear the reaction. Being honest was my responsibility; the reaction was not—I couldn't control that; I was powerless. The great paradox of recovery: releasing control, accepting powerlessness, giving up the struggle—all of which leads to empowerment, and the power of choice.

You have to accept whatever comes, and the only important thing is that you meet it with courage and with the best that you have to give.

—Eleanor Roosevelt

CHAPTER 34

Healing

ONE EVENING EARLY in April, my middle son, Shaun, who was now fifteen, began complaining of severe body aches. At first it seemed as if he merely had the flu, but after twenty-four hours, and 800 milligrams of Ibuprofen every six to eight hours, everything we were doing to relieve his symptoms had been totally ineffective, I knew we had a problem. His wrists, hands, and knees were becoming swollen. He could barely move from the couch or take care of his personal needs.

The next morning, I took him to his pediatrician. They suspected an unusually acute onset of juvenile rheumatoid arthritis (JRA). This was not the typical way that JRA presented, so they did a battery of blood tests to rule out other things, such as Lyme disease, rheumatic fever, and other autoimmune syndromes. We left the doctor's office with a prescription for a drug that would help alleviate Shaun's symptoms. That night, he was no better than he had been the previous one, so the next morning, he was admitted to Children's Hospital in Hartford for further testing and to receive intravenous steroids to arrest the pain and swelling.

It tore my heart out to see my child in this much distress, to see my usually uncomplaining, very active, very independent fifteen-year-old son crying in pain every time he moved. Hadn't he already been through enough this year worrying about me, his father being away, and his grandfather so sick in the hospital? It must have seemed sometimes that his world had fallen apart—and now this.

He tried to be brave, but he told me how afraid he was that he would end up like Grampa—disabled, unable to walk, and in constant pain, and at such a young age.

Pat Rzewnicki was very understanding of my need to take time off work to care for my child. Thank God I was restricted from having access to narcotics that first year at work, and that I had to give random urines. At times like these, these safeguards really gave me another layer of protection. Early in recovery, external controls help a lot.

IT WAS DETERMINED THAT Shaun was suffering from a rare complication of Salmonella poisoning. At Easter that year, we had gone to a restaurant for dinner, and over the next few days, Shaun had diarrhea which cleared up spontaneously. However, in his case, the Salmonella went right to his joints causing a widespread arthritis syndrome.

Within twenty-four hours of his being in the hospital, he was feeling much better and was able to come home, and within a week he could return to school. He was on a medication to keep his symptoms at bay, and eventually the swelling in his joints went down and he regained his full range of motion. He had to have one of his knees drained twice, and he periodically suffered from achiness, but after three months, the symptoms of the Salmonella poisoning were virtually gone.

Our whole family, especially Shaun, was very happy and grateful that Shaun's problem was due to a temporary condition. He still experiences achiness in his joints from time to time, however.

I am so grateful to have had the support and guidance of my friends in recovery during this period. I could cry about my fears, and they'd remind me, once again, that I was powerless, that I had to trust my Higher Power to see us through this, and that even if Shaun's troubles turned out to be JRA, his Higher Power was with him, too.

MY FATHER WAS DYING. He had developed methicillin-resistant *Staphylococcus aureus*, MRSA, a virulent, antibiotic-resistant, bacterial infection The source of the infection was the catheter that had been inserted in his upper chest for his dialysis. He was counseled that it was his choice to be on the dialysis, but he chose to continue with it.

The circulation in his legs became so bad that both of them were amputated further, this time above the knees. The infection made him feel so miserable that he could no longer raise his hands to his face to feed himself. He was in isolation from others, so that the chance of the infection spreading to anyone else was diminished. Because of Shaun's sudden illness, which made him susceptible to infection, I was not permitted to visit my dad in the last weeks of his life. He had been in and out of the hospital for ten months and had suffered so much. He was dying in bits and pieces. I prayed that God would take him. After all, he was more than ready.

ON MARCH 24, MY father's last grandchild was born in the room directly above his, to my brother and his wife.

On April 14, God took Dad home.

The guilt returned: I should have been there. Was he scared? Was he in pain? I should have been there.

At the request of my brother, they didn't send Dad to the morgue until I got to the hospital. My sister was on vacation with her family, so she was unable to be there. When I walked into the hospital room I found my three brothers crying. I hugged each of them, and then went over to my dad. He was ashen, gaunt, a deflated shell of the man I had loved my whole life.

At that moment, I had no doubt that he truly was not there, in that body. I kissed his forehead, and in my heart I asked him to forgive me again — for the addiction, for not being with him when he died, for any way I may have disappointed him. I was stroking his cheek as I silently continued to talk to him. *I guess He's finally finished with you, Dad.*

I remembered once when he and I were watching TV, one of his favorite shows, *Mother Angelica Live,* was on. Mother Angelica said that she was ready for whenever the Good Lord would take her, because then she could see the face of Jesus, and how awesome that would be. My dad was now in the presence of that face.

I felt at peace during the wake and the funeral. I never thought that I could have this kind of peace at the death of one of my parents. I did not then nor do I now feel that death has separated me from my father. He is very close to me, and to my brothers and my sister. I frequently dream about him, and I awaken from those dreams knowing that I have been blessed by a visit from him.

I have since come to know that I was grieving my father long before his death, the father I had already lost while he was living with us, while I was taking care of him. Watching him become weaker, and more incapable of caring for himself, was more than I could bear. I was not aware of this at the time, but the loss of him for me was part of the reason for my drug use. Losing the strong, capable independent man I knew to be my father was like a death for me. I was grieving that. I was numbing that.

My sister told me of a dream she had about a month after Dad died: He was in his hospital room and had just died, when he opened his eyes one last time and said to her, "Tell everyone thank you," and then he closed his eyes again.

Thank you, *Dad.*

There is a bit of good in the worst of us,
and a bit of bad in the rest of us.

—*Denial Is Not a River in Egypt,* by Sandi Bachom

CHAPTER 35

It's All about Me

I NEEDED TO KNOW the big "Why?" I knew there was a core reason somewhere inside of me that had made me become an addict that didn't have anything to do with taking care of my father or my lack of sleep. I knew that somewhere within me was something basic to my nature that had led me to make the choices I made. With his intuitiveness and innate sense of pacing and timing, Adam began to help me peel away the layers of that onion to reveal that core. Just like an onion, every layer we peeled back brought on the tears.

External events and influences can bring us to a crisis and force us to look within ourselves. We then have the choice to transcend and transform, or not—to stay stuck in regret and anger. I had to learn what my role was in life and how I'd co-depended, how I'd taught others how to treat me. I needed to take responsibility for my actions, the only actions I can be responsible for.

By assuming responsibility for myself, I was learning how to set my boundaries, learning to say no if I had to. I no longer had to be all things to all people, or worry if someone else thought I was wrong. I had to trust my own senses, and know that I could make decisions for my own best interests. If I wasn't sure, then I had my Higher Power and all that He had sent my way: Adam, my sponsor, my recovery connections.

LIFE WAS FINALLY ROUTINE for a while: I went to work; I came home; I did housework (well, sometimes). I decided that I would work nights. I was used to this routine, and once again I could be available to the boys during the day if they needed me. My oldest son was now eighteen, and he was in charge of making sure that everything was okay when I wasn't there. When I left the house, our dog, Oreo, would "man" her post by the back door.

There are no coincidences, only situations where God chooses to remain anonymous.

—*Denial Is Not a River in Egypt,* by Sandi Bachom

CHAPTER 36

F-Words

JULY 3, THE ONE-YEAR anniversary of my recovery. Imagine that! It had gone by so fast. I felt intense gratitude. Yes, I was grateful, grateful and proud, that I was a recovering addict. Most of the guilt and shame I'd felt for so long was now gone, or going. I really didn't care who knew I was in recovery, because I had nothing to hide. I had received such positive responses from everyone I told, which had given me the courage to continue to tell my story. Some people may have talked behind my back, but that wasn't something I could control, nor did I care to. I had the opportunity to "put a face to this disease."

One night after a meeting, Sue asked me if I felt I was ready to be a sponsor. "I'm not ready for that. I haven't worked all of the steps, and I still feel like a baby in this myself. How do I know if I'm ready for that responsibility, or if I even want it?"

"You have a really solid recovery," she reassured me. "I think you would make a good sponsor. You have so much to offer, and I'm in awe of your spirituality, your connection to God. Pray about it. You're not in this alone, you know. I'm always here for you. You know we only 'keep what we have by giving it away.' Just pray to see signs of His will."

So I prayed about it. I really loved being supportive of new nurse-addicts, and knew that I had something to offer, but the thought of being a sponsor *scared the shit out of me*. When new people asked for a sponsor, I never raised my hand. I certainly considered myself far from ready, and anyway, I figured God would let me know when the time was right.

SINCE I HAD EXPERIENCED such support from work, I decided to start telling my friends about my addiction. A very close friend to whom I had not confided my story, Dede, had worked with me at Middlesex Hospital for 12 years. She was one of the best labor and delivery nurses I'd have ever worked with, and her knowledge and expertise extended to other areas of OB: the nursery and the postpartum unit. We had a very intuitive relationship. When we worked together, each "knew" what the other needed without the need for many words. We were on the same wavelength in our sense of humor, too.

Our relationship extended beyond work. We talked on the phone regularly. I'd been in her wedding, and was with her through the labor and birth of her son. Hell, I knew she was pregnant before her husband did! She called me her big sister. And yet, I hadn't been able to tell this close friend what I'd been going through, for the same reason that I hadn't told anybody: I was too ashamed, and thought that I could go through all of it without anyone knowing. But I needed Dede in my life.

"Why don't you just do it?" Erin asked me. "You know she'll understand. Judy understood. People at work understand. It's time you told Dede."

"I know that, but she always sounds so tired, and... I don't know... sad or something. I think she's going through a hard time. She's been healing from surgery; her son has been diagnosed with ADHD. Maybe that has something to do with it... and besides, I don't want to burden her with this."

"I think you're just afraid you'll be a disappointment to her or something. You should just do it. The longer you wait, the harder it'll be."

I had to admit she was right. I wanted my friend fully back in my life, and if she was going through a rough time, then perhaps she needed me as much as I needed her.

ON JULY 22, THE DAY after my birthday, I called her. I was going to teasingly harass her for not having called me and wished me a happy birthday. I was also going to tell her all about the past year. *Hey! Guess what I did on my last summer vacation?* As I listened to the phone ring on the other end of the line, I felt nervous, and was prepared to cry, even though she was a worse crier than I ever could be. (She always swore that her tear ducts were connected to her kidneys.) I was braced for whatever reaction she might have. Shock? Disappointment? Whatever I had to say—how sorry I was I hadn't told her about my addiction for a whole year—would be okay.

Yes, Dede and I were best friends, but the conversation we had that afternoon was something that neither of us—no matter how much intuition we had for each other—could have predicted:

I flopped on the bed as she picked up the phone. "I called to give you a hard time for not wishing me a happy birthday," I said.

"Hi, um…yeah…I'm sorry about that. I didn't forget, but, I… I…something happened at work…" She was beginning to wheeze and hyperventilate, and I could tell she was crying, or just about to.

"What? What's the matter?" I said, truly alarmed. *What was the matter with my Dede?* The first thought I had was that she'd made a big mistake and a baby had died.

"Well, I'm kinda, like, on a medical leave. Well, not really medical. It's something else…and I'm so scared…"

Could it be? Impossible!

"No fucking way…" was all I could say, so softly that it was really to myself.

"Yeah...um..." I heard her light up a cigarette. "Oh! Patty!" She was definitely crying now. "I kinda 'borrowed' some Stadol from work and now I'm in a drug treatment program...and..."

"No fucking way!" was all I could repeat, a little louder.

"Well, they didn't fire me. They said they just wanted me to get better. These guys from Drug Control..."

"No fucking way!" a little louder, a little more astounded.

Now she was talking faster and faster, and crying harder and harder. "...came to the hospital, and they have video of me...and I don't know how much trouble I'm in with my license..."

"No fucking way!" I was unable to say anything else. I was so stunned, stupefied, actually. My best friend! The same drug? I was right in thinking she'd been going through a hard time, but this had been totally off my radar.

"Oh, Patty. I know what you must think of me. I'm so sorry. I...I'm really scared..." She was sobbing now.

"Dede—"

"Oh, what am I gonna do? I'm so scared. I wouldn't blame you if you never wanted to speak to me again."

"Dede, honey—"

"You must hate me! I—"

"*Dede!* Shut up a minute. It's okay. That's what happened—"

She was sobbing so hard now that it was difficult for me to get her attention. I knew she was interpreting my "no fucking ways" as disapproval, and not as expressions of shock and stupefaction.

"Dede!"

Sniff, sob. "What?"

Deep breath. "Dede, it's okay. That is what I have been going through for the last year. The same thing happened to me at VMMC!"

Silence. No crying. No wheezing. No puffing. No breathing.

"Dede? Are you all right?"

Silence.

"Dede? Dede? Are you still there?"

Continued silence. Then her stunned response: "No fucking way!"

It was like two tractor trailers hitting head on in the middle of the night, in a fog. We were both dumbfounded as the impact of what we had just told each other sank in. When I recovered my sense of time and space again, I told her that I could help her. I asked her if she'd received information about Nurses for Nurses, and she said that she had. It quickly became apparent that we had way too much to discuss in a phone call. It was difficult for either of us to have the privacy we needed, so we decided to meet in the commuter parking lot near where I worked.

WHEN I ARRIVED AT the parking lot, I got in her car and we hugged each other and cried for a long time. I knew her pain and fear. She told me that since her being confronted by Drug Control, she'd been in treatment in a small facility in West Hartford, and that she was amazed at what she was learning about addiction.

"Why didn't we know? Nurses don't know what it really means to be an addict. Patty, I never thought it would feel like this! Those patients we criticized for being addicts. I'm one of them! I feel so bad I was so angry with them. I didn't understand that they just couldn't stop! I still can't really understand why I couldn't stop. And when I did want to stop, I didn't know what to do. I didn't know where to turn. I couldn't tell anybody. Who was I going to tell? I was so afraid of being caught, but I knew I would be eventually. Patty, I used someone else's Pyxis code, and she almost got in trouble. I don't think I can ever face her again; she never did anything to me. How could I have done this to her? I didn't want to lose my license. I couldn't tell anybody I had stolen drugs from work. They would have fired me."

Through her tears, she poured out the whole story of her use, abuse, and addiction to Stadol, and the stresses in her life that she felt may have led to her feeling isolated and alone. She had had surgery to repair an area of her C-section incision that had developed a hematoma. This incision also did not heal well, with areas of it breaking down entirely. Her doctors had decided that it had to heal by granulation—that is, from the inside out. This made for a slower, but more complete and stronger, healing process. What had happened, however, was that it only healed on top, and not underneath, thus giving doctors the illusion that it had healed.

In the process, Dede had to scrub her incision several times a day to keep it from getting infected, and also to keep the site raw and bleeding to promote the growth of new tissue. In order to bear the pain of doing this, she began using Stadol Nasal Spray before carrying out this procedure. This was the beginning of her addiction. Before long, she began diverting vials of Stadol from work. Dede, also being a diabetic, did not have any fear of injecting herself with it.

Her story was that of the quintessential nurse-addict who feels she has to be all things to all people—her spouse, her child, her family, her patients—and who loses herself in the process. The ultimate caregiver and a very reluctant care receiver using a drug for the right reasons. But that drug then altered her brain, giving her that obsession to obtain and that compulsion to use. Addiction had bitten Dede in the ass.

For a long time we sat in that commuter parking lot and cried our eyes out. We still couldn't believe this had happened to both of us. I asked her if she'd gotten a lawyer yet. She said she hadn't; the people at her treatment facility advised her that since this was her first offense, she had nothing to worry about and that the board of nursing would "go easy on her." *Why do people who know nothing of the process try to give advice about it?*

I told her the truth: that it was like going to court, and the Department of Health had a lawyer who was going to try to screw her over, so she had a responsibility to herself to ensure there was a level playing field. This started a whole new round of tears for her. Just like me, she didn't know that going before the board was going to be such a big deal. I offered to call Marilyn for her, if it would be too difficult for her to do herself. I remembered that first day when someone called her for me and how much that had eased my mind. Dede agreed.

I was *so* grateful that I could be there for my friend. I wanted to impart to her all that I had learned in the last year, and how wonderful recovery was going to be. I wanted to tell her all about Adam, and how important he'd been to helping me rediscover myself. I wanted to tell her about Sue, and how much she would love Nurses for Nurses. I wanted her to meet Erin.

I wanted to tell her everything now! I wanted her to be as happy as I was, but I knew that she had to experience her own pain and learn from it. This was her journey, and she could only do one thing, one day at a time. I was sad for her, but my heart was soaring. It was like watching her when she was in labor with her son: I knew what that pain was going to feel like. I could help and support her while she did it, but I couldn't do it for her. I couldn't take away her pain, but I could comfort and encourage her.

"One of the things I know I need is a sponsor. Could you be my sponsor?" Dede timidly asked.

YIKES!

I told her that I had never sponsored anyone yet, and I didn't know if I was ready for it, but I reassured her that no matter what, I would always be there for her. I asked her to let me think and pray about it; I wanted the best for her, and for me, and if my Higher Power didn't think it was a good idea—or even if He did—He would let me know.

THE NEXT DAY, I called Erin and told her all about what had happened to Dede. Erin was in state of shock almost equaling mine. I don't remember the conversation we had, but I'm sure that the phrase "No fucking way" was part of it. I called Marilyn, as I had promised. The only *F*-word she used was *flabbergasted*. I called Sue and told her, too. After the appropriate "No fucking ways," I told her that Dede had asked me to be her sponsor.

"Great!" Sue responded. "Isn't it amazing that we were just talking about that, and God is letting you have this wonderful opportunity now?"

"So you still think it's a good idea? You think I would make a good sponsor?"

"The most important thing you need is the desire to be a sponsor, a good sponsor. It has to be a good fit, you know. You have to think you'll get along with the sponsee, and you have to have at least one year clean. You should be actively working on the higher steps. You know, it's so good for your own recovery to be a sponsor. It helps keep it fresh, helps keep it green. It reminds you to surrender.

"You won't be able to do her recovery for her; you're only a guide. Maybe that's the only thing you'll have to be aware of: setting your boundaries in your own mind. That can be problematic when the person is a good friend, but I think you can. And don't forget: I'm here, and the group is here. None of us does this alone."

I was afraid people would say, "What gives you the right to be a sponsor? You haven't been in recovery long enough." But, of course, again, that was only me talking to myself in my own head and assigning my insecurities to what others may think of me.

I prayed about it. I didn't have to pray very long, because God sent the answer to me very quickly. It was just a knowing and a feeling that it was "right." I wrote Dede a long letter saying that I was humbled that she'd asked me and that I would be honored to be her sponsor. I was apprehensive, but I knew that I had the best resources: Sue, my recovery, and God.

The next week, Dede joined me for her first Nurses for Nurses meeting.

Regarding bad things happening to good people:
First of all, things aren't that bad
And you're not as good as you think you are.
—*Denial Is Not a River in Egypt,* by Sandi Bachom

CHAPTER 37

Sweet Pee

WHAT A DIFFERENT summer I was having from the one I'd had the previous year! Even the weather was better: warm, sunny days and very little rain. The passage into fall was just as mellow and gradual. The warm weather persisted into September, almost as if it were making up for the cold and dreary summer of the year before.

The oak tree had come full cycle. It was resplendent in its beauty with the exhibition of its green, healthy leaves. It was about to put on its best show yet as it matured into the autumn, when it would give back the gifts of the summer to revitalize the soil to preserve its own health.

Sponsoring Dede was proving to be one of the best decisions I'd ever made. I was maturing in my recovery. I could give back. One of the paradoxical tenets of recovery is that the only way you can "keep what you have is by giving it away." Helping her in her early recovery kept it all green for me. It is recommended in recovery to go back to the basics every so often, and sponsoring is the best way to do that.

ON SEPTEMBER 23, I was off from work. It was finally cooler now, after the warm autumn we'd been experiencing. As a matter of fact, it seemed downright cold in our house. I went downstairs to check the oil level, and there wasn't any. What an annoyance this was! I called the oil company. They said that they would not be able to supply us until after three o'clock. *Shit.* I decided that since I had to see Adam at noon, I would spend the day doing errands such as banking and grocery shopping. Besides, the van would be warmer than the house.

I took a lukewarm shower and got into the car by nine o'clock. I normally would have been in a pissy mood the rest of the day because of this situation, but I decided to practice taking life on life's terms and not letting it affect me so much. In the car I formed a gratitude list in my head and stuck to positive thoughts. Having no heating oil was not the end of the world—at least I could pay for it, now that I had a job. Now, there was gratitude.

Erin always had her appointment with Adam just before mine, so I was looking forward to seeing her for a few minutes at that time. After my session, we planned on meeting at Lena's for lunch. After that, I would head home, connect with my kids after school, and wait for the oil man. So it was going to be a good day after all.

I arrived at Adam's office right on time. Usually, Erin and he would still be in session, and I would wait until they were through. When I got there, however, the door to his office was open, and there was no Erin to be seen. Adam ushered me into his office immediately and quickly sat back down in his chair. I sat in my usual place on the couch. He had a very serious expression on his face and he was drumming his fingers on the arm of his chair.

This was the complete opposite of his usual calm demeanor. The hairs on the back of my neck were at attention as I wondered why he was so nervous. Was Erin all right? Or was it something personal? He seemed hesitant to say anything to me at first. His legs were crossed and his foot was swinging to and fro; his eyes were fixed and stern; his mouth was tight. I felt as if he were looking through me! This all took place in a span of a few seconds as I sat down. Was he mad? If so, at what? He definitely was concerned, or disturbed, and I was becoming very fearful.

"How are you today, Patty?" he began, but he did not say it in the normal way; it was a very pointed and direct question.

"I'm okay. Other than I let the furnace run out of oil and they can't deliver it until after three."

"Nothing else?"

"No, not that I... Why?"

"You're okay? There isn't anything you want to tell me?"

Now I *was* scared! What was he hinting at? "What's wrong?" I demanded. "What are you talking about?"

"I just got a call from Marilyn," he began, as his expression changed to one of concern. "Did you get any phone calls this morning?"

"No. I haven't been home because it was too cold, so I did some errands."

"Well, she has desperately been trying to contact you, so she called me because she knew you had an appointment with me at noon. I just got off the phone with her. I cut Erin's appointment short because Marilyn said that this was serious."

I swallowed hard.

"Patty, Jeff Kardys from the Department of Health has been trying to get a hold of you. He couldn't, so he called Marilyn and asked her to tell you that you had a urine report that came back positive for alcohol."

"A what?" I said in an almost whisper. "Alcohol? How could I have a urine positive for alcohol?"

"I don't know. Why don't you tell me?"

"Adam!" I looked right at him. "Alcohol?" I said again quietly and dumbfounded. That was the last thing I'd expected to hear from him. At first I thought he must be kidding! It obviously was a lab error, because

I hadn't drunk any alcohol. Adam would know that, of course—or would he?

"Adam, I did not drink any alcohol. I have no idea why this urine is positive." I put my hand to my mouth and started to cry, even though I really wanted to scream. I had to stay as calm as I possibly could. *Why should he believe me? I'm an addict! Addicts are not to be believed or trusted. Addicts are manipulative and sneaky. No one would believe me...not even Adam.*

But I desperately needed him to believe me. He continued to look intensely at me. His mouth remained rigid and now his hands were tented in front of his face. His foot was not swinging as fast as it had been. Then very deliberately, he leaned over, placing his elbows on his knees, his feet planted firmly on the floor. I started to shake. Was he going to tell me that I couldn't be his client anymore? Was he going to ask me how I could have done this, if all of our therapy had been a sham? I pictured myself pleading with him, promising him that I was clean and sober, and begging him not to abandon me.

"I believe you," he said softly. His expression was of genuine compassion and concern. "I have not seen any evidence objectively or subjectively that you have relapsed in any way, and I think I would know from your behavior in this room. If you'd told me you'd been drinking, I would have been very surprised. Do you have any explanation for this?"

I sat staring out of the window at the oak tree. The panic over the idea that he would terminate our therapy, that he would abandon me or admonish me, was subsiding. I had been listening to the escalating fear. He would never abandon me when I needed him the most, even, or especially if I had relapsed.

"No!" I answered. My tears quietly began to flow as the impact of what this would mean to me became clear. If this was made known to the lawyers at DPH, they would act first and ask questions later.

My brain was racing less now, and I was able to detach from the emotion as I began to problem-solve. Was it something I'd eaten or come in contact with? Was there any reason for this positive result? *Think logically, Patty,* I told myself.

"Maybe it's the alcohol solution I wash my hands with," I said. "When I do a med pass, I wash my hands thirty to forty times in the span of about two hours. I don't not know if it's ethyl alcohol, the kind you drink, or isopropyl alcohol, rubbing alcohol. If it's isopropyl, then maybe there's a cross-reaction."

Adam turned his chair toward his desk. "Let me call the lab in New York to see if they might have an explanation."

He dialed the number, and after all of the electronic directions, he was finally in contact with an actual human. He asked if there was could be any reason, other than the ingestion of alcohol, for a positive result. The human on the other end said that he did not know of any. Adam then asked him if the test was definitely positive for ethyl, as opposed to isopropyl, alcohol, and the answer was that it was, without a doubt, ethyl alcohol. Adam then asked him if isopropyl alcohol, which is generally used for hand-washing, could break down to imitate ethyl alcohol, and again the answer was a definite no.

Adam continued to ask about other factors that might explain the positive result: Were they sure the chain of custody had been maintained? If it had not, then it could mean that it wasn't my urine that had been tested or that my urine had been contaminated with someone else's urine. The person on the other end of the line gave Adam the company line about how their quality control followed the utmost standards, blah, blah, blah... Well, we were getting nowhere here.

Adam asked how we could get the urine retested by another lab. This person could not answer this question at all, and did not know, or was not willing to help direct us to, the someone who did know.

Adam hung up the phone very frustrated with the lack of cooperation from the lab. Of course they were not going to believe that I hadn't drunk, and they were not about to say that their wonderful lab had made an error.

"I told Marilyn I'd call her back to let her know that you were okay, and to let her know that you haven't been drinking. Is that okay with you?"

"Yeah, that's fine. But I'll talk to her when I get home." While Adam left her a message, I stared out at the oak tree, trying to suck up that strength. The fear that I had initially felt was now mixed with anger, and staring at that strong, beautiful tree kept me from screaming.

Adam and I talked for a long time after that. He reassured me that he would help and support me in any way he could. He reminded me to try to face this with grace and ease, and to pray for the truth to be revealed. He reassured me that I had a good recovery, with wonderful people in my life who would support me through this. He asked me to have a passion for the process and to leave the outcome up to God.

"I don't know what the board of nursing is going to say or do if they get this report, Patty. But I do know that you will move through this and be intact. I want you to call me anytime you need to."

For most of the time he was talking to me, I stared out of the window at the oak tree, alternating between crying and anger. I didn't leave his office until almost three o'clock, and then drove home in a daze. I found a bill from the oil man on the back door.

I LEFT A MESSAGE for Marilyn that I was home and safe, and that I was okay, and would be there until she called back. About fifteen minutes later, she did.

I immediately started to cry.

"Oh Patty!" A few seconds went by before she continued. Her next words were cautious and deliberate. "Do you have an explanation as to why this urine was positive for alcohol?" Those were her words, but I know that she wanted to say, while looking me in the face and shaking my shoulders, was: "Have you been drinking?"

"No," I quietly responded. "I didn't drink, Marilyn." I heard her finally breathe again.

"Good. I was hoping you would say that. I do believe you. In fact, when I was talking to Jeff Kardys at the Health Department, I told him that this had to be a false positive, because I had been in regular contact with you, that I had had lunch with you on several occasions and I never saw any indication that you'd been drinking, and that you were a diabetic, so if you had been drinking you would probably have needed medical care."

"Was this the last urine I did?"

"Yes, it was collected on September eighth."

"September eighth! Gee, it took them long enough to get the results."

"That was surprising to me as well. It makes it difficult to remember conditions and pull facts together. Can you remember anything about that day?"

I closed my eyes very tightly. First one and then several memories came tumbling forth.

"Marilyn! That day I was at work! I was with people all day long. It was busy and I barely even got any lunch break." I wracked my brain trying to remember other details.

"Good, good," Marilyn replied. "You're going to have to remember that day in vivid detail: what you did, who you interacted with, and times. You'll need to get statements from these people. I'll call Jeff and ask him to hold off on this as long as he can, but I'm not promising anything. It's only because he's a good guy that this isn't being sent over to the legal department immediately. Patty, they'll look to summarily suspend your license, and they'll move on that very fast, like by the next meeting of the board, which will be on October second, so I want you to concentrate on that day." One thing about Marilyn: she was direct and honest. Sparing my feelings was not important at a time like this.

When I got off the phone, I closed my eyes, lay on the bed, and concentrated on the day in question, September 8: I'd gotten up at six and gotten ready for work. Part of my morning routine was taking my insulin. The first person I talked to at work was the night nurse. Her brother was an active alcoholic and she had opened up to me previously how scared and sad she was about him. That morning I sought her out in the med room, leaned across the med cart, and asked her how he was. It was a very private conversation. We were practically nose to nose, so that we could talk in very low tones. After that, I got change of shift report in a very small room with two other nurses. This was good. People interacted with me very closely and could be witnesses to the fact that I did not smell like alcohol when I arrived at work that day.

I was assigned as the treatment nurse in the morning and the medication nurse in the afternoon. I remembered that around ten, I didn't feel well and decided to see if my blood sugar level had anything to do with that. I used my Accuchek machine, and found that the level was 199. Even if it was elevated in the morning, the insulin should have brought it down by now, especially since I hadn't eaten anything since breakfast. I continued with my work and then, about an hour later, checked my blood sugar again. I had to use the facility's machine because I had run out of test strips for mine. The result was even higher: 225! I was concerned but not alarmed at this point. I remembered that I had experienced a urinary tract infection about a month prior, and I wondered if it was recurring.

One of the responses to illness in a diabetic is elevated blood sugar. I also was just getting over a vaginal yeast infection because I had been on antibiotics for the urinary tract infection—another gift of being a diabetic. At about 12:30, I took my lunch break and then went to say hello to Pat. I told her about my high blood sugar and that I was not feeling all that great. We talked for a little while, and she asked me to go for a urine toxicology screen and possibly a urinalysis to see if there was anything amiss there.

When I left Pat's office, I went back to the third floor and did the afternoon medication pass for the forty patients, and then charted and chatted with the other nurses.

At about 2:50, I had a ten-minute conversation with the other nurse in recovery, who was just coming in to work. I punched out a little after 3:00 and went directly to the lab and gave my specimen. That was the day.

I HAD TO TELL Pat about the positive urine screen as soon as possible. I decided I would tell her in the morning, before I went home. This was not going to be easy. Was she going to believe that I had not drunk alcohol? I had so much affection and respect for this woman who'd given me a second chance, so thinking she might see me as a burden, and would regret her decision to hire me, was more than I could bear.

I was perplexed about how alcohol could have gotten in my urine, provided that my specimen had not been contaminated. Could it have had something to do with my blood sugar level that day? Chemistry has never been my strong suit, but I have a very logical mind. I'm not the kind of diabetic who would normally produce ketones, a dangerous by-product of high sugar levels, but since I was most likely spilling sugar into my urine, and ketones are closely related to alcohol chemically, I wondered if that's what happened.

I wasn't going to be able to nap before work, and anyway, I needed to do some research on this. Since we didn't have a computer at that time, I went to a bookstore and pored over any information I could find on lab results, alcohol, and diabetes and tried to tie some of this information together. One of the key things I found out was that alcohol consumption lowers blood glucose levels, so the greater danger is not hyper- but rather hypoglycemia. The day I gave my specimen, September 8, my blood sugar had been high, so that alone was evidence that I had not been drinking. I bought two books that had the most information on the topic, and went home.

I was exhausted when I went to work that night. The first person I told what had happened was the nurse I had had the conversation with the morning I gave the specimen. She was amazed that this could have happened, and that my license could be taken from me as a result. She immediately agreed to write any kind of letter I needed that would help. I did not want to share this news with anyone else until I told Pat. I gathered some more information from nursing texts at work. Somehow I got through the night.

IN THE MORNING I called Pat from home. "I had a urine report that came back positive for alcohol. But Pat, I did not drink." I started to cry. "This really sucks."

"Are you telling me the truth, that you did not drink? Did you keep your promise to me?" Pat asked.

"Yes, I did," I blubbered back.

"Then don't worry. You still have a job here. You've been doing so well here, and I'm so impressed with your recovery. The whole thing is ridiculous. Lab errors happen all the time, but of course the Health Department may not see it that way. Try to calm down. Unless they tell me otherwise, you don't have to worry about your job here. What do I have to do to help you? Can I call Jeff Kardys? He's a pretty decent guy."

How did I deserve all of these wonderful people in my life?

"I don't know yet. I have to talk to Marilyn about what she wants to do next."

"Well, you just let me know what I can do."

I was so relieved, so grateful.

MARILYN CALLED ME later on, after I woke up. "I called Dr. Wu at Hartford Hospital. He is the head of the Hartford Medical Lab. He has given testimony before the board, so he has a lot of credibility with them. He was a huge help. He said that in order for there to be a positive urine for alcohol without ingesting alcohol, there have to be three factors: heat, a microorganism, and time for incubation. It fermented. Your little bottle of urine was its own brewery! I called the lab in New York. Did you know that it took four days for your urine to get to New York?"

"Four days!"

"It goes by regular mail, and then it was another eight days before it was tested!"

"How come it took eight more days to test? They should be testing it as soon as it gets there. How can the results be reliable?"

"That's my question, too. It was so warm that week; it may have been sitting in the back of a postal truck for the four days. So, I have to ask you if you had a bladder infection or a yeast infection at that time."

"I had finished a course of antibiotics about two weeks before, and then I got my usual yeast infection."

"Thank God. I mean it was too bad that you had a yeast infection, but we have all of the factors that made it ferment."

"Well, the other thing is that it wasn't a sterile specimen, just a regular collection. I peed in a Styrofoam coffee cup, and then poured the pee into the container provided by the lab, because that one is too small for a woman to aim for, so even if I didn't have a bladder or yeast infection, I'm sure that bacteria were present from the way I had to collect the sample."

Marilyn then gave me my orders. I was to get written statements from everyone I interacted with that day, especially the first nurse I saw that morning, and the last nurse I talked to that afternoon. I had to obtain a copy of the printout of the times I punched in and out. I had the glucose result from that day in the memory of my Accucheck machine, and Marilyn asked me to see if it could be copied. If not, I was to show it to Pat. We decided that Marilyn would come to the convalescent center to talk to Pat personally about what should be in her statement.

OVER THE NEXT COUPLE of days, I explained my predicament to the nurses I'd interacted with on the "day in question." Everyone I asked gave me a great statement. Most of the reactions were of surprise, with comments on how ridiculous it was that I could lose my license over a lab error. One of the nurses declared, "Well, that is just bullshit," and she composed a letter of support right then and there.

With Marilyn's help, Pat wrote a very supportive letter that verified my blood sugar readings of the day in question, stating that I had not left the premises that day and there was no evidence that I was any way impaired. In the last sentence of her letter, she stated that she was sure I had kept my promise to her.

I was totally humbled by everyone's response to this crisis. My fear was that they would see me as an addict who, if perceived to have relapsed, was not to be believed. I was living in fear again, and that fear, again, was false evidence appearing real. It was not reality. I was in the care of my Higher Power, a Higher Power who was speaking through other people to let me know that I was loved and cared for, even when I thought I'd be abandoned.

All of this, along with an affidavit from me and a three-page explanation authored by Marilyn, was sent over to Jeff Kardys at the Department of Health. A few days later, he told Marilyn that all of the documentation we'd provided was satisfactory, and the case would not go any further. The subject of fermented urine would be brought up at the board of nursing as an issue, but my nursing license was no longer in jeopardy. A lab error was not going to steal my nursing license.

As a result of this, I was ordered to test my urine at the time of collection for the presence of sugar so that if there was alcohol in my urine at the time of testing at the lab two weeks later, they would know that the sugar might have caused it to ferment on the way there. So easy!

None of the nurses in my Nurses for Nurses group, nor anyone in the other Nurses for Nurses group in New Haven, were aware that something like this could happen. At the next meeting, we discussed how people could spill glucose into their urine for reasons other than their being diabetic. For example, a pregnant woman might develop gestational diabetes, a situation where she could have glucose in her urine. People who needed to take steroids for arthritis, asthma, or a host of other reasons might have glucose in their urine, since steroids raise blood sugar levels. People with primary kidney disease were also at risk. There were other conditions that might bring about the presence of glucose in the urine. We agreed that what had happened to me had probably happened to others—and they'd probably lost their licenses as a result.

We all felt the sting of injustice, and the fear that something like this could happen to any one of us. I was lucky, oddly enough, that I had an established diagnosis of diabetes. I was lucky that the day Pat had asked me to do a urine test was a day I was around people who could confirm that I had not been drinking.

In the broad picture, I know that God had allowed me to be the guinea pig, in order to bring this important information to the light of the Department of Health and the nursing board—and that was okay with me. In their role of monitoring nurses' impairment by urine drug testing, and the impact a false positive could have on their lives, those entities *should* have known that this could happen, and they should have *all* nurses test their urine for glucose at the time of collection. They still don't.

Only with Adam's help was I able to make sense out of what this crisis had meant to me personally. It seemed so stupid in a way, but I really suffered terrible emotional turmoil that I felt I didn't deserve, because I hadn't done anything wrong. However, in the process, I learned that I always have the ability to choose love over fear. I learned the hard way that experiencing fear truly is a choice, and for several weeks, I had chosen fear. I'd been afraid to listen to the love and support from everyone. Fear was the familiar route. I needed to see the end for myself before I could relax. God was with me all through this ridiculous situation. I will experience fear again, but hopefully I will be able to choose love and not live in the fear for so long.

Fear of feeling the pain is worse than the pain itself.

—*Denial Is Not a River in Egypt,* by Sandi Bachom

CHAPTER 38

Blessings in Disguise

DEDE'S JOURNEY THROUGH the disciplinary action of her license was different from mine. The Department of Health decided that they would offer consent orders (CO), a kind of plea bargain arrangement. This would mean that she would not have to go for a full hearing, or have a summary suspension, but the board of nursing would have to approve the terms, which would be the same as if she had gone through a full hearing. For some reason I don't fully understand, a consent order was not being offered to nurses at the time of my board action. The only consistency with the Department of Health was their inconsistency.

Dede and Marilyn, along with the prosecutor, had to attend a compliance conference, an informal information-gathering session at which the prosecutor gets a sense of how the nurse's recovery is proceeding, and offers her a CO outlining the terms of her probation. I went along as a support person. Dede's prosecutor was the same one that Erin had had (the one who thought that Erin would be on birth control pills for the rest of her life).

Dede was so nervous at the conference. She recounted her ordeal concerning the care of her incision, and how painful that was to endure. She told the prosecutor that she'd needed to medicate herself just to withstand the pain of the scrubbing and the change of dressing. He seemed to have difficulty understanding the whole process: He didn't know what a hematoma was, and had a hard time grasping the concept even after it was explained to him. He needed to have "healing by granulation" explained to him, and why it took so long. He repeatedly asked what Dede meant when she said that she had to scrub her incision. I was again amazed at the lack of medical knowledge in an attorney who represented the Department of Public Health.

His lack of understanding of addiction was even more obvious than at Erin's hearing. He actually asked Dede why she'd needed to steal the drug from her workplace, and why she hadn't just obtained more prescriptions from her doctor. Afterward, Marilyn said she'd wanted to scream at him, "Because she's an addict!" I'd wanted to do the same thing.

Nonetheless, Dede did a great job of patiently explaining everything to him in as simple terms as possible, and Marilyn jumped in to clarify when necessary. After he had received all the information he needed, he flipped his notepad over to reveal the terms of Dede's CO, already written out. Marilyn took down the information, and the meeting ended with thank-yous all around. We left the conference room and sat down at a table in the hallway.

Dede was blown away by the fact that the prosecutor had asked her all those questions, put her through that inquisition, when all that time the terms of her probation were already written. "What was this? Just an exercise in torture?" she asked crying hard as the tension was finally released.

"That is just the way they operate, Dede," Marilyn said. "You did a great job."

I rubbed her shoulders. I couldn't do much more to help her feel better, but I knew that things would be better for her. She was just going to have to experience this torment, and then grow and learn and transcend. That prosecutor had just been doing his job; he was just a cog in the wheel of a punitive management that was still in the Dark Ages about nurses' addiction, was unwilling to learn, to the extent of employing a lawyer ignorant not only about nurse addicts but about the health field in general.

IN NOVEMBER, DEDE'S consent order was presented before the board of nursing. Since there are no coincidences, only synchronicities, Faith also had her CO the same day. I chauffeured them to Hartford. Even though their appearance before the board would be brief, and they wouldn't have to testify, it was just as bewildering and upsetting for them as it had been for me.

We arrived at the Legislative Office Building in Hartford bright and early. Dede's and Faith's cases were the last on a list of seven or eight to be heard that day. Dede was so tense and the expression on her face was so strained. Faith, being seven months pregnant, looked tired and uncomfortable. Marilyn was reassuring and confident. The morning dragged on as the board discussed each case. Some nurses were there with their attorneys; others were not even present for the decision regarding their licenses.

It was approaching lunchtime. The only two cases left were Dede's and Faith's. We were almost done. Zombie-like, Dede flipped through her 12-Step Prayer Book, waiting for her turn, just wanting to be out of there.

"Oh boy. What time is it?" the chairperson of the board of nursing suddenly exclaimed. "I think we should break for lunch now, and then continue after lunch."

What? *What the hell was this?* There were only these two cases to go! Maybe another ten minutes! I looked over at Dede, and *she was mad.* Her face was bright red, as she grabbed her coat and purse to get up to go to lunch. Lunch? Who could eat? Marilyn's jaw was so clenched that I thought she would never get her teeth apart. Faith just looked weary.

We went to the cafeteria and ate lightly. I tried to reassure Dede and Faith that it would soon be over. This was so unfair: to have them here all day when they were scheduled to be done before lunch, and then have the audacity to break for lunch with only these two very short cases left.

"All they have to do is approve our COs, right?" Dede asked Marilyn in a sudden attack of insecurity.

"Yes. You're absolutely right," Marilyn responded. "They have no idea what it's like to have to go through this, and whatever compassion they may have had went out the window. They saw you both sitting there all morning. They saw that Faith is largely pregnant. I'm telling you, I'm very angry with them for this." She leaned across the table and did her best to reassure Dede and Faith. "But it will soon be over and this will be in the past. It has nothing to do with either one of you personally, so try not to process it that way. Everything's going to be all right."

AT ONE O'CLOCK WE reentered Room 2A. After about ten minutes the board was ready to proceed. Faith's case was first. They accepted the terms without amendment and wished her good luck, and a healthy baby. Dede's case was last. She looked like every emotion she was feeling at that moment: fear, shame, humiliation, and anger generated by the rudeness and insensitivity of the poorly timed lunch break.

The board read over the documents that Marilyn had helped Dede prepare. They were the same type I had had to prepare for my own hearing.

"Is there a motion to accept the consent order?" the chairperson asked the members of the board. Several members raised their hands, but one member asked for a change.

"I think that since she's returning to the same place where she obtained her drugs, instead of decreasing her urines to twice a month after one year, we should extend the frequency of weekly urines for six months after her key restriction is lifted." The rest of the board agreed with that suggestion.

Marilyn leaned over to ask Dede if she wanted to accept this change. Dede, with a stunned expression, just shrugged her shoulders. Marilyn indicated to the board that they would accept the change. The board voted to accept this amended consent order. They wished Dede good luck and then concluded their day.

Dede was finally able to shed all those tears she'd been suppressing all day. We returned to the cafeteria to have a cup of coffee. Marilyn told Dede and Faith how proud she was of them and that now they could get on with their lives. Dede was so spent she didn't have the energy to respond with anything more than a nod. I knew exactly how she felt as I remembered my day in front of the board.

THE DRIVE BACK TO my house was very quiet. Dede continued to look tense and troubled. After Faith was gone, she asked, "Patty, why did they change my consent order and not Faith's. Why did I look worse to them than she did?" She was crying really hard now.

"They did *not* see you as worse. They saw you as being in a situation that needed more monitoring, not less, after your key restriction was up. They said you were returning to the environment where you obtained your drugs, and when you have access to narcotics again, that may be a dangerous time for you. They have to protect the public, and one of the ways they do that is to monitor us in some concrete way, such as with urine screens. It's actually a good move. It's a safety net for you, too, because that may be a difficult time for you after a year without access to narcotics.

"See it as a positive thing, Dede!" I continued. "They actually had your best interest in mind. This was always in God's hands and *He* is protecting you. Faith isn't going back to her place of employment, so it wasn't the same issue for her. Hey! She doesn't have employment to return to. You do! She has different blessings and burdens. So try not to compare yourself to her."

Dede sighed. "It's hard not to see yourself as pond scum on a day like this. I just want to go home and hug my boy. I need to have his little arms around me so I can feel 'normal' again."

I gave her a long hug, we both cried some more, and then she went home. Her CO would take effect on December 1. She didn't have to wait the three or four months as I had after my hearing.

Just as I had to, I knew she would process this day in her own way. I would be there for her, just as my sponsor was there for me, and my recovery was there for me.

If we look closely, we will see that we are given even amounts of blessings and sorrows.

—*Denial Is Not a River in Egypt,* by Sandi Bachom

CHAPTER 39

Eyesight

MARCH WAS USHERING itself in the way it was supposed to: like a lion. The air was changing. I could smell the faint aromas of spring that the strong winds were stirring up. The barren oak tree outside of Adam's window was again the illusion of itself. Deep within, hidden from view, the forces of nature were thawing the juices that would nurture the tree back to life, to hope, to the continuation of itself, and the assurance of another generation of its own. The miracle of life, survival, presence, and permanence was continuing its heavenly ordained cycle. The tree stood resolute, trusting the cycle, trusting God.

I was preparing mentally and emotionally for my husband to come home. Eighteen months before I could not wait for him to leave. I was so ashamed of what I had done that I wanted him away so that I could keep my secret. I knew that the separation was our Higher Power taking care of both of us. We had become so co-dependent in our relationship that we couldn't see ourselves as ourselves, only as a reflection of each other's actions and reactions.

"You're a different person now," Adam reassured me. "You've worked very hard on yourself. You have a higher level of awareness,"

"I know, but I've developed that without Fred being home. I hate the thought of going through another period of adjustment. The one thing I'm sure of, though, is that I would not have been able to concentrate on my recovery if he'd been home. We needed a separation without all the legal entanglements to save our marriage."

I needed the time and the guidance to find my authentic self again. I needed to know and take responsibility for my part in this co-dependent dance.

"Do you know what co-dependency really is?" Adam asked.

"Enabling someone else's bad behavior to continue, mostly by protecting them from the consequences of their bad behavior."

"That's only part of it," Adam said. "Co-dependency is actually a dysfunctional relationship with the self. Think about it. You and your husband are always tiptoeing around each other's reactions. You stated that you felt that you were walking on eggshells much of the time. I know that we can't speak for your husband, but I imagine that he is as well. You have a choice to continue with this dance or not. Awareness is the beginning. You're at the first step in preparing for Fred to come home and have a new or different—better—relationship, if that's what you truly want."

"But I'm having trouble with that definition of *co-dependency*."

"Co-dependent people actually live through one another. They attempt to control others or blame others, have a sense of victimization, or try to 'fix' others. Some of what I'm saying may feel true to you and some may not. But if you're willing to take an honest look at yourself, then you'll be able to see what applies to you and what does not. I'm not saying you're not, or have not been, willing to take an honest look at yourself. On the contrary, I think you've been very willing, but that effort has to continue. The more of an effort you make, the clearer it all becomes, and in the process, you begin to lose your fears about facing yourself. You're responsible only for your own thoughts, feelings, actions, and reactions, for 'your side of the street.' The only way you can change the dance, is if you change *your* footwork."

It was a beginning, and only a beginning, of a whole other process, another layer of that onion that needed to be peeled. In the following weeks, Adam and I continued to plow through the deep and ingrained patterns that had come to define Fred's and my marriage, and where I was co-dependent in the relationship. I loved my husband. There was no question or doubt in my mind, but love was just a foundation. I had so much difficulty letting go of the anger I felt toward Fred, his emotional absence, and how lonely I'd felt the time my father was in my care.

Now that the shame and guilt about my addiction were no longer an issue, I had unresolved resentments about other stuff that was rising to the surface. I had a continuous feeling of rage in the center of my being. But just as I could no longer live in that shame and guilt, I could also no longer live in this anger.

"The roiling rot of rage—that is what I feel inside," I told Adam. "I don't want to feel this way anymore."

"You have that choice, Patty,"

"How?"

"Fred is the panther," Adam stated.

"Huh?" *What the hell are you talking about, Adam?*

"A panther is a panther. It does not have the ability to be anything else. If a hungry panther were in your path, no matter how much you didn't *want* that panther to attack and eat you, it still would make an effort to do that. Your being angry is not going to change the panther's behavior. *You* have to take your own responsibility to save your life, to protect yourself. Is this making any sense to you yet, Patty?"

"Uh-huh...sort of. Keep going."

"Just like the panther, Fred is who he is, and you are who you are. You can only be you."

"Yeah, but I'm still not sure who I am! I mean I know what I am, but not who." The tears were starting.

"You do know who you are, you really do. You're in the process of tapping into and trusting what your higher self is telling you about who you are. Somewhere you lost the ability to 'see' yourself because you've been wearing someone else's glasses, sometimes your husband's, sometimes your mother's, sometimes your friends', but not your own. If we wear someone else's glasses, we cannot see clearly, can we? We can see clearly only through our own glasses."

It took a while, but in fits and starts, the rage that I'd carried around with me began to dissipate. It was attached to my self-esteem, which was directly related to my ability to see myself through my own glasses.

LIFE WAS SETTLING INTO the kind of pattern I imagined normal people experienced. Nothing dramatic was happening. We were just waiting for the day when our whole family would be together again. The boys were very happy that Fred was coming home for good. They never complained too much, but I could tell by their behavior that they were happy to have this chapter in their lives come to a close, and that, as a family, we were coming through it intact.

At work, I was the night supervisor and also responsible for a floor with forty patients. The work was not hard. Many nights I had a significant amount of downtime. I worked on my true passion — my recovery, and learning as much as I could about the disease of addiction. If there was ever a reason God wanted me in this job, then it was for this. It was not necessarily for the job that I was being paid to do; it was the people I needed to interact with for my own growth and transformation. It was a time to incubate. It was a time to feel true gratitude in a place I would have never thought possible in my 'former' life. I didn't need the energy-sapping climate of a high stress, fast-paced job right now. I needed to work on seeing myself and the world through my own glasses.

Believe more deeply.
Hold your face up to the Light,
even though for a moment, you do not see.
—*Denial Is Not a River in Egypt,* by Sandi Bachom

CHAPTER 40

Emptiness

DURING THIS PERIOD, Erin and I talked frequently and saw each other every week at the Nurses for Nurses meeting. She told me she was feeling cravings while at work, and someone at the meeting challenged her as to why she was still at her place of work if it wasn't safe for her.

"The ER is the only nursing I love," she said. "I can't imagine doing anything else but ER work. I'm grateful that I still have my key restriction, and I have to pee in a cup."

Joan said, "I think it's always risky to work around your drug of choice. If you're having cravings, then it is probably the wrong place for you now. I know no job is worth my life, and my recovery comes before my family, my marriage, and my work. If I don't have my recovery, then I don't have any of the things I love."

One of the maxims of recovery is "Whatever you put in front of your recovery you will lose." But did that mean that Erin had to leave the ER? Maybe she could just redouble her recovery work and she'd be alright. I was afraid that if she had to leave the ER, she'd relapse from the grief.

ERIN'S OVARIAN CYSTS were recurring because she was in the process of switching birth control pills. Because of the cysts, she was having back pain and low-grade fevers. During one of the visits to her ob-gyn, to evaluate her cysts, she found out the reason for the discomfort.

"Patty?" You'll never guess. I'm in a state of shock. *I'm pregnant!*"

"You're preg—are you sure?"

"Yes! I had to switch birth control pills, so they did a routine pregnancy test on me... and I am six weeks P-R-E-G-N-A-N-T!"

This was so hard to believe. I was so happy for my friend. This is what she had wanted her whole life. The back pain was being caused by the stretching and loosening of globs of tissue that her endometriosis had produced over the years. After about a week, she was able to return to work. Everyone at Nurse for Nurses was overjoyed for her. And she was glowing.

A couple of weeks later, Erin's doctor was concerned that the fetus was not growing properly, and its heart rate was low. Erin was panic-stricken. At our Nurses for Nurses meeting on Monday, she reached out for prayers and support. They were going to repeat her ultrasound on Thursday. I prayed so hard for her. She was constantly on my mind. I was afraid for her if she lost this baby.

THE THURSDAY ULTRASOUND INDICATED that the baby Erin had so desperately wanted was no longer living. Erin started to hemorrhage a few hours later, and underwent a D&C to stem the bleeding.

I called her the next day. Her voice was flat, monotone, absent of inflection, void of emotion. She said that she was physically okay, and she asked me not to worry about her; she would get through this. I sensed she was trying to move herself through the necessary stages of her grief as quickly and as painlessly as possible, to reach a false level of acceptance.

"I am so sorry," I told her.

I heard her mournful sobbing on the other end of the phone, "It's gone, Patty. The one thing I wanted more than anything else, and God took it away from me."

"I know…I know how much you wanted this baby. And I am so sorry," I sobbed back. "But you have to know I love you and I'm here for you."

"I know. Thanks."

It made no sense to me.

ERIN TRIED TO PUT the sadness behind her, but there was nothing to replace it. When I next saw her, her eyes were vacant. I wanted to enter that void and find the real Erin and pull her back to us.

"Where is she?" I cried to Sue. "She's not 'there.'"

"I know. I'm worried about her too. But it's not our job to rescue her. She has to work her way through this, and find herself. God has a plan for her. She is seeing Adam; that is the best thing. We need to do the only thing we can in these kinds of situations: just be there for her and pray for her."

The Monday after her D&C, Erin went back to work. She hemorrhaged again, and had another D&C. Three days later, she returned to work again. She thought she was better, but that was an illusion.

She said that she believed that God had abandoned her; she felt numb and empty. She said that her cravings were still there, and that maybe the ER was not the place for her to continue to work, but she had no energy to look for another job, start something new.

ONE NIGHT WHILE SHE was working, a patient refused a prescription that had been written out for her. Erin put the filled-out prescription form in her pocket. When she got out of work, she went to a pharmacy and had it filled. She'd memorized the woman's address and date of birth, but not her phone number, so she gave her own. Unfortunately (or fortunately) the pharmacist knew the real patient, so he called Erin's hospital and then called Drug Control. She was confronted a few days later, and because she was under a "return to work" agreement, she lost her job in the ER.

THE GRIEF SHE'D BEEN experiencing was now compounded by this loss. Her anxiety level was so high that it was, in Erin's words, intolerable. She called her psychiatrist to help her cope with this dangerous level of emotional anguish, and she prescribed Ativan. I was afraid for Erin, going on this drug, but she said it was just a temporary solution until the anxiety lessened.

The Department of Health wasted no time in seeking to suspend Erin's license.

"Just like that—poof—and I'm not a nurse anymore," she said dazedly after her appearance before the board. When I brought her home, she stated that she was really tired and was going to bed. I felt uneasy leaving her, but she said Paul would be there in about an hour, so not to worry. Paul was helping her financially until she could support herself again.

I thought all was going to be okay until I received a phone call at one o'clock in the morning at work.

"Patty, he left me. My Prince Charming left me. I don't know what to do. I can't tolerate another loss. I don't want to live if I lose Paul, too! Can you come up here? You're the only one I can call…" Her voice trailed off and was replaced by hysterical sobbing.

"Are you sure? Maybe he was just angry. Try to calm down, Erin. I'll call you right back."

I didn't know what I was going to do exactly. I called the on-call nurse and told him I had a family emergency. I thought of calling Sue, but when my relief came, I just got in the van and went to Erin's house. I prayed for clarity, strength, and wisdom.

Almost out of gas, I arrived at Erin's house. The back door was unlocked. Buster quietly greeted me. The only light on was the one over the sink. I didn't find Erin her where I'd expected her—on the living room couch. She was not in the bathroom.

"Erin? Erin?" No answer. I walked straight ahead to the dark computer room. The door was about three quarters closed. With heart pounding and my knees feeling like jelly, I opened the door and approached the daybed. The only light was that from the kitchen, so it took me a minute for my eyes to adjust to the darkness of the room. I saw a lump on the bed. I bent down very close.

"Erin?" I shook her shoulder. "Erin?" I was very alarmed and trembling now as I shook her again. "ERIN?"

"Huh?" was her sleepy response. "Patty, what are you doing here?"

"What the hell do you mean what am I doing here?! You called me hysterical that Paul had left you and you didn't want to live!" I angrily replied.

"Oh my God. It's all coming back to me now." She sat up and started crying, as reality sank in. "I have to go to the bathroom." I watched her walk to the bathroom swaying with each step. She stumbled to the living room, sat on the couch, and lit up a cigarette.

"Erin, where are the rest of the Ativan, and I want them *all*."

"I'll get them for you."

"Does Paul have any of them?"

"No, he never had them. I always had them." She returned to the bathroom and brought me two prescription bottles. They were both for Ativan. The prescribed amount in one bottle was for thirty pills; the other was for ninety. They'd both been prescribed by the same psychiatrist, and within only one week. I couldn't believe she'd prescribed a depressed addict thirty, and then ninety highly addictive tranquilizers! I opened both bottles. One had only two pills left and the other had only three pills left!

"Erin! Where are the other pills? Did you take them all? Did you take this many Ativan in just five days? And how many did you take tonight?"

"I don't remember how many I took tonight," Erin replied with the slurring, sluggish, and drowsy speech of the stoned. "The psychiatrist told me to take them sublingually if I was having a panic attack. I may have kept popping them, because the panic never went away." She began crying mournfully. "What am I going to do? Paul left me; he just left me. I'm really all alone now. No baby, no Paul, no job that I love. Patty, don't send me to that ER. I'll be okay."

She told me that she and Paul had gone to a meeting and she'd had a meltdown. She was lying on the floor crying, and Paul had had to carry her out of there. He brought her home, and then he said he couldn't take it anymore and he left. Knowing what state she was in, why hadn't he brought her to the ER, or called her psychiatrist?

It was already three o'clock in the morning. Erin had settled herself on the couch and eventually fallen back asleep. Now that I had assessed the situation, I had a plan. I would monitor her respirations and pulse frequently, and wake her up to check her level of consciousness. If I became at all concerned, I'd call an ambulance.

I stared at Erin as she slept that dangerous sleep of the "sick and suffering" addict: the sleep that could kill. I thought about this disease of addiction, the embodiment of evil, that seduced the vulnerable. An opportunistic and invasive predator, it lay cloaked and waiting until a flaw in the defenses, a lapse in faith, an emptiness to fill, came its way. Then it disguised itself as the answer, the release, and relief for the anguish, enticing its victim as powerfully as nectar draws a bee.

Once the victim was caught, the disease continued to cajole and flatter and distort, convincing her that she had no other choice, convincing her that life was too painful, too unfair, but meanwhile stealing all that was true and meaningful and precious in life. Now this addiction, this materialization of the devil himself, had gleefully achieved its objective and entrapped my friend the addict in her own hell on earth, as she slept the dangerous sleep.

AT ABOUT SEVEN, I woke Erin up. Before I left, I made her call her sister, Eileen, who assured me she was on her way. I threw the Ativan down the drain. I was fairly certain that Erin would be okay until Eileen got there. I *had* to go home to my own family.

I was angry all the way home. How could that psychiatrist have been so stupid? Ninety pills? "Here's the cure. Just take these and you'll be all better. Now go away and feel better." Needing 90 Ativan for an acute episode of unbearable and debilitating anxiety should be its own red flag! And Paul had left her there to die! How could he have done that? How could he have left her like that? What a selfish bastard. Why hadn't he at least taken her to a hospital?

I would remain angry with Paul for a long, long time. I hoped he would have nothing more to do with Erin. By that afternoon, Erin was on her way to a psychiatric hospital.

In the aftermath of Erin's relapse, I felt emotionally hung over. I had become so enmeshed in her struggles that I had had a hard time separating from it all. I was so afraid for her and so powerless to help. Sue reminded me that Erin and I had been together from the beginning. For so long, her struggle had been my struggle, and vice versa.

"I know it's hard to see someone you're close to get sick," Sue said, "but you have to give her to God. She has her own path now. She's going to have to find that strength she had before. She's going to have to learn to be honest about her pain, and not hide it or hide from it."

SOME MONTHS LATER, DEDE was telling me about one of her sessions with Adam and how she'd had to explain to him "healing by granulation," which means allowing the body to heal from the inside out which is a more complete, stronger, and stable process. This is what she'd had to endure when she had complications from her C-section. He thought it was a good metaphor for what an addict has to do to heal completely. I thought of Erin and how she gave the impression that she was all "fixed." But she only had the appearance of healing. As time went by, however, the structure that should have been supporting her caved in. Things looked good on the surface, but no one knew that she was collapsing underneath.

Erin needed healing by granulation—from the inside out—something strong, a solid base on which to build. It would be painful, but the pain would be part of the healing, part of the granulation process, and it would subside when the healing was accomplished.

There are only twelve inches between your head and your heart, but they are not always connected.

—*Denial Is Not a River in Egypt,* by Sandi Bachom

CHAPTER 41

The Answer

ALTHOUGH WE HAD visited Fred many times over the last two years as a family, I had never gone up to Buffalo alone. We decided that since the company he worked for would pay for one more flight, I would fly up there to see him, alone, no kids. I was looking forward to this mini vacation after Erin's drama and turmoil that had been such a big part of my recent life.

I asked God for a sign that Fred and I had enough love to continue as a married and committed couple. I knew I was willing to do my part, and there were many indications that Fred was, too. I had an almost insatiable need to be forgiven by him for my addiction. He'd already told me that he'd forgiven me, which made me feel great, but I had such a hard time actually believing it.

ADAM SAID THAT IF Fred had not forgiven me he would not have been able to come back to the marriage. The reality was that I had to forgive myself. I wasn't aware that I hadn't fully forgiven myself until the nearly obsessive need to be forgiven by Fred surfaced. I had taken that need for myself and transferred it to my husband, the one I felt I had hurt the most, besides my children and myself. Adam reminded me that this might be the most difficult part of healing.

"What are those lines in your favorite song, Patty?" Adam said. "'What He forgives, He forgets'? If God has forgiven you, then the next step is for you to forgive yourself. Only then can you transcend and move forward."

"All you have to do is be willing," Sue reminded me. "Do the footwork and trust God to do the rest."

I BOARDED THE PLANE and took my seat near a window. No one sat next to me, which was good, because I didn't want to talk to anyone. As the plane climbed into the clouds, I felt that thrilling sensation in the pit of my stomach, as well as the slight feeling of fear that goes along with it. I watched the world disappear behind the low clouds. I was flying away from what was. I pressed my forehead against the window and stared down at the dark earth between the gaps in the clouds. This was a short flight, so we weren't very high, and I could see the cars going along the ribbons of highways, the buildings, the trees, fields, and lakes. My life "down there" seemed so far away.

When the plane reached its cruising altitude, I looked up to the sun, in the west, not quite set, and watched how the colors danced so beautifully over the clouds. The disorienting vastness of this heavenly landscape was as intoxicating as a drug, an escape.

How easy it is to forget all of my problems down there. How easy it is to forget, ignore, and neglect, and to live in a nebulous world of flight and evasion. I did that. I tried to fly away—into a vial.

Sue's words came to mind, "Look back but don't stare. We all have things in our past we can obsess about; that is our nature. Look forward and stay in God's will."

I saw the vastness of God up there in those magnificently beautiful clouds. I pictured my father experiencing this beauty as he passed from this life.

Ascendance to transcendence.

I MET MY HUSBAND in the terminal. It was good to see him. I'd missed him. While I was in Buffalo, he treated me to a wonderful dinner at a first-class restaurant. We browsed through an antique show, and we went to a road at the end of the airport runway where planes took off right over our heads. We took a drive up the Niagara River on the Canadian side and went to the Canadian Falls, which was my favorite thing to do when I was up there. We went up to Lake Ontario and then took a leisurely route back to his apartment. We talked and planned about his coming home. Only another month.

HE BROUGHT ME BACK to the airport on Monday. As I boarded the plane and took my seat, I was suddenly overwhelmed with a panicky, sickening, guilt-ridden feeling in the pit of my stomach. *This is not right! This is distorted! Reality is twisted. Why is he staying here? It is so wrong! He should be here in the seat next to me, going home! He should not be here, in Buffalo, all alone!*

As I looked over at the terminal's huge window, I could see the small figure of my husband watching the plane taxi out to the runway. He loved us so much. He missed the boys terribly. How lonely he must have been the last two years being away from his family. He said that sometimes it felt like one long nightmare. It was time for him to come home.

I leaned back in the seat and closed my eyes. The feelings of guilt and panic slowly subsided. We were going to be a couple again, a family again, with good times and bad, but with a deeper appreciation for the gift of each other. At times, while I was struggling with my recovery, I wondered if I still loved him. I knew that I did now, because the image of him standing in that window, so alone, so far away from home and the family he loved, broke my heart, and filled me with longing for him. I had my answer.

The sun was setting in the west as the plane headed east, for home. I put my head against the window and again marveled at the spectrum of colors with which the sun bathed the endless mountain peaks of clouds. It was always a beautiful day up here. I could have gazed at those clouds forever, but as the plane banked to begin its approach to Bradley Airport, I lost my heavenly view. I closed my eyes to lock in the memory of the clouds and the colors. I wanted to be able to retrieve that memory if I ever needed it for the times that were gray and foggy. I faced forward and rested my head against the back of the seat, preparing for landing. The plane broke through the clouds. It was a damp, gray evening and there was a light mist. With a thud I was back on earth in Connecticut.

As I drove home, I thought about the beautiful day up there in the clouds, a thought that reminded me of a memory of another beautiful day down here on earth, two years before, when I wanted time to move at an accelerated pace to bring me to the future. I shuddered when I thought of that day, when I was so alone and so afraid. Yet, here I was living in that future, and through the intense process of this profound experience, I had learned that I could live *through* intense pain and fear and not lose my mind, or my life. I could not circumvent, elude, bypass, or anesthetize my life, because that is not a life.

One good thing about repeating your mistakes is that now you know when to cringe.

—*Denial Is Not a River in Egypt,* by Sandi Bachom

CHAPTER 42

Back to Normal?

IN JUNE OF 1998, we went up to Buffalo and moved Fred back home. I still had some anxiety about how it was going to be with him at home again. I had developed my own routine with work and the boys and meetings and therapy, a routine he wasn't used to. I didn't want to fall into the same patterns of avoidance, walking on eggshells, and acquiescing to keep the peace.

"That is fear-based, don't you think?" Adam asked the week Fred was coming home.

"These are my fears," I responded.

"Well, then, how are you going to change that? You can't change Fred. So what are *you* going to do?"

"Part of the problem is that I was so sick when he left. My drug use was the center of my existence, so I naturally avoided him so he wouldn't find out. I had to keep the peace because I didn't want any attention on myself, and also because my father was there. I didn't want him to know that Fred had so much resentment about him living with us. So, I have difficulty remembering how much of those dynamics were there before the drug use. I'm not afraid of repeating the interactions we had when I was using, because I'm not that person anymore. I'm afraid of the ones in the relationship we had before that, those years leading up to my drug use."

"No, Patty, you are not that person anymore, but you are not the person you were before you picked up a drug, either. You have a much greater insight into yourself, and what led you to your drug use, as well as new tools to help you deal with life on life's terms. I'm not predicting whether your marriage will survive or not, and I'm not here to tell you what to do about your marriage. That will be your decision. I'm here to help you sort out the feelings you may have, and I'm here to help you develop ways to help change your part of the 'dance' you and Fred learned over the course of your marriage."

I never was a great dancer.

So, I didn't have to lose myself in the relationship with my husband. I had to learn not to be so reactive, or not to react at all to things that were said or situations that might be frustrating, until I could be in touch with the healthy part of myself, and express myself from that center.

ALL THINGS CONSIDERED, it was good to have Fred home again. The boys were thrilled. I had had to be so self-centered over the last two years, in order to heal, that I was not truly aware how they'd felt about their father being so far away. We always assured them that we would be together again as a family, but I knew it was hard for them. I knew they were worried and sad. I hoped that I was always able to convey that I was there for them if they needed me. But just watching them interact with Fred when we were all home, together, was reassurance for me that they were okay and that that chapter of our lives was over.

Home was going to mean a new address. The big ten-room house was too much for us financially. We had to start fresh and get our finances in order. By November of 1999, we found a great condo to rent on the north side of town with three big bedrooms, and the condo administration was going to allow us to bring Oreo. Our last Christmas in the home where we raised our kids was the last one of the old millennium, too. A week later we watched TV as the world welcomed a new age. The Hollorans were welcoming a new beginning.

Twenty-five years of our lives packed in brown boxes lined the first-floor walls of our new home. I leaned over the counter staring at them and around at the space where our lives would now be. I was at peace. This would be a house of healing for us.

I KNEW THAT MY time working at the convalescent home had to come to an end. I had only one more year on my probation. Pat Rzewnicki was no longer the DNS there. Things were changing at work and within myself. I looked around the day room one morning, at the elderly people sitting around the nurse's station waiting to eat or be fed, living in happier times past. Befuddled, toothless, heads back snoring, heads down drooling, crying or laughing for no reason, mumbling or yelling, some asking to go home, some thinking they were home—and I realized I was done with old people.

I needed to do nursing that fulfilled me more than this. I couldn't go back to labor and delivery yet, maybe not ever. So I thought substance abuse was a place where I could be happy. As things never happen by accident, one day, while getting a ride from Dede, I glanced down and saw, on the floor of her car, a nursing journal opened up to the classifieds section. Reid Treatment Center was looking for a nurse. *What did I have to lose?*

IN JULY 2000, THE DAY of my interview for the treatment center, I walked up to a sprawling, casually haphazard building in the upper-middle-class town of Avon. Set back from the road with a very large yard with a volleyball net (normal rehab landscaping), the main building was a two-story brick house. The rest of it looked as if every time somebody had had a new idea for its use, another appendage had been added to it. The insides needed some updating, but the atmosphere was casual. Around the corner was the nurse-tech station. I introduced myself to Roslyn, a small woman with a British accent, and she summoned the director of nurses. While waiting for her to arrive, I looked around the place and noticed many AA and NA quotes and sayings scattered around on the walls around the hallway by the nurse's station.

These are my people, I mused.

The director of nurses arrived and brought me to her office. I was hoping so hard I would get this job, but I knew that my probation might prevent them from hiring me. I didn't know when to bring it up. At the beginning? The end? Maybe I could sneak it in in the middle, real quick, and then she might not notice. I decided to let her get to know me a little first. My anxiety was building up more and more as we talked.

When it seemed like the interview was just about over, I said, "There's something else I have to let you know. I am on a consent order until next June because of diverting meds and becoming dependent on them. I have been in recovery since 1996, and I haven't had a relapse or anything. I can get letters of support and recommendation for you."

"That shouldn't be a problem at all," she said as she waved off what I'd just said.

Oh my God. They "get it." They know what addiction is, and what recovery is!

Two weeks later, I was in my new job. And it was as natural to me as water was to a duck.

I thank God for my handicaps, because through them
I have found myself, my work, and my God.

—Helen Keller

CHAPTER 43

Giving Back

DEDE AND I ARE no longer *anonymous* members of the community of those recovering from addictive disease. In 1999, the Connecticut Nurses Association formed a legislative committee to introduce a bill to the Connecticut General Assembly that would establish an alternative to the archaic disciplinary system, as it pertains to impaired nurses, and I asked to be a part of it. Marilyn was also a member of the committee, and eventually Dede joined, too. The Connecticut Nurses Association's efforts to get such a bill passed dated back to the 1980s, and had been defeated every time.

The ideas contained in our proposed bill were not new concepts. Alternative programs had been working quite well in most other states in the country, in many cases, for years. Polly Barey, the new executive director of the Connecticut Nurses Association, assured us at our first committee meeting that this bill was a top priority.

Our committee met every month, beginning in the winter of 1999. We used as a template for our bill a previously proposed bill from 1995, changing the language of some key parts. We spent many, many hours on research. What we discovered was the following:

Alcoholism and addiction have an enormous impact on healthcare. They are frequently the root cause of so many other conditions. Too often, only neurological, cardiovascular, pulmonary, and liver diseases are treated aggressively. The addiction may be a component of the clinical picture, but it is not given the treatment priority it needs.

This crucial area of medical education and nursing education is sorely neglected, not only in the institutions that educate doctors and nurses, but also in the ones that employ them. The medical and nursing community has shoved this major pandemic to their educational back burner.

Healthcare workers see only the very dramatic and negative sides of active addiction. What has resulted is a community of healthcare workers who are allowed to "treat" patients with the disease of addiction through the prism of their own prejudices. If a nurse ever treated a cancer, cardiac, or diabetic patient with the same lack of concern or the same unethical manner, there would certainly be professional consequences.

With this attitude toward the disease of addiction, it is no surprise that nurses are even less tolerant of those in their own profession who suffer from addiction. Before 1996, I was one of those nurses. Due to my lack of education about the disease, my attitude always got in the way of my treating patients. Yes, I'd been told that addiction was a disease, but like all of the nurses I knew, I never fully understood what that meant—that is, until the day I had to say, "Hi, I'm Patty, and I'm an addict."

During the course of our research, some statistics we learned included:

- At least 10 percent of the general population is victim to the disease of addiction/alcoholism. The percentage of nurses who have this disease reflects that of the general public, but some estimates have placed it as high as 20 percent.

- There are about 55,000 licensed APRNs, RNs, and LPNs in Connecticut, about 45,000 of whom are actively practicing their profession. This translates to at least 4,500 nurses who are addicts, and who may be practicing while impaired.
- The Department of Consumer Protection, Division of Drug Control, can investigate only about 100 cases a year.
- The nursing board can adjudicate only 40–50 of those cases every year. The board of nursing does the best it can with the tools it has. (The board of nursing is 100 percent behind Connecticut having an alternative program.)
- The relapse rate for addiction in general is about 50 percent. The relapse rate in well-constructed alternative programs is 10 percent or less.
- The National Council of State Boards of Nursing recommended as far back as the late 1980s that states set up alternative programs.
- The American Nurses Association passed a resolution that supports alternative programs, and addresses this as part of the profession's responsibility to fixing the problem.

WHY ALTERNATIVE PROGRAMS work is simple: they address the problem, and they function in the solution. When a nurse is discovered to be impaired by drugs or alcohol, she signs a contract, tailored to her situation, agreeing to stop working. She agrees to be evaluated by a treatment program, and enters treatment at the level recommended by that program. The nurse is then evaluated for fitness to return to work. The program would be run by mental health and addiction professionals and nurses in solid recovery.

This program would not be a safe haven for nurses trying to avoid discipline. In fact, the monitoring in this alternative approach would be more structured, and thus relapse behaviors could be identified earlier rather than later. And the program is not just for addicted nurses but also for those with psychological or physical conditions that may be impairing their practice.

A vital component of an alternative program is the confidentiality of the participants. No nurse looking for help will self-refer—that is, voluntarily enter a program—where DPH is privy to information on the program participants. In such a scenario there is too much risk for nurses having their licenses threatened, regardless of how compliant they are in their recovery.

If a nurse refuses to get evaluated immediately, if she chooses not to contract with the alternative program, or if she does not remain compliant with the program, she will have to endure a disciplinary process. The disciplinary process DPH has in place will apply for those nurses whose cases have additional factors that render them ineligible for the alternative program: nurses who have sold drugs or harmed a patient. Any other legal ramifications of a nurse's drug use (e.g., theft charges) will not be mitigated by her participation in the alternative program, and will be her responsibility.

One of the major components of our program would be ongoing education about addiction, for all levels of nursing practice and the student nurse. Educational formats would be developed for employee assistance programs and human resource personnel of healthcare facilities as well.

In contrast, the current outdated, DPH-controlled disciplinary process involves the following:

- Nurses who find themselves in the downward spiral of addiction wish that they had a place to turn to, a place to get help, but they don't know what to do for fear of losing their licenses. So most run from or ignore the help that they should be receiving, all the while getting sicker in their disease.

- There is no mandate for the nurse to get treatment she needs when confronted.
- The usual time it takes for a nurse to have her case decided before the board is six months (as it was in mine). Then weeks or months go by until the red tape is untangled and the nurse's practice is actually monitored. During this time, there is no direction, management, or supervision of the nurse's practice from DPH before the probation is in place.
- Once the probation is in place, the monitoring of the nurse's practice is managed by people with no education in or understanding about addiction or recovery.

DPH, THEREFORE, HAS BEEN an *active participant* in preventing nurses with the disease of addiction from receiving the help they need, an *active participant* in putting the public health of the State of Connecticut at risk.

MUCH OF OUR INFORMATION came from the oldest program in the country, the Intervention Program for Nurses (IPN) in Florida, which has been a success since 1984. It is the model for programs all over the country. In April of 2001, we went to Florida to attend the IPN/FNA convention as invited guests. Adam was the keynote speaker. There we met the people we'd been emailing for months, and we learned more about how their program worked. Dede's mother, Marie, and her son, Dylan, were also along on the trip, so when the convention was over we had a mini vacation, and ate most of the lobster in the greater Tampa/St. Petersburg area.

The Connecticut Nurses Association introduced our bill in the 2001 session. It bill passed every committee it was sent to and was ready to be voted on in the Senate. The senator who sponsored it informed us that it looked like it was going to pass. All the members of our committee were ecstatic that our bill was moving forward so quickly.

But the Department of Public Health, the perceived sentinel of the safe functioning of the healthcare systems of Connecticut, was skulking in the dark corners, ready to pounce and strike at our most vulnerable moment. At the eleventh hour they proposed an amendment to our bill that eviscerated it. Among other things, they did not want any of the confidentiality that is so important to attracting self-reporting nurses. The timing was perfect—for DPH. We had no time to fight their proposed amendment.

By the end of May, we decided to pull our bill. It was better to have no program than a bad one or, just as bad, a program that DPH had their grubby hands all over. The language DPH put in their amendment would have made the system even *more* punitive, which we hadn't thought humanly possible.

We were very disappointed, but we knew we were not defeated. We were determined to continue to pursue what we knew to be the right thing.

THAT JUNE, MY PROBATION with the State of Connecticut was over. A very short letter from DPH confirmed that I had completed all the requirements. No "good job." No "congratulations." But I didn't need or want such sentiments from them anyway. I had my family, Dede, Marilyn, and my Nurses for Nurses friends, who were truly happy for me and proud of me. No more peeing in a cup twice a month. No more fear of something being in that cup that wasn't pure pee. Over the last year I had mentally and emotionally prepared myself for this moment. Now it was all up to me and my recovery.

In October, Dede and I were asked to be presenters at the Connecticut Nurses Association's annual convention. "The Impaired Nurse: Why Didn't I Know?" was the most highly attended session of the convention. Then, during the next year, we went to various nursing schools and facilities to gather support for our bill, which was to be reintroduced in the 2002 legislative session.

DEDE WAS DRIVING the two of us to a Nurses for Nurses meeting the night we found out that we were being asked to give our presentation to Drug Control! For about half the trip, we were lost in our own thoughts. Staring straight ahead at the road, I started thinking out loud. "Hey Dede, we're going to meet with Drug Control, voluntarily, on our own. We're looking forward to it, with no fear. *We're* going to *them*. I can't wrap my head around it. What are your thoughts?"

Without breaking her straight-ahead stare, she responded, "No fucking way."

During the break in our presentation to Drug Control, I came face-to-face with the man who'd changed my life that June morning in 1996, John Gadea.

"Hi," I said to him. "Do you remember me? You confronted me at VMMC in '96."

"Yes, I remember you, "he responded as he shook my hand. "Dick and I were there that day. Dick has since retired. We thought you were going to shoot us."

"*Shoot you?* What on God's green earth would make you think I was going to shoot you? I've never even held a gun!"

"Well, at one point in the interview you reached down below the table, and we thought you might just shoot us under the table in the cajones, so we kinda slid back and closed our legs." He shook his head, smiling. "We were pretty relieved when we saw that glucometer."

"Talk about full circle," Dede said in the car on the way home.

My answer was a clear, "No fucking way."

WE REINTRODUCED OUR BILL at the 2002 legislative session. Again it passed through all of the committees it was brought to. The legislators who raised the bill practically hand-carried it to the Senate floor. Members of our committee met with key members of DPH, and compromises were discussed. We were determined to have the bill that was needed, and we would not give in, especially when it came to the confidentiality issue. Members of our committee also met with Lieutenant Governor Jodi Rell, who was shocked at DPH's position, especially after hearing all of the research we had done about the success of these programs in other states, and how they were much more efficient in protecting the safety of the public health. She said she was going to let the commissioner of public health know that she was in support of our bill.

EVERY WEEK WE PRAYED at Nurses for Nurses that our bill would pass. More days went by. The bill was on the Senate floor and therefore ready to be voted on. We were coming down to the wire.

Then in May, during the last week of the 2002 legislative session, Polly Barey announced that the Commissioner of Public Health was not going to support our bill. The legislator who'd raised our bill said that it had no chance of passing if the commissioner was opposed to it. Polly put our bill at the bottom of the Senate agenda, so that it had no chance to be voted on, thus saving it for another time.

Another defeat, not for our committee, but for the nursing community, and the safety of the public health of Connecticut. The commissioner of public health had summarily dismissed our bill without knowing anything about it. His *only* information had come from those who potentially had something to lose—those who prosecute and regulate. In the interest of self-preservation, to maintain the status quo, and in ignorance and arrogance, DPH had entitled itself to spend taxpayer money literally to fight that which it claims to be its mandate—to protect the health of the citizens of Connecticut—by keeping a bad system in place.

But we will not give up. We will have an alternative program.

In 2004 and 2005, our bill was knocked down again. In 2006, Dede and I were asked by the new commissioner of DPH to participate in an ad hoc committee to research the feasibility of an alternative-to-discipline program. On the committee was representation from DPH, the Department of Mental Health and Addiction Services, the Connecticut Nurses Association, and others. It was the most frustrating committee I ever had the displeasure of serving on. The people from DPH didn't have a clue what a program was supposed to be composed of. They had done no research on something they were so vocally opposed to, and they really didn't care.

Under the guise of compromise, they presented information that was blatantly a manipulation of information. They were there just to serve the same interests of DPH they had served all of the previous years we'd tried to get our bill passed. Their goal was simply to report back to the commissioner that our bill was unfeasible. *They* wanted the control, but we would never let that happen. The committee met until January, when the 2006 legislative session was about to begin, and DPH submitted its report.

BUT BEHIND THE SCENES that January, a covert operation was taking place. Doctors' organizations and other groups were watching the progress of our legislation very carefully. They figured that if the nurses got a good, confidential program, then they could, too. The doctors had a program, but DPH was basically in control of it, so doctors who could afford expensive treatment out of state did not self-report, thus keeping their drug use a secret. So, the Connecticut Academy of Physician

Assistants, the Connecticut Nurses Association, the Connecticut State Dental Association, the Connecticut State Medical Society, and the Connecticut Veterinary Medicine Association formed a coalition and began authoring legislation for an alternative program for all licensed by DPH.

As with our bill, this new bill got all the way through to the final vote in the Senate, the last stage needed for passage, then some senior senator got a bug up his ass about a personal affront he'd heard in passing from one of the lobbyists working for the coalition, and he sent the bill back to the Public Health Committee of the Connecticut General Assembly with only three days left in the session, which essentially rendered it dead.

I thought this was my *representative government, not your tool for revenge!*

Pissed off but undeterred, the coalition reintroduced the bill in 2007. Key members of the House and Senate coddled and nurtured it. Meeting after meeting was held with the coalition, DPH, and the Public Health Committee.

In retaliation, DPH drafted its own bill, which looked good on the surface but was just as duplicitous as their basic nature. They tried to market it to all of the licensing boards, but it really promised nothing, and was a just bogus way to get funding for DPH. *We have money for your program. Yeah, bullshit. You just want control. Same old story, different day.*

Our supportive senators and representatives assured us that DPH's bill was not going to get off the ground, not even going to get on the runway, and that our bill would pass. The coalition was guardedly optimistic. So many times we had been shot down at the last minute.

ON A HOT JUNE 12, 2007, Dede and I were ushered into the inner office of Governor M. Jodi Rell as 17 of the people involved with the bill surrounded the governor's desk for the official picture and signing of HB 7155, thus making it Public Act 07-103: An Act Concerning a Professional Assistance Program for Health Care Professionals. Dede and I stood together facing each other right behind Governor Rell's chair. We held, actually squeezed, each other's hands and tried not to cry as our bill was signed, cameras flashed, and small talk ensued. It was a surreal experience. HAVEN (Health Assistance interVention Education Network) was born.

DPH DID RETALIATE, not directly to the legislation, but in the most depraved and destructive of ways: by attacking the individual recovering nurse doomed to have to endure the disciplinary process. With the assistance of an attorney from the attorney general's office (who used to work for DPH), DPH drafted a ruling that stated that unless a nurse signed a release allowing the disclosure of *all* of her medical records to them, she would not be allowed to present her defense.

Arguments were brought forth from Marilyn and another attorney, Martha, who represents nurses, citing the confidentiality laws in place. They argued that it is the privilege of the patient alone, per federal law, not to allow the disclosure of private and confidential and sensitive conversations or medical issues she has had with her counselor, psychologist, therapist, or doctor.

DPH's motion would allow every detail of intimate information, such as whether a nurse's parents, siblings, or children are or have been substance abusers or suffer from mental illness; when the nurse had her first period and when was her last period; her first intercourse; whether she has been a victim of incest or other sexual abuse or assault or a victim of other physical, psychological, or emotional abuse as a child or adult; whether she is sexually active; if she practices safe sex; what her sexual preference is; what her history of sexually transmitted diseases and abortions is; if she has had suicidal thoughts or any attempts; her previous inpatient or outpatient mental health admissions (even as a child or teenager); how she is sleeping lately; all of her past and present medical conditions and any medications she is or has been on; her HIV and hepatitis status; and on and on.

The privacy laws are there to preserve the therapeutic relationship between client and therapist. The loss of confidentiality results in a destroyed therapeutic relationship. Without that confidentiality, there is no longer a safe place to confide problems, issues, or fears and get a therapeutic response. The privacy acts allow for the release of this information in legal and administrative proceedings, but only if the client signs a release or if a court order is issued, and then only the *least amount* of information needed is to be released. With DPH's intrusion in this manner, most certainly a nurse will die as a direct result of the fear of losing her license. She might act on a suicidal thought, accidentally overdose, or not receive treatment for fear of public disclosure and therefore suffer a fatal withdrawal. To not allow a nurse to present her case unless all of this information is disclosed is against the nurse's constitutional right to privacy.

In response to DPH's actions, the board of nursing held a closed (secret) session to discuss the ruling. When the board needs to submit a ruling, they are supposed to hold hearings related to the issue. To the dismay of the attorneys, the nurses in the recovery community, and the nurses yet to face the nursing board for their own cases, the ruling went forth, and was signed by the chair of the nursing board, at the advice of the same assistant attorney general. The battle will be ongoing until this unconstitutional ruling is hopefully reversed in Superior Court.

DESPITE THIS SETBACK, WE will continue to advocate for those recovering nurses who choose to remain anonymous and for those who show incredible courage, character, and strength while feeling vulnerable, ashamed, and dispirited while they are being humiliated, attacked, and abused by the bullies at the Department of Public Health.

There are many recovering nurses whose own stories demonstrate much more courage than mine. Mine is only a variation on a theme. There are the similarities: the guilt, the shame, the fear, the sudden realization of being an *addict.* Most of us fit the profile of an addicted nurse at the beginning of this book. Most of us came to realize that what we knew about addiction from our nursing education could not fill a med cup. Most of us have denied the depression, tension, and stress in our lives. Most of us are the best and the brightest the profession of nursing has to offer.

The differences among us lie in our personal stories and histories. Some of us suffered from physical, emotional, and verbal abuse our whole lives; others of us, not. Some of us have that predisposing factor of genetic predisposition; some, not. Some of us "need" to relapse, and some don't. Some get recovery, and some don't. Some stay sick. Some die.

I am one of the lucky ones. I have the disease of addiction. I have a physical, social, mental, and spiritual disease, and I have never been so grateful in my life. This disease and its recovery have given me 100-fold more than it ever tried to take away. The day my life inexorably changed, I asked my Higher Power to point me in the right direction, and He pointed me down the road of recovery. His road signs were, and continue to be, the people in my life who are my recovery network.

St. Teresa of Avila once said, "Christ has no body on earth now but yours; yours are the only hands with which he can do his work, yours are the only feet with which he can go about the world, yours are the only eyes through which his compassion can shine." I find the true presence of my Higher Power every time I attend a Nurses for Nurses meeting. I have the privilege of witnessing the body, hands, feet, eyes, and compassion of my Higher Power in that room every time I interact with a nurse in the grip of active addiction, or struggling with the fear and confusion of new recovery, or experiencing another miracle of recovery, or imparting the experience, strength, and hope of a recovery long embraced.

Now when I raise my hand and say, "Hi, I'm Patty and I'm an addict," I have nothing to be ashamed of. I know I'll have nonjudgmental acceptance and love no matter what I have to share. I will not get wrapped up in a warm and fuzzy blanket of enabling approval. That is not love. But I will receive guidance and support to do the next right thing. Then it is up to me. I will do the footwork and get out of the way so that my Higher Power can do the rest. I never have to hide or keep secrets or experience waves of fear. The choice is mine, and every time I make a choice, I predict my future.

When I was helpless, I asked God for help. When I was hopeless, I reached out for His hope. When I was powerless over my addiction, I asked to share His power. Now I can honestly thank God that I was helpless, hopeless, and powerless, because I have seen a miracle.

—*Denial Is Not a River in Egypt,* by Sandi Bachom

EPILOGUE

I STAND AT THE FOOT of the birthing bed as the young mother labors and pushes her daughter into the world. As I watch this miracle, indescribable emotions well up inside of me. I am so grateful to be doing the work I love once again. I reflect back on the day I was led away from my moms and babies twelve years before. I have gained so much.

I have often said that June 28, 1996, was both the worst and the best day of my life. God did for me what I couldn't do for myself. The grace of God allowed me to connect to the people I needed in my life to propel me into recovery. I had to learn to let go. I could no longer believe I could fix everything for everybody. And I could no longer feel guilty when I couldn't. There is one person I have had difficulty letting go of, however.

Part of Erin died when she lost her baby. I never again saw the Erin I knew in those two years after IOL. She never got her nursing license back. She stated many times that she was going to petition the nursing board to lift the suspension on her license so she could get a nursing job, but she never did. She got a good non-nursing job at an insurance agency, but her job was eliminated after a few months.

Paul was back in her life. He moved in. He was not working, either, and they were living off his investments. Physically he was not well, suffering from repeated bouts of pancreatitis. Erin was involved in his health and "running the show" in that regard. When she shared at Nurses for Nurses, it was always about Paul's health and how frustrated she was with his doctors. We asked her many times how *she* was doing, but the subject always went back to Paul.

Over the next few years, Erin and Paul relapsed on and off. They were arrested for stealing OxyContin from a home where Erin was working as a health aide. She received a sentence of treatment in lieu of jail, but jail was the only option if she relapsed. She signed up for outpatient treatment and was attending that program. She also had a job in a doctor's office, as an office manager. Paul was supposedly out of her life "for good."

I have not heard from Erin since then. I pray for her every day. I hope she is healthy, happy, and safe. I miss her.

THERE HAVE BEEN OTHER painful losses and changes. Oreo came to the end of her ability to have a good-quality life. I looked into the brown, trusting, unconditionally loving but now blind eyes of our friend, our protector, who was telling me that she was ready to go to God. We decided as a family when we would bring her to the vet to grant her wish. We wrapped her in the blanket we all used from the couch, so she would know her family was with her as she passed. We all thanked her and kissed her. We placed her in the care of the vet staff and hugged and kissed her again. Neither Fred nor I chose to be with her as they put her to sleep. We could not bear to see those brown, loving, and trusting eyes close forever.

I have continued in my steps toward recovery. Recovery is about owning my responsibility, getting past the guilt and fear, and making amends. And there was one big amend I had to make. I visited Linda Spivak at the hospital and told her how sorry I was for what had happened. I think she was very surprised. She probably thought I was going to tell her what a terrible person she was or that I was suing the hospital. I asked her permission to have Nurses for Nurses meetings at the hospital, and she enthusiastically agreed. We have a very strong group there now. Linda is one of Nurses for Nurses strongest advocates.

My family continues to heal and grow. Our sons are all adults now. Our middle son, Shaun, got married to his longtime girlfriend, Kate, who has been a part of our family now for about seven years. The wedding was held in August of 2007, at her uncle's golf course in Plymouth, Massachusetts. The ceremony was outside on the first tee. The reception was outdoors as well, in a party tent. If there was ever a sign from God that our family was whole and healthy again, it was this day. The weather was perfect. The ceremony was perfect. The party was perfect. I don't mean that everything went off without any minor glitches. Not that kind of perfection. But surrounded by our extended families and friends and seeing everyone having such a good time was just wonderful. For me it invoked a deep feeling of serenity. My children had grown to be healthy in mind, body, and spirit. They loved being together. I was proud of them. I watched Fred on the other side of the dance floor observing the festivities. Was he thinking the same thing? He glanced over to me and smiled, and I knew he was.

And in terms of my life as a nurse, after working in substance abuse for eight years, I knew it was time for a change. Changes in administration and policy made it difficult for me to work there. I knew I couldn't stay, but where would I go? I really wanted to get back to hospital nursing, so I scanned the Internet for jobs that would appeal to me. And I was drawn back to my first love, labor and delivery. Did I dare think I could go back?

I shared this thought with Nurses for Nurses. We talked about the fact that anything we put in front of our recovery we would lose. I couldn't fool myself into thinking I was cured. The members of the group challenged me about my motivations for wanting to go back to labor and delivery work. No matter where I worked, or what life threw at me, my recovery was my responsibility. I needed to stay intimately connected with my recovery support network. Sue assured me that I had a strong recovery and told me to pray to see signs of God's will. I prayed and meditated and decided to pursue this job. And I was hired. During the hiring process I felt at peace with my decision. I was supported and congratulated by all.

I was struck once again by how awesome recovery is. What other disease gives one the opportunity to share her deepest fears or greatest joys, her successes or failures, and be met with love, understanding, and true advisement? What a blessing are the people I have known in recovery. I could not have made this decision without them. If they had said no, then it would have been no for me too.

AND NOW HERE I AM. The beautiful baby girl emerges, crying, gasping, and protesting. She tries to figure out how to survive in this strange place. Wrapped in a warm blanket and placed in her mother's arms, she stops to take a look around, at the faces of the people who will love her forever. Everything is going to be alright.

I feel my Higher Power in my soul and I know I am home again.

The miracle of life beginning, the miracle of life enduring.

Stay clean and sober and I will show you how wonderful it can be.

To all of us "going down the same river,"
although our boats may be different,
this book is dedicated to "us."

The Pearl

There is something deep inside you that is brighter than a star.
No one can touch it, tear it, or take it. It is the essence of who you are.

Your humble spirit knelt meekly before the Lord above,
And you received His essence; a drop from His ocean of love.

It's opalescent beauty, so gentle, so fragile, so pure,
Belies the strength it possesses and ability to endure.

This sanctified endowment, bestowed in advance of your birth
Is your pearl of serenity and truth for your sojourn to earth.

As an infant you were essence predominant; innocence in sweet-smelling skin.
Looking into your eyes thus beholding the proof of heaven within.

Growing into adulthood, you built upon your dream.
Molding your life and future, presumed thrust by your own steam.

Time and pride uplift your confidence, your pearl becomes concealed
Suppressed beneath life's layers, struggling to be revealed.

Your successes drive you onward; you are clever, well-mannered and kind,
The pearl of your essence forgotten; to that wonder and beauty, you're blind.

Your pearl tries hard to remind you of the luminosity you deny,
Like displaying the splendor of nature, and heaven in a baby's eye.

Insidious, pernicious enticements, addictions, impiety and sin,
Coerce you to stumble downhill, to a nightmare thus trapped therein.

You cry out in desperation, lost and afraid and alone,
Unconscious of the pearl of heaven, as if it were never known

Your misery is felt by your essence, and knows you need its care,
Starts tunneling its way to the surface, as you collapse in prayer.

"Please heal me!" you cry as your pain grows, and as tears are drenching your face.
And your crushing desperate emptiness gradually fills with grace.

Essence speaks through your misery, "Quiet, my love, do not fear."
And you recall the drop from His ocean as your essence's voice says, "I'm here."

—Patricia Holloran

ACKNOWLEDGMENTS

To Ricky, Shaun, and Michael:
Thank you for your unconditional love.
Words cannot express how I cherish the three of you.

To Fred:
Thank you for growing and learning with me,
and for loving me through this. I love you . . . more.

To Mom and Dad:
Thank you for your love and solid values that formed
the bedrock of my morals, my ethics, and my judgments.

READER'S GUIDE

1. While working demanding hours and taking care of her father, Patty told herself that she could handle all her responsibilities, although it was soon revealed that she needed help. Do you agree with her that this attitude is typical of nurses?

2. As Patty's understanding of her addiction changes over the course of her recovery, what new realizations does she make regarding how she became an addict?

3. Why was it so difficult for Patty to admit that she's an addict? What did she gain, if anything, when she was able to make the admission?

4. After admitting to her addiction, Patty said she still had to "thoroughly assimilate and incorporate addiction into my identity." How did she approach this task? How is it different from simply admitting that she's an addict?

5. Patty said she needs to "take an active role in my recovery." How did she do this, apart from simply resolving not to abuse drugs?

6. When Erin returns to work after detox, she decides not to tell her boss, and Patty is in agreement; then, not long after returning, she relapses. How would telling her boss have helped her control her addiction? What other things does Erin do which, contrasted with Patty's experience, make her recovery more difficult?

7. Several passages in *Impaired* deal with the support and strength Patty took from religion. How does Patty's belief in a divine presence in her life help her to control her addiction and continue with her life? Why do her therapist and her support groups, none of whom are ecumenical, encourage this?

8. Patty describes her hearing before the nursing board in detail, and in doing so, she reveals a grueling, bureaucratic procedure. Yet she told her Nurses for Nurses group that it was "one of the most spiritual experiences of my life." Why does she see it as a spiritual experience?

9. At the hearing, when the nurse ahead of Patty tells the board that she's learned from her recovery and won't abuse drugs again, Patty and Erin know that this isn't what the board wants to hear. What does Patty say about her recovery that makes a better impression on the board?

10. Patty writes, "One of the maxims of recovery is 'Whatever you put in front of your recovery you will lose.'" This applies to Erin and her job. In the case of Patty, is it realistic to expect her to put her recovery in front of her other responsibilities—not just her career but her marriage, her children, and her ailing father? What does she gain by doing so?

ABOUT THE AUTHOR

PATRICIA HOLLORAN, RN, has been a nurse for more than 30 years. She has served as Chairperson of the Recovering Nurse Community of Connecticut, a committee that oversees the anonymous support group, Nurses for Nurses. She speaks regularly about issues of addiction as a guest lecturer for various levels of nursing education and at conventions. She lives with her husband in Connecticut, and has three grown sons.